QUICK.ESCAPES®
St. Louis

"*Quick Escapes: St Louis* is a great getaway resource even if you don't live in St. Louis. There are so many out-of-the-way, interesting, historic places to go and enjoy in and around Missouri, and this book tells you where they are and what to do when you get there."
—*Missouri Life* magazine

Help Us Keep This Guide Up to Date

Every effort has been made by the authors and editors to make this guide as accurate and useful as possible. However, many things can change after a guide is published—establishments close, phone numbers change, facilities come under new management, etc.

We would love to hear from you concerning your experiences with this guide and how you feel it could be improved and kept up to date. While we may not be able to respond to all comments and suggestions, we'll take them to heart, and we'll also make certain to share them with the authors. Please send your comments and suggestions to the following address:

> The Globe Pequot Press
> Reader Response/Editorial Department
> P.O. Box 480
> Guilford, CT 06437

Or you may e-mail us at:
> editorial@globe-pequot.com

Thanks for your input, and happy travels!

QUICK ESCAPES® SERIES

QUICK ESCAPES®

St. Louis

*25 Weekend Getaways
from the Gateway City*

SECOND EDITION

JULIE MOBLEY GUSTAFSON
and
LINDA F. JARRETT

The Globe Pequot Press

GUILFORD, CONNECTICUT

Text design by Nancy Freeborn
Maps by M. A. Dubé

Photo credits: pp. 61, 150: courtesy of the Convention and Visitors Bureau of Greater Kansas City; p. 69: courtesy of The Greater Saint Charles Convention and Visitors Bureau; p. 88: ©H.K. Barnett/Westminster College; p. 122: courtesy of Lake of the Ozarks Convention and Visitors Bureau; p. 163: courtesy of Big Cedar Lodge; p. 169: ©Dennis A. Hermann/Southwestern Illinois Tourism and Convention Bureau; pp. 184, 232: courtesy of Southwestern Illinois Tourism and Convention Bureau; p. 206: courtesy of Branson/Lakes Area Chamber of Commerce and CVB; p. 216: courtesy Memphis Convention & Visitors Bureau; p. 227: ©Gregory Thomas/Evansville Convention and Visitors Bureau; p. 241: compliments of the Mt. Vernon Convention & Visitors Bureau; p. 259: courtesy of Springfield Convention & Visitors Bureau; and p. 266: courtesy of Historic New Harmony. All other photos by the authors.

ISSN 1542-5525
ISBN 0-7627-2475-7

Manufactured in the United States of America
Second Edition/First Printing

This book is dedicated to my wonderful husband, Bob, my beautiful children, Isabelle and Ben, and my parents, Robert and Susan Mobley. Thank you all for your loving support and encouragement.

JMG

I dedicate this book to my wonderful husband, Bob, who will soon write his own book on TV dinners; my children, Mike, Robin, and R.J., and my extended family of friends. Thank you all for holding me together!

LINDA

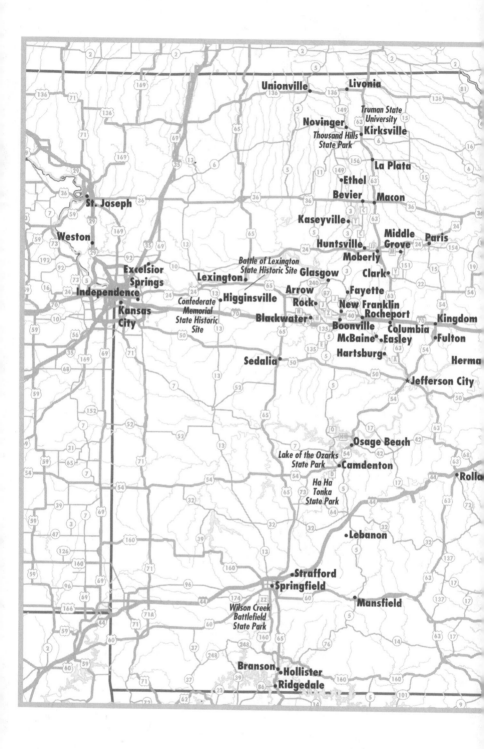

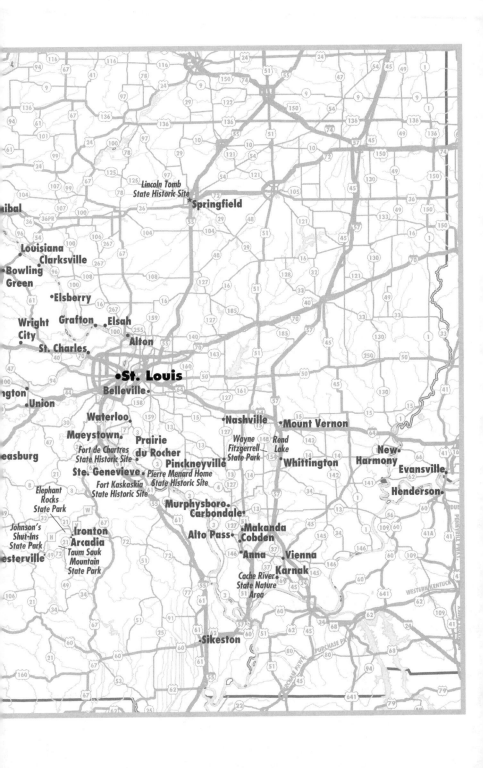

CONTENTS

The prices and rates listed in this guidebook were confirmed at press time. We recommend, however, that you call establishments before traveling to obtain current information.

ACKNOWLEDGMENTS

The authors wish to acknowledge the invaluable assistance they received from the departments of tourism and convention and visitors' bureaus of the cities and towns mentioned in this book. A special thank-you to the owners of the many B&Bs who made our stays so enjoyable and gave us much-needed insight into each area.

INTRODUCTION

When presented with the opportunity to write a travel book on getaways from St. Louis, we leaped at the chance to combine our love for travel with our skills as freelance writers. Who wouldn't want to hop in the car and head out of town for a quick getaway? we reasoned. But when reality set in and we had to come up with twenty-five destinations, we asked ourselves, "Where in the world are we going to go?"

We knew the obvious getaways from St. Louis, like The Lake of the Ozarks, Kansas City, and Branson, and we knew some of the attractions these towns had to offer. But where else should we go? Many maps, miles, and nights away from home later, we discovered that Missouri and its surrounding states had many more hidden gems than we realized. In many cases, the destinations we discovered often delighted us and surpassed our expectations, giving us a whole new appreciation for the Midwest. And as an added bonus, all these places are easily reached within a one- to six-hour drive from St. Louis.

We hope you'll benefit from our extensive research and enjoy some of these getaways yourself. While it's not necessary to try to do everything listed for each destination, you can feel confident that we've organized each itinerary in a logical way to make the most of your time. For example, we assume most trips will be taken on the weekend, so we've paid particular attention to the hours of operation for stores, attractions, and restaurants. If a place is closed on Sunday, we've included it in Day 1 of the itinerary, since more than likely this day will be a Friday or Saturday.

Most of the restaurants and lodgings recommended in this book are moderately priced. We have included options for couples wanting a romantic weekend away as well as for families who want to have fun without going broke. As an added convenience, with many of the restaurant descriptions we've provided price ranges for entrees per person: Restaurants considered "inexpensive" have entrees under $12; "moderate" generally includes entrees between $12 and $18; and "expensive" covers entrees

$18 and up. For the most part, the lodgings we've chosen are bed-and-breakfasts or lodges, and are listed because of their unique qualities. However, we've tried to include alternate choices such as chain hotels, particularly if a bed-and-breakfast does not allow children.

For us, packing for these trips became rote. Some of the handiest things we learned to take included binoculars, a camera, an umbrella or poncho, walking shoes, a cooler bag with snacks and drinks, sunscreen, bug spray, a hat, sunglasses, and detailed maps. Because the directions and maps provided in this book are general, it's always best when possible to get a detailed map of the area in which you'll be traveling.

Also, a word about safety. Always trust your own judgment when deciding whether an excursion or activity will work for you. We've included things for all ages and abilities, yet some may be more rigorous than you or your children should undertake. You know your and your family's limitations best, so use good judgment.

Before you take a trip based on our suggestions, however, you should know a little something about us and our preferences. One of us, Julie, did her traveling with her husband Bob and two young children, Isabelle and Ben. The other, Linda, also traveled on some trips with her husband Bob. Because of this, we've looked at these destinations from varied perspectives—the eyes of a young family as well as those of empty nesters. Regardless of our differences, we both like the same things: a comfortable bed, a clean, modern bathroom, exceptional food, cold iced tea, and warm, friendly people. We enjoyed uncovering hidden gems, learning interesting stories about the places we visited, and discovering activities that not everyone knows about.

Along the way we also culled our own quirky little list of "Bests."

Best place to get away from franchises: New Harmony, Indiana

Highest pie: Cowan's Restaurant, Washington, Missouri

Best fish sandwich: Fin Inn Aquarium Restaurant, Grafton, Missouri

Best French fries: Addison's, Columbia, Missouri

Best Missouri River view: Les Bourgeois Winery, Rocheport, Missouri

Best Mississippi River view: Anywhere along Highway 79

Best stuffed animals: Bass Pro Shop in Springfield, Missouri

Best little-known museum: Cedarhurst and the Mitchell Museum in Mt. Vernon, Illinois

We could go on and on, but we'll leave it up to you to discover your own favorites.

No matter what your interests might be, we're sure more than a few of these escapes will surprise and delight you with all they have to offer. We hope we've uncovered some new things for you to enjoy or have shed a new light on destinations you've already discovered yourselves.

Bon voyage and happy traveling!

NORTHERN
ESCAPES

Alton, Illinois

St. Louis's Neighbor to the East / 1 Night

Hidden gems can be found at every turn on a trip to Alton. This sleepy little river town of about 30,000 people just over the Mississippi River is still very much connected to its past. Once home to some of the area's

☐ Historic sites

☐ Antiques

☐ Shops

☐ Mississippi River

wealthiest business tycoons, Alton boasts an abundance of beautiful older homes and a plethora of history. From its key role as a supply station in the Civil War and its numerous stops along the Underground Railroad, as the former home of abolitionist and editor Elijah P. Lovejoy to the tallest man in the world, Robert Wadlow, Alton has quite a story to tell.

Day 1 / Morning

The best way to get to **Alton** is to head east on Highway 270 toward North County. Take the State Route 367 exit toward Alton. Cross over the Clark Bridge and you're there. Once over the bridge, make a left onto Landmarks Boulevard for most shops and attractions. Depending on where in St. Louis you're coming from, the trip to Alton should take about an hour.

Start your day at the corner of Piasa and West Third Street. Make a right onto Piasa from Landmarks Boulevard, then left onto West Third Street. Parking is on the street.

One hundred one West Third Street is home to **The Frontier Furnishings Company,** (618) 465–8868. Breathe in that wonderful aroma of fresh-cut wood as you browse this store full of finished and unfinished solid wood furniture. Open Monday and Friday 10:00 A.M. to 7:00 P.M., Tuesday through Thursday 10:00 A.M. to 5:00 P.M., and Saturday 9:00 A.M. to 4:00 P.M. Closed Sunday.

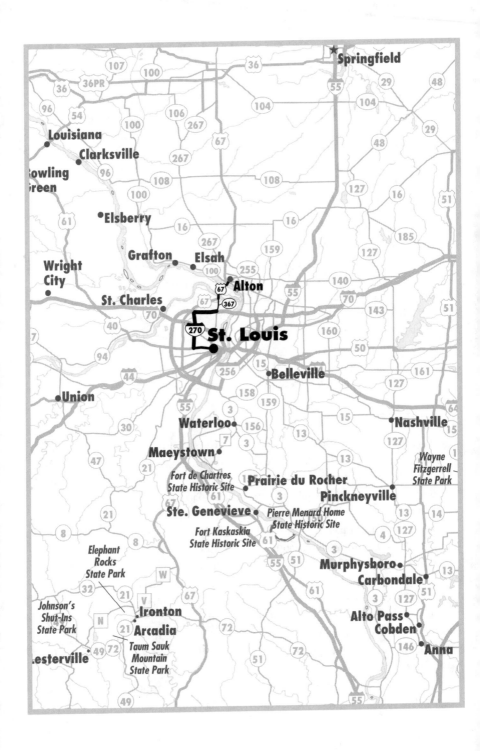

At 108 West Third Street is **Patchwork Plus,** (618) 462–8565, filled with hundreds of charming quilt fabrics. Open Monday to Thursday 9:00 A.M. to 5:00 P.M., Friday and Saturday 9:00 A.M. to 4:00 P.M., and Sunday noon to 4:00 P.M. **Dian's Reflections and Treasures** at 110 West Third Street, (618) 465–4891, specializes in gifts from around the world, including antique reproductions of home accessories and a fun collection of nautical gifts. Open Monday to Saturday 9:00 A.M. to 5:00 P.M., Sunday noon to 5:00 P.M. **Towata Studio Gallery,** 206 West Third Street, houses original pottery, sculpture, and paintings. Open Tuesday to Saturday 10:00 A.M. to 4:00 P.M., Sunday 1:00 to 4:00 P.M. Closed Monday.

LUNCH: Sweet Olive Café, 100 West Third Street, (618) 465–7669. A trip to Italy by the cafe's owners was the inspiration for this little restaurant. Family owned and operated, Sweet Olive Café is dedicated to providing healthy, fresh foods with unsurpassed guest service. Lunch items include salads, soups, and sandwiches, including a special made-from-scratch chicken salad that only has seven grams of fat! There's even a tofu wrap for vegetarians and a tried-and-true kids' menu that's sure to please. Check out the ever-changing dessert menu if you have a sweet tooth. The cafe is open 7:00 A.M. to 4:00 P.M. Monday through Friday, 8:00 A.M. to 4:00 P.M. on Saturday; closed on Sunday. Inexpensive.

Afternoon

Take a trip back in time on the **Underground Railroad.** The Mississippi River and Alton played an important role in this secret grass-roots movement. Although this "railroad" had no cars or tracks, it was the path to freedom for escaping slaves whose ultimate destination was north into Canada. Its location just across the river from the slave state of Missouri made Alton an ideal location to begin the journey. J. E. Robinson Tours will take individuals and families on a tour of these historic "stops" on the railroad, which include The College Avenue Presbyterian Church, the Alton Museum of History and Art, the Lyman Trumbull House (Trumbull was the U.S. senator who wrote the Thirteenth Amendment, which abolished slavery in America), and Josiah White's Log Cabin. One-hour walking tours for individuals and families cost $25 and are conducted year-round. Driving tours in your car are also available. Contact Eric Robinson, owner of J. E. Robinson Tours, in advance of your trip at (618) 462–5590.

Double-back down Landmarks Boulevard south toward the Clark Bridge and continue about 2 miles on what is now called Highway 143.

Go right at the light on Lock and Dam Way to the **Melvin Price Locks and Dam #26** for a tour of this amazing feat of engineering. Did you know that there are twenty-nine locks and dams on the Mississippi River between St. Louis and Minneapolis? These "stairways" of water make otherwise treacherous river navigation possible between the two towns. Free public tours are available at 11:00 A.M. and 2:00 P.M. daily Labor Day through Memorial Day. From Memorial Day through Labor Day, tours are conducted daily at 11:00 A.M. and 2:00 and 5:00 P.M. Make sure you dress appropriately for the weather as you'll actually be walking on top of the lock. For safety reasons, tours of the locks and dam are restricted to persons thirteen years and older. Visitors under thirteen can view the structure from inside without actually walking across the locks. Contact the Melvin Price Locks and Dam at (618) 462–6979 or toll-free at (888) 899–2602. Reservations required.

DINNER: Tony's, 312 Piasa Street; (618) 462–8384. Tony's is a mainstay in Alton, and for good reason. Guests can enjoy charbroiled steaks, seafood, pasta, or pizza at reasonable prices in a comfortable atmosphere. Appetizers include homemade tenderloin-beef vegetable soup, shrimp cocktail, and mozzarella cheese sticks. The signature entree is Tony's Pepperloin, which is tenderloin marinated and rolled in cracked black pepper. The restaurant also offers filet mignon, chicken cacciatore, veal Parmigiano, and just about any pasta dish you can imagine, as well as their renowned pizza. A fairly substantial wine list is also available. The restaurant is open daily and accepts reservations. Moderate.

LODGING: The Beall Mansion, 407 East Twelfth Street; (800) 990–2325 or (618) 474–9100; www.beallmansion.com. The Beall Mansion was formerly the home of Senator Edmond Beall, who made his living as an industrialist, financier, and politician. He's best known, however, as the four-term mayor of Alton who brought the town out of the mud, leading the rally cry to pave the then-dirt streets with brick. The home is now owned by former St. Louisans Jim and Sandy Belote, who have spent the past three years completely renovating this architectural gem. Rooms, which range in price from $119 to $189, include private baths, most with whirlpool tubs, and some king-size beds. Other amenities include a complimentary glass of champagne or wine upon arrival and nightly turndown with chocolates and fluffy robes. Spend some time perusing the before-and-after pictures of the mansion. Sandy has compiled two photo albums, and both she and Jim delight in telling stories of the mansion's

The Beall Mansion, Alton

transformation. Ask them to tell you about the gorgeous woodwork next to the first step of the stairway or the story of the gold-colored radiators. If you want to ensure quiet as well as privacy, request the third-floor room and have the television set removed.

Day 2 / Morning

BREAKFAST: At The Beall Mansion. The toughest decision you'll need to make is whether to have breakfast in bed or in the dining room. You can expect breakfast to include such delights as Tortuga rum French toast with praline sauce, or yeast-raised Belgian waffles with real maple syrup. You won't want to miss a glass of Mississippi Sunrise; it's so refreshing and a nice change of pace. Fresh fruit, cream cheese, and caviar are also favorite menu items.

After breakfast check out of the B&B and head down to Broadway for some serious antiquing. Alton has more than sixty dealers, which will keep you busy for hours. Head south down Henry and make a left on Broadway and you're there. Parking is ample and free, so grab a spot and start shopping. Our favorites include **Mississippi Mud Pottery,** 310 East

Broadway; (618) 462–7573. Ken and Brenda Barnett started their business in 1983 and have been growing ever since. Here you'll find the potters working daily making dinnerware, lamps, vases, planters, casseroles, Raku pottery, and custom-designed items. The building also houses the Mudd Gallery, which displays the works of regional artists. Store hours are Monday through Saturday 10:00 A.M. to 5:00 P.M. and Sunday noon to 4:00 P.M. Other shops include **Alton Antique Center,** 401 East Broadway, on the lower level (618–463–0888), **Steve's Antiques and Reproductions,** 323 East Broadway (618–465–7407), and **Heartland Antiques,** 321 East Broadway (618–465–6363).

LUNCH: Cane Bottom/My Just Desserts, 31 East Broadway; (618) 462–5881. In keeping with the antiques theme, have lunch in on old building surrounded by antiques while overlooking the Mississippi River. Grab a seat by the back windows for a view of the "Mighty Miss." Order the delicious spinach salad with homemade poppyseed dressing; it's exceptional. The grilled chicken spinach wrap is also tasty. The chicken salad is a local favorite with its interesting ingredient: green olives. But the best reason to eat here is the desserts. Don't leave without enjoying the mouth-watering Mrs. Ledbetter's Pie, a German-chocolate creation, or the Mystery Pecan Pie with its layer of cream cheese. If you ask nicely, you may just come away with a souvenir postcard complete with Mrs. Ledbetter's chocolate-pie recipe. The restaurant is open daily from 11:00 A.M. to 3:00 P.M. Inexpensive.

Afternoon

Finish up your shopping and then head back home by heading south on Landmarks Boulevard (it's just south of Broadway) and cross over the Clark Bridge. Follow the signs for Highway 270.

There's More

Alton

Alton Little Theatre, 2450 Henry Street; (618) 462–3205. Take in some quality community theater while you're in town. For little more than the cost of a movie, you can enjoy wonderful live entertainment. Past performances of this more-than-sixty-year-old theater company have included *Kiss Me Kate, The Marriage Fool,* and *Hay Fever.*

Alton Museum of History and Art, 2803 College Avenue; (618) 462–2763. Learn more about the Lewis & Clark Expedition, Elijah P. Lovejoy, the area's black pioneers, and more. Open Monday through Friday from 10:00 A.M. to 4:00 P.M., Saturday and Sunday from 1:00 to 4:00 P.M.

History and Hauntings Tour. Local author and "ghost researcher" Troy Taylor will take you on a tour of "haunted Alton." The town is considered one of the most haunted small towns in America, and Troy shows you why. Many locals scoff at the haunted reference, but it makes for an interesting tour. Troy's tours depart from his bookstore, **Riverboat Molly's Book Company,** 515 East Third Street; (618) 465–1084. Call for tour times and rates. Individual tours are held spring through fall. Bookstore hours are Monday through Friday 10:00 A.M. to 6:00 P.M. and Saturday 10:00 A.M. to 4:00 P.M. Closed Sunday.

Nan Elliott Memorial Rose Garden located in the **Gordon F. Moore Community Park,** 1211 Henry Street. If your idea of a great getaway includes communing with nature, take a stroll through Alton's premier park. This 1,600-bush rose garden is a wonderful focal point of this park, which also includes an oriental garden, a fishing lake, a nature trail, tennis courts, and baseball, softball, and soccer fields.

Special Events

Fall. Fall Color Caravan. Drive along the Meeting of the Great Rivers National Scenic Byway for a glimpse of fabulous fall foliage. Call (800) ALTON–IL for more information.

December through March. Eagle watching. All along the river are wonderful opportunities for spotting the magnificent bald eagle and other majestic birds. During winter many area businesses offer a variety of bird-watching packages. Contact the Alton Convention and Visitor's Bureau at (800) ALTON–IL for more details.

May. Memorial Day Parade. Enjoy a historic spring celebration through upper Alton. Call (800) ALTON–IL for more information.

Other Recommended Restaurants and Lodgings

Alton

Fast Eddie's Bonair, 1530 East Fourth Street; unlisted phone. Fast Eddie's is like no other—what other bar do you know that doesn't give out its phone number? If you want good, cheap eats and cold, cold beer, Fast Eddie's is the place. Expect a crowd whenever you go as well as good music on the weekends. Don't be surprised to see Fast Eddie himself dancing and hamming it up with the crowd. Because it's first and foremost a bar, children are not allowed. Hours are Monday through Thursday 1:00 P.M. to 1:00 A.M. and Friday through Sunday 11:00 A.M. to 1:00 A.M. Inexpensive.

The Jackson House Bed and Breakfast, 1821 Seminary Street; (618) 462–1426 or (800) 462–1426; www.jacksonbb.com. This graceful house has been owned by three generations of women, which is evident in the details throughout the house. Each of the three guest rooms is wonderfully decorated and very relaxing; some have a fireplace and/or whirlpool bath. A generous former barn out back is now a comfortable suite, perfect for a romantic getaway or suitable for families with children. Limited accommodations for pets. Rates range from $95 to $125 and include pie with breakfast—a Jackson House tradition!

Godfrey

Josephine's Tea Room, 6109 Godfrey Road; (618) 466–7796. Hop on Highway 67 and head toward Godfrey, about fifteen minutes away, for an out-of-the-ordinary treat at Josephine's. Enjoy freshly made salads, soups, and desserts in a beautifully decorated restaurant. Browse in the elaborate gift shops and the exceptional Christmas shop next door. The fruited chicken salad is a specialty. Definitely worth the drive. The tearoom is open 11:00 A.M. to 2:00 P.M. Monday through Friday and until 3:00 P.M. on Saturday; closed Sunday. The gift shop is open 10:00 A.M. to 5:00 P.M. Monday through Saturday, noon to 5:00 P.M. Sunday. Inexpensive.

For More Information

Greater Alton/Twin Rivers Convention & Visitors Bureau, 200 Piasa Street, Alton, IL 62002; (618) 465–0491 or (888) 227–9612; www.alton cvb.org.

NORTHERN ESCAPE TWO

Elsah/Grafton, Illinois

Riverside Discoveries / 1 Night

The mystery of the Mississippi River has enchanted many people over the years. Its power and size are most evident just north of St. Louis near the town of Grafton, Illinois. Grafton is at the heart of the Meeting of the Great Rivers National Scenic Byway, which begins in Alton and ends at

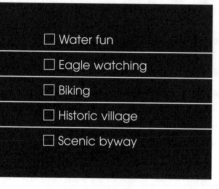

☐ Water fun

☐ Eagle watching

☐ Biking

☐ Historic village

☐ Scenic byway

Kampsville. One of the newest of the national byways, Grafton is where the Mississippi, the Missouri, and the Illinois Rivers merge. The byway stretches some 50 miles, but because of Grafton's location at the rivers' meeting point, it has developed into a sleepy yet charming little town that's a great hub to visit while exploring all the area has to offer. From the glorious foliage in spring and fall to the many boating and water activities in summer to eagle watching in winter, Grafton has something to do and see year-round.

The byway drive is very picturesque, with the steep, jagged bluffs on one side and the deceptively calm water on the other. You'll be amazed at how far you can see up and down the river. It's reported that at some points you can see for miles. No wonder the eagles love it here. The river is a natural "highway" for American bald eagles, who make Grafton and the surrounding areas their home during winter. Their magnificent presence atop bluffs or balancing on chunks of ice in the river is glorious, and a sighting of one of these keen-eyed predators is known to make otherwise calm adults as excitable as kids in a candy shop.

Day 1 / Morning

The easiest way to get to Grafton is to head east on Highway 270 toward North County. Take the exit for State Route 367 to Alton. Cross over the Clark Bridge and go left on Landmarks Boulevard. Follow the signs for

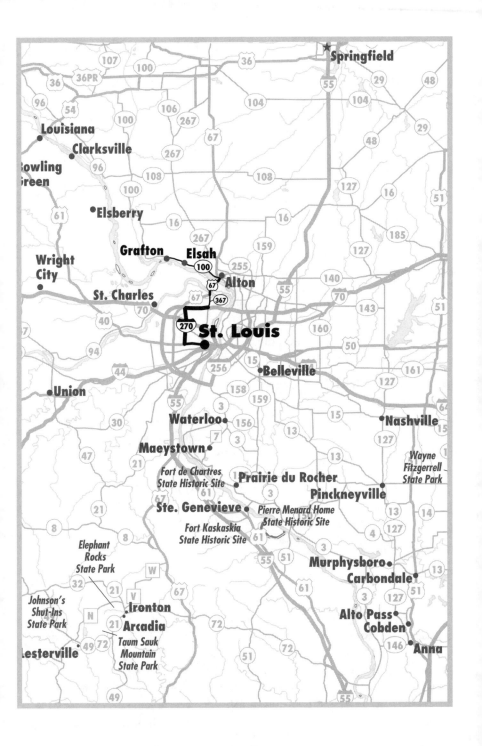

Highway 100, also known as the Great River Road, and stay on Highway 100, which will take you directly to Grafton. Depending on where in St. Louis you're coming from, the trip should take about an hour and a half.

On your way up the river road, take a little detour in the town of **Elsah** before reaching Grafton. This charming New England–like village was the first town in the nation to be listed in its entirety on the National Register of Historic Places and is well worth a leisurely drive or stroll. Strictly a residential community, this little village is nestled snug into the hillside and is full of wonderful old stone buildings, a couple of churches, and a handful of bed-and-breakfasts.

After you've circled through town, go back to the first cross streets for a little side trip to **Crocker & Springer pottery shop,** 40 Beltrees Road. Take a right onto Maple Street and drive 2 miles to the shop, which will be on the right. This little nondescript workshop is located down a scenic, winding road and is home to some wonderful salt-glazed stoneware. The shop is open from 10:00 A.M. to 6:00 P.M. Tuesday through Saturday and 1:00 to 6:00 P.M. on Sunday; closed Monday. (618) 466–8322.

Once back in Elsah, leave the little village and continue heading north on Highway 100 until you come to Grafton.

LUNCH: Michael's Restaurant, 420 East Main Street (618–786–SOUP), is the first building you see on the right as you enter Grafton. Formerly The Elsah Landing Restaurant, Michael's serves breakfast, lunch, and dinner, and the food continues to be as delicious as ever. Stop in for a French dip sandwich and a bowl of baked French onion soup, or try the Cowboy, a sandwich of shaved roast beef brisket, grilled onions, and barbecue sauce smothered with cheddar and Monterey Jack cheeses. The restaurant is open 10:00 A.M. to 8:00 P.M. Tuesday through Thursday, 10:00 A.M. to 9:00 P.M. Friday, 7:00 A.M. to 9:00 P.M. Saturday, and 7:00 A.M. to 8:00 P.M. Sunday. Inexpensive.

Afternoon

Spend a leisurely afternoon strolling down Main Street in Grafton. Stop in at the little shops up and down the street. Of particular interest is **The LaMarsh House,** 25 East Main Street (618–786–2438), a historical stone house filled with fun little gifts, garden accessories, candy, and gourmet foods. **The Wood Worker's Wife,** 13 East Main (618–786–3244), is a wonderful shop with handmade wooden items. Stop in at **Piasa Winery,** 211 West Main Street (618–786–WINE), for a little wine tasting; enjoy a glass of wine along with gourmet snacks on their deck overlooking the river. If you're ready for a sweet treat, stop in at **Country Corner Fudge Store,** 321 East Main (618–786–3700). More in the mood for a **bike ride?** Country Corner Fudge Store will rent a bike to you for $15 for a half day. Pick up a free bike-route brochure and tool up and down East Main. Or better yet, head over to the bike path that follows the river for an exceptional view.

If you're more interested in the former residents of this river area (we're talking about those who lived here thousands and thousands of years ago), head up to Kampsville to the **Center for American Archeology.** Located about forty minutes north of Grafton on Highway 100, this little town is home to the CAA, a leader for more than forty years in contemporary archeology in the Midwest. Many people consider Kampsville to be one of the richest archeological regions in the country. In fact, some twenty-five years ago, the town was home to an excavation that received considerable national media attention for its discovery of ancient Native American artifacts. Spend some time in the visitor center, which contains artifacts, exhibits, and displays that explain how archeologists learn about the past as well as some incredible artifacts from the area. The visitor center is in the historic Kamp store, situated on Highway 100, and is open April through November, noon to 5:00 P.M. Sunday through Friday, Saturday 10:00 A.M. to 5:00 P.M. For more information or to find out about archeology classes for kids and adults, call (618) 653–4316.

Reverse your steps and head south on Highway 100 back to Pere Marquette Lodge, where you'll be staying for the night. Check in, then head to the dining room for dinner.

DINNER AND LODGING: Pere Marquette Lodge and Camping, Highway 100, Grafton; (618) 786–2331. Situated on the Great River Road just north of Grafton, Pere Marquette Lodge is a warm and rustic pairing of gorgeous scenery and comfortable, easygoing accommodations. Originally built in the 1930s by the Civilian Conservation Corps, the lodge has been expanded and updated in the past fifteen years, yet has retained many of its original features. You'll love the large lobby area, with its life-size chessboard, exposed timbers, and stone fireplace. It's a great place for kids as well as adults. And the view is wonderful through the enormous glass window that overlooks the Illinois River. Rooms are clean and hotel-like; some overlook the indoor swimming pool and whirlpool spa. There's also an exercise room, a sauna, tennis courts, and a variety of outdoor activities. Rates are $99 per night. The lodge is very popular with families and key weekends are filled up to a year in advance, so it's wise to make reservations.

You'll love the rustic atmosphere in the lodge's restaurant, not to mention the food. People come from miles around for the fried chicken, and once you taste it, you'll understand why. It's crispy and juicy and comes with enough sides to feed an army. Relax in the comfy chairs and enjoy the friendly, easygoing service while gazing at the impressive 700-ton stone fireplace. Inexpensive.

Day 2 / Morning

BREAKFAST: Pere Marquette Lodge. The lodge serves an outstanding breakfast buffet on Sunday that's not to be missed, or you can order off the menu of typical breakfast fare the other days of the week.

Although many groups offer excellent eagle tours, the **Ruebel Eagle Tour** is delightful, thanks to entertaining and very knowledgeable guides. Board a minisize tour bus in front of **The Ruebel Hotel,** 217 East Main Street, and you're on your way. While there's never a guarantee you'll see these awesome creatures, you can be sure you'll enjoy trying. Ruebel's guides are personally interested in the eagles and make a concerted effort to ensure guests get at least a peek, yet they're very respectful of these birds' privacy and never get too close to their nesting areas. Call the hotel at (618) 786–2315 for departure times and dates. Half-day trips run about $25.

If the eagles aren't in town, spend some time enjoying the water. *Grampa Woo III* offers **river excursions** for sight-seeing on the river. Cruises and prices vary. Call (334) 421–4211 for dates the boat will be in town as well as pricing information.

LUNCH: Fin Inn Aquarium Restaurant, located on the Great River Road (618–786–2030), is quite an experience and a great place to come if you like fish—both watching them and eating them. This restaurant is reminiscent of a 1960s-type themed eatery you'd expect to see in some Doris Day movie, but therein lies its charm and popularity. On a recent Sunday afternoon, the crowds were hanging out the door waiting for their turn to slide into a long wooden booth next to one of a dozen or so gigantic aquariums that are home to Mississippi River fish, loggerhead turtles older than your great-grandparents, and a catfish the size of a six-year-old child. The best part is that the food is even better than the atmosphere. Try a mouthwatering walleye fillet sandwich with coleslaw or the ever-popular buffalo fritters. If you've left room, indulge in a piece of homemade Kentucky Derby Pie (made by one of the owners' mothers). It's like eating a warm chocolate chip cookie, only better. Inexpensive.

Afternoon

Head back to St. Louis by going south on Highway 100. Make a right onto Landmarks Boulevard in Alton and head south. Cross over the Clark Bridge and follow the signs for your highway home. The trip home should take about an hour and a half.

There's More

Grafton

Hiking. Pere Marquette State Park has some wonderful trails for novice as well as experienced hikers. Stop in the park's visitor center just north of the lodge for an overview of the trails as well as general information on the park. The visitor center is open daily 9:00 A.M. to 3:30 P.M. and can be reached by calling (618) 786–3323.

Horseback riding. Pere Marquette Park's riding stable is open year-round, but reservations are required November through April. Call the stable for more information at (618) 786–2156.

Raging Rivers Water Park, 100 Palisades Parkway; (618) 786–2345; www.ragingrivers.com. If you want to play in the water, this is the place for warm-weather fun. Raging Rivers has water slides, a wave pool, tube floats, children's area, and more. Open Memorial Day through Labor Day. Hours vary. Admission is $15.95 for ages nine and above, $12.95 for ages three to eight.

Special Events

January and February. Bald-eagle watching. Grafton. (618) 786–2315.

April through October. Riverside Flea Market. Grafton. Held every second and fourth weekend (9:00 A.M. to 5:00 P.M.) at the Boatworks building, 400 Front Street; (618) 462–8210.

July. Art Fair. Grafton. (618) 786–3338.

October. Gathering of the Waters Rendezvous. Grafton. A reenactment festival for the whole family. (618) 786–3344.

Other Recommended Restaurants and Lodgings

Grafton

The Brainerd House Bed and Breakfast. Located above Michael's Restaurant, 420 East Main Street; (618) 786–2340. The Brainerd House B&B boasts two cozy bedrooms and a shared sitting room decorated in charming English country style. The owners paid considerable attention to detail, from the beautiful quilt and antique carved wood bed in the Bill Brainerd room to the tasteful tulip lamp and cheerful wallpaper in the C. B. Rippley room. Both have private baths, and the Rippley room has a whirlpool tub. Because of the shared sitting room, this B&B would make for a fun getaway for a family (children twelve years and older are welcome) or two couples traveling together. Rates are from $110 to $135 and include a full gourmet breakfast at Michael's Restaurant.

Brainerd's Village Inn, 308 East Main Street; (618) 786–2282. If you want biscuits and gravy and other down-home breakfast fare, this is the place. Also serving lunch and dinner. Inexpensive.

The Ruebel Hotel, P.O. Box 638, 217 East Main Street; (618) 786–2315. If you love cowboys and western history, the Ruebel is the place for you. Enter the lobby and you feel as if you've stepped back in time. The owners have lovingly restored this twenty-two-room hotel and brought it back to life. Kick off your cowboy boots and relax in one of the modern hotel rooms before sauntering downstairs for a bit of grub in the saloon/restaurant. If you're looking for a little more leg room, consider the Ruebel cottages located across the street and high up on a bluff. The cottages include Jacuzzis and minikitchens as well as gas grills on the deck. Hotel rates start at $59, and cottages start at $119. Most Saturday evenings the hotel also puts on a murder-mystery dinner theater, which is a real hoot. If you're visiting in summer, you can enjoy musical and theater acts at the amphitheater nearby. Call in advance for reservations.

For More Information

The Greater Alton/Twin Rivers Convention and Visitors Bureau, 200 Piasa Street, Alton, IL 62002; (800) 258–6645; www.visitalton.org.

Grafton, Illinois Chamber of Commerce; www.grafton.il.us.

Hannibal/Louisiana/Clarksville, Missouri

The Mighty Missouri / 1 Night

River towns never fail to relax visitors, and these towns are no different. Each has its own personality and ways of attracting people. Hannibal has Mark Twain and his stories of Tom Sawyer and Huckleberry Finn. Perched on bluffs overlooking the Mississippi River, Louisiana has its antiques shops, and its entire downtown district is on the National Register of Historic Places. Clarksville has become known as the place for watching eagles. This only takes place in January and February, but it has popularized this little burg as a haven for a quiet getaway.

- ☐ Mark Twain
- ☐ Riverboat cruise
- ☐ Caves
- ☐ Antiques shops
- ☐ Eagle watching
- ☐ Scenic drive
- ☐ Old cemeteries

Day 1 / Morning

Grab a sack of bagels and a cup of coffee and jump in the car around 8:30 A.M. Hannibal lies 110 miles north on Highway 61, a short, easy drive. (Take I–70 west to Highway 61.) As you drive in, don't be put off by the fast-food chains and retailers along the highway. Once you follow Business Route 61 into town, the buildings and houses all take on the character of an old, comfortable river town, bursting at the seams with stories to tell.

Start with a tour of the thirty-two-room **Rockcliffe Mansion,** 1000 Bird Street (573–221–4140), from whose stairwell Mark Twain was welcomed by Hannibal society in 1902. The grandeur and elegance of this restored mansion, built in 1900, cannot be understated. Tours cover the first three floors and, for those visitors willing to climb, the fourth-floor observatory, from where one gets a magnificent view of three counties and the Mississippi River. Open daily 10:00 A.M. to 3:00 P.M. except Thanksgiving,

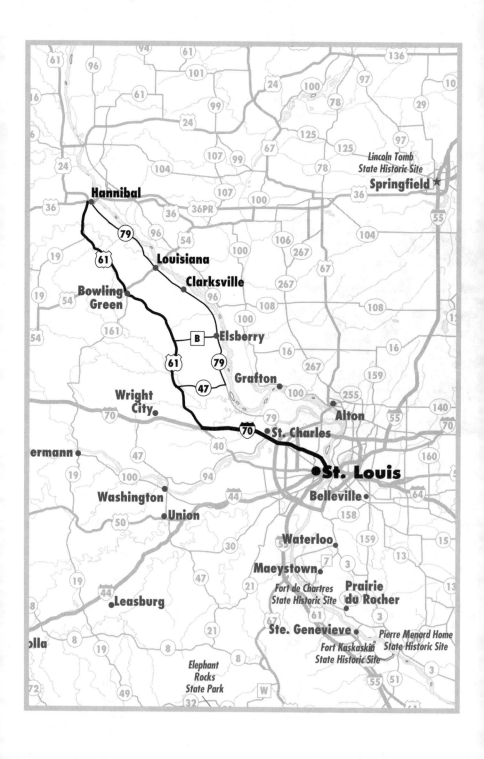

Christmas, and New Year's Day. Admission: adults, $6.00; children six through eleven, $3.00; children under six, no charge.

Time to get some Mark Twain history. The **Mark Twain Boyhood Home and Museum,** 208 Hill Street (573–221–9010), consists of six buildings. The tour begins in the **Mark Twain Museum Annex** adjoining the home and museum. Watch the video and see photographs of the people from whom Twain modeled his characters. Next comes the **Mark Twain Boyhood Home,** the two-story dwelling where Twain became inspired, and the **Mark Twain Museum and Gift Shop,** with Twain's famous white suit. **Grant's Drug Store/Pilaster House,** which dates back to the 1830s, is at the corner of Hill and Main Streets. The Clemens family lived upstairs, and Twain's father, Judge Clemens, died there. **J. M. Clemens Law Office** is across the street from the boyhood home. **The New Mark Twain Museum,** on Main Street south of Twain's home, features a replica of a steamboat pilot house complete with a whistle, fifteen original Norman Rockwell *Tom Sawyer* and *Huckleberry Finn* paintings, and historic Hannibal memorabilia. Open daily June, July, and August 8:00 A.M. to 6:00 P.M. and May 8:00 A.M. to 5:00 P.M. November through February open Monday through Saturday 10:00 A.M. to 4:00 P.M. and Sunday noon to 4:00 P.M. In April, September, and October, open 9:00 A.M. to 5:00 P.M. daily. In March open Monday through Saturday 9:00 A.M. to 4:00 P.M. and Sunday noon to 4:00 P.M. Admission: adults, $6.00; children six through twelve, $3.00; children under six free.

LUNCH: The large windows at the **Riverview Cafe** (573–221–8292), at **Sawyer's Creek Fun Park,** Highway 79 South (573–221–8221), looking out on the river, provide a perfect spot for lunch. Start with the Haystack Onion Rings, thinly sliced and fried to crispy perfection, or the spicy buffalo chicken wings. The South Pacific Tropical Salad—chicken breast, tropical fruits, and toasted almonds over crisp greens with either poppyseed or honey lemon dressing—is a delight. It's large enough to share, but you might not want to. Or try the Riverboat BBQ, a mound of shredded beef on a large bun. Under $10. Open 11:00 A.M. to 9:00 P.M. daily; closed January, February, and March. www.sawyerscreek.com.

Afternoon

After lunch walk through the rest of **Sawyer's Creek.** Feed the koi in the fish pond. Try the bumper boats or arcade. Play miniature golf on a course

The Mississippi River from Highway 79

that winds through ponds and fountains. Browse through the many gift shops, including wonderful Christmas shops. Free admission to the park. Open daily at 10:00 A.M.; closed January, February, and March.

Drive back to Main Street and spend the rest of the afternoon browsing through the shops and chatting with Hannibal residents, who are eager to tell you about their town and its history. Stop at the **Hickory Stick Quilt and Gift Shop** (573–221–4538), with its three historic buildings filled with quilting, embroidery, and cross-stitch supplies and other stitching needs; **Show-Me Antiques,** where you can find old soda bottles (remember Wink?), old postcards, buttons, thimbles, and other items you might find very interesting; and **Angels & Inspirations,** where you'll find angels everywhere.

The **Native American Trading Company and Gallery** features many handcrafted items from cultures including Navajo, Zuni, Hopi, Cherokee, Sioux, and others. Find blankets, mandalas, dream catchers, kachina dolls, jewelry, and many other items. A peek into **Bankhead Chocolates** means you won't go away without their famous "turtles," made from the same recipe since 1919. Stop for a cappuccino at **Fresh**

Ayers, look at the pottery, and then walk up to **Ayers Pottery Co.,** 103 North Third, to see the potter in action.

For an unbelievable view of the river, walk past the statue of Tom and Huck and up the 186 steps of Cardiff Hill. At the top stands Memorial Lighthouse, the farthest inland lighthouse in the world and built in memory of Mark Twain. Visitors not wanting to walk can drive through **Riverview Park** along North River Road. Follow the signs for some amazing views for miles up and down the river.

On your way back visit **"The Unsinkable Molly Brown" Birthplace and Museum,** Highway 36 and Denkler Alley; (573) 221–2100. See memorabilia from Molly's rags-to-riches story. She became known as "unsinkable" after she survived the maiden voyage of the *Titanic.* Open June through August 9:30 A.M. to 6:00 P.M. daily; in April, May, September, and October, open weekends only 10:00 A.M. to 5:00 P.M. Admission: adults, $3.00; children, $2.00. www.mollybrownmuseum.com.

D I N N E R : For a real river experience, go aboard the *Mark Twain* riverboat for a dinner cruise. The evening cruise lasts two hours and includes a buffet dinner with a cash bar. Sit on the deck and watch a barge chugging its way up or down the river for distant ports or watch birds skimming the water for food. Cruises are offered Memorial Day through Labor Day daily; during May and October only on Friday and Saturday; and in September, Tuesday to Sunday. Starting time is 6:30 P.M. Prices: adults, $26.95; children five to twelve, $18.95.

One-hour day cruises are also available and include commentary on river history, legends, and sights. Two-hour jazz cruises are available on Saturday nights. Board thirty minutes ahead of departure. Call (573) 221–3222 about times or visit www.marktwainriverboat.com. Rates: ages thirteen and up, $7.50; children five to twelve, $6.50.

L O D G I N G : Another residence visited by Mark Twain will be your house for the evening, **Garth Woodside Mansion;** (888) 427–8409. Awarded as one of the Top Ten inns in the county by The Romance Channel and *Country Inn Magazine,* the mansion will provide an unforgettable experience. Built in 1879 and nestled in thirty-nine acres of woods and meadows, it gives the feeling of truly being away from everyday stress. Relax on the wide veranda and listen to the breeze and sounds of the country. Eight rooms with private baths. Rates: $109 to $195. No pets. No smoking. Children over twelve welcome. www.hannibal-missouri.com.

Day 2 / Morning

BREAKFAST: At Garth Woodside Mansion. Come down to breakfast in the nightshirt provided by your hosts. Visit with other guests over a breakfast of home-baked breads, gourmet egg casseroles, juice, and fruit. Hosts John and Julie Rolsen spare no details in serving a breakfast in keeping with the manner of the mansion.

Start your day with a visit to a place that played a large part in Tom and Huck's adventures—**Mark Twain Cave,** Highway 79 South; (573) 221–1656. A guide explains all the legends on the sixty-minute tour and points out markings on the walls made by actual long-ago visitors. The temperature is about 52 degrees, so bring a light jacket. Summer hours are 8:00 A.M. to 8:00 P.M. daily; April through May, 9:00 A.M. to 6:00 P.M. daily; September through October, 9:00 A.M. to 6:00 P.M. daily; November through March, 9:00 A.M. to 4:00 P.M. daily. Admission: adults and high school students, $12.00; children in eighth grade or under, $6.00.

Before you leave town on 79, drive up to **Lover's Leap,** ½ mile south of Hannibal, for another sweeping view of the river. Legend says that two Indian lovers from warring tribes leaped to their deaths from this point to avoid being separated.

The 42-mile drive south to Louisiana is one of "America's Scenic Drives," and it's no surprise. The road winds through the hills bordering the river, then swoops down into long valleys. Along the way are various turnoffs with amazing river views.

For a different activity, try all or part of the Pike County **Tombstone Tours.** Listing fifteen of the more than 150 cemeteries in Pike County, their tour map shows the way to cemeteries that serve as a history lesson for this area. Here lie buried statesmen, Revolutionary and Civil War soldiers, and Indian massacre victims and leaders. There are Jewish, Protestant, African-American, community, and family cemeteries. The tombstones tell of fire, sickness, and other family tragedies. Contact the **Pike County Tourism Commission** at (573) 324–2077 for the map.

One of the most interesting cemeteries is located in Louisiana. **Riverview Cemetery** contains more than 14,000 graves, many of which are those of Pike County pioneers and soldiers. The cemetery steps lead up to a bluff overlooking the Mississippi River—a breathtaking view.

Founded in 1818, Louisiana is known for its antiques shops, and you can spend many hours in the historic downtown district just browsing in the many shops that line North Main Street. The town is also known for its many antebellum and Victorian gingerbread homes, giving Louisiana the reputation of having the most-intact Victorian neighborhood streets in Missouri.

Following Highway 79 South, Clarksville, Missouri, is the next stop, 9 miles downriver. Located on the Mississippi Flyway, visitors have the opportunity to see all types of waterfowl and other birds. The most popular are the bald eagles that feed and nest near the lock and dam. In January and February, when the water is cold and ice-filled, the water near the lock is in constant motion, bringing fish to the surface and within easy reach of the eagles.

Visit the **Clarksville Eagle Center** in the **World Bird Sanctuary** on the north end of town on the river side of the road. Besides an eagle, owls, and other birds, they have a Madagascar Hissing Cockroach and non-venomous snakes on display. Park down on the riverfront, walk out to the overlook, and enjoy the river. You might be lucky enough to see a barge go through the lock and dam.

LUNCH: The Book Nook. 105 Front Street across from the Mississippi River. You can't miss it; you'll smell the basil and oregano wafting along the street. Walk in and peruse a wide selection of new and used books, then lunch at little bistro-type tables. The specialty sandwich is a "Nook Nak"—a loaf of French bread filled with sandwich goodies that rises, then bakes, steaming and cooking the filling. Finish off with the signature apple strudel dessert or homemade baked sugar pecans. Open Tuesday through Saturday 9:00 A.M. to 5:00 P.M., Sunday 10:00 A.M. to 5:00 P.M. Lunch is served from 11:00 A.M. until 2:00 P.M. or "while supplies last."

Afternoon

After lunch browse through some of Clarksville's shops, such as **Stoney Creek** for antiques and primitives, **Bee Naturals** for natural bath and body supplies, **A.S.L. Pewter Foundry** for handcrafted pewter, **Clarksville Pottery** for wheel-thrown stoneware, **Brentwood Furniture, Ltd.,** and **Harlequin Antiques.**

Clarksville is the last stop before home. You can follow Highway 79 for 44 miles into St. Charles, get off at Elsberry on Route B, and cut over to Highway 61, or you can get off at Winfield on Route 47 and go 13 miles to Highway 61. Either way, taking Highway 61 south will lead to St. Louis.

There's More

Hannibal

Amish Community at Bowling Green. Bowling Green is 30 miles south of Hannibal on Highway 61. The community is located south and west of Bowling Green, and all through this area are shops where the Amish sell such handcrafted items as cabinets, quilts, rugs, and baked goods. Call The Pike County Tourism Department at (573) 324–2077 for a map of the area.

Becky Thatcher Home & Bookshop. 211 Hill Street; (573) 221–9010. This bookshop occupies the main floor of the former home of Laura Hawkins, Mark Twain's childhood sweetheart, known in his writings as Becky Thatcher, Tom Sawyer's sweetheart. This shop features the largest selection of books by and about Mark Twain to be found. No admission fee.

Cameron Cave at Mark Twain Cave; (573) 221–1656. In Missouri's newest show cave, visitors can carry lanterns and explore for ninety minutes. Tours daily from Memorial Day to Labor Day at 10:00 A.M., noon, 1:30 P.M., and 3:00 P.M. Admission: adults and high school students, $14.00; eighth-grade students and under, $7.00.

Golf. Norwoods Golf Club; (573) 248–1998. This eighteen-hole course has carts, lessons, a driving range, and a concession and pro shop. Daily fees: nine holes, $9.00; eighteen holes, $13.00. Weekend and holiday fees: nine holes, $10.00; eighteen holes, $15.00; cart fees, $6.00.

The Haunted House on Hill Street Wax Museum, 211 Hill Street; (573) 221–2220. Watch Mark Twain's characters "come to life." See the Skull Room, Corpse Room, and the Spooky Graveyard, all on one level. Open daily March through day before Memorial Day 8:00 A.M. to 5:00 P.M., Memorial Day through Labor Day 8:00 A.M. to 8:00 P.M., day after Labor Day through November 8:00 A.M. to 5:00 P.M. Admission: adults, $5.00; children six through eleven, $3.00.

Main Street Theater, 200 North Main Street; (573) 231–0746. Entertainment, food, and dancing in Hannibal's downtown historic district. Food entrees include choice of lemon pepper catfish, roast pork with rosemary sauce, or roast beef with gravy. Shows run Tuesday through Saturday starting at 5:30 P.M. Admission: $26.95; children ten and under, $17.95.

Mark Twain Outdoor Theatre, Highway 61 South; (573) 221–2945. A two-hour pageant with twenty-five actors tells the story of Mark Twain and his story characters. An all-you-can-eat buffet at Huck's Homestead Restaurant next door is extra. Performances run May through September at 8:30 P.M. Monday through Saturday. Dinner/theater combinations: adults, $23.95; children nine and under, $13.95. Theater only: adults, $14.00; children nine and under, $8.00.

Train Tours with Twainland Express, 400 North Third Street; (800) 786–5193. See all Hannibal has to offer aboard a comfortable "choo-choo" on wheels. Two choices: one and a half hours of Historic Hannibal, or a forty-five-minute minitour. Tours start at 10:00 A.M., noon, 1:30 P.M., and 3:00 P.M. during May on Saturday and Sunday; Memorial Day through Labor Day daily; and during September and October on Saturday and Sunday. Rates for the train ride are $7.10 for adults, $5.10 for children five to sixteen.

Louisiana

Henderson-Riverview Park, crest of Main and Noyes Streets. Picnic tables, benches, playground, and a magnificent view of the river.

Special Events

January. The Masters of the Sky. Clarksville. Demonstrations of free flight of birds of prey. (573) 242–3132.

Eagle Days. Clarksville. Live eagles on display with programs given by the Missouri Department of Conservation and the Eagle Center. The Army Corps of Engineers also sets up spotting scopes and tents along the river for viewing eagles. (573) 242–3132.

May. Mississippi River Art Fair. Hannibal. Midwest artists and artisans display their wares, crafts, and works in a two-day festival with food booths, children's activities, and entertainment. Historic District. (573) 221–6545.

June. Regional ICS Chili Cook-Off. Clarksville. Regional cooks compete to see who has the best chili. (573) 242–3132.

July. National Tom Sawyer Days. Hannibal. Held for more than forty-five years, this nationally known festival features National Fence Painting Championship, a frog-jumping contest, Tomboy Sawyer Competitions, Mississippi Mud Volleyball, plus many other activities. Also food booths, bingo, and entertainment, plus a huge fireworks display on the Fourth. (573) 221–2477.

September. Big River Days. Clarksville. A family weekend event featuring a pre-1840 campsite with traders and period artisans creating their crafts. Visitors can take a forty-five-minute barge ride on the Mississippi River. Period museum in Golden Eagle River Museum. Music, crafts, kids' activities. (573) 573–3771.

October. Applefest. Clarksville. Parade, art show, fiddler contests, chiropractic sessions, food and craft booths.

Autumn Historic Folklife Festival. Hannibal. Artisans demonstrate lifestyles and crafts of the mid-1800s. Street musicians, storytellers, food prepared over wood fires, plus other food booths and activities. Historic District. (573) 221–6545.

Colorfest. Louisiana. A two-day festival during the third weekend in October held downtown. Events include a parade, car show, a Civil War Reenactment Group, and gem and mineral show. Also a Kids' Alley, quilt show, and historic-home tour. Food and craft booths.

November. Land of Mark Twain Bluegrass Festival. Hannibal. See some ol'-time pickin' and grinnin' as talented musicians compete for championships and provide bluegrass demonstrations. Hannibal Inn. (573) 221–6610.

Other Recommended Restaurants and Lodgings

Clarksville

Carroll Inn Bed & Breakfast, Highway 79; (573) 242–3957. Spend a relaxing weekend in a 120-year-old home listed on the National Register of Historic Places. Two rooms in comfortable settings. Guests get cookies, cakes, or brownies served in the evening. Wake up to a full breakfast such as egg casseroles, homemade cinnamon rolls, and fresh fruit. Children welcome. Smoking permitted outside. No pets. Rate: $75.

Clarksville Inn, Highway 79; (573) 242–3324. Inn with seventeen rooms overlooking the river and lock and dam. Rates: $43 to $53. Two rooms include kitchenettes, $63. In-ground pool; children welcome. Smoking permitted. Breakfast not included.

Daniel Douglas Bed & Breakfast; (573) 242–3482. Built in 1859, this brick two-story Greek Revival Italianate house sits on Second Street in the heart of historic Clarksville. Three guest rooms with two full baths, one with a large old-fashioned tub, and one with tub and shower. Original pottery, furniture, and folk art crafted by local artisans fill this delightful home. Relax and read or play chess in the living room after a day of antiquing or walking along the river. Large country breakfast with fresh fruit and muffins, with coffees, teas, and juices starts the day. No smoking, pets, or children. Open Friday and Saturday. Rate: $75.

The Doug Out, 105 Front Street; (573) 242–3829. Situated along the river, The Doug Out serves home-grilled hamburgers that rank among the best, along with the French fries—both served very hot. The hot ham and cheese is also a winner. Lunch for two with drinks under $10.

Hannibal

The Gilded Age Bed & Breakfast, 215 North Sixth Street; (573) 248–1218. An 1871 Italianate house on the National Register of Historic Places with three marble fireplaces. Six rooms with private baths and some with refrigerators. Coffee for early risers. Breakfast includes gourmet cinnamon rolls or coffee cake, tea breads, biscuits, fresh fruit, quiches, breakfast meats, and juices. Rates: $55 to $90. No smoking. No pets. Children welcome. E-mail: gildedag@dstream.net.

Hannibal Inn, Highway 61 and Market Street; (573) 221–6610 or (800) 325–0777. 242 rooms. Free continental breakfast and free morning coffee. "Fundome" with indoor heated pool, whirlpool, and sauna. Also game room. Restaurant and lounge. Teens stay free with parents. Rates: $60 to $95.

LulaBelle's Restaurant and Bed & Breakfast, 111 Bird Street; (800) 882–4890. Once an infamous bordello, LulaBelle's now enjoys a new reputation. Steaks, seafood, beef, and pasta from $12.95 to $21.95. The B&B has six rooms with such names as Jaded Jewel, Gypsy Rose, and Bird of Paradise. No smoking, children, or pets. Rates: $50 to $90.

Mark Twain Campgrounds, Highway 79 South at Mark Twain Cave; (800) 527–0304. RV sites with hookups; also tent sites. Shower house, Laundromat, camp store, and snack bar. Rates: full hookup, $18; tent sites, $14.

Mark Twain Family Restaurant, 400 North Third Street; (573) 221–5511. Serving Hannibal since 1942, this hometown restaurant features the famous Maid Rite and the Mississippi Mud Malt (don't bother with a straw). Also sandwiches such as Cajun tenderloin, Mexican tenderloin, burgers, and a catfish sandwich. Very reasonable prices.

Ole Planters Restaurant, 316 North Main; (573) 221–4410. Daily specials include meat loaf, barbecue beef or pork, catfish, and chicken. Big burgers. Dinners include Chicken Celesto, pepper steak, and catfish. Specialty homemade pies include German chocolate and blueberry cheese. Prices are low to moderate.

Sixth Street Guest Haus, 407 North Sixth Street; (573) 248–0082. Five upscale apartments include fully stocked kitchens with continental breakfast, fresh fruit, coffee, and teas. Relax in the hot tub surrounded by gardens. Extras include two robes in the room and turndown service with chocolates. No children, pets, or smoking. Rates: $125 to $185.

Louisiana

Beldane's Restaurant, 321 Mansion; (573) 754–6869. Hometown restaurant with large variety for lunch and dinner. Sandwiches include Cajun prime rib with sautéed mushrooms or Philly beef. Dinner features prime rib, steaks, pasta, and seafood. Reasonable prices.

Eagle's Nest Winery, Inn, and Restaurant, 221 George Street at the corner of Highway 79 and Georgia Street; (573) 754–9888. Located in an old 1880s bank building, this lovely establishment will feed and bed you. Dinners include rack of lamb with roasted honey and garlic glaze ($18.95) and smoked pork loin topped with brandied apples ($14.95). People travel miles for the signature lunch, bacon, potato, and cheddar soup served in a sourdough bowl ($3.95), and ham, roasted red pepper, and goat cheese sandwich with tomatoes and pesto on focaccia bread ($6.95). The in-house bakery offers all types of pastries, plus omelets or biscuits with sausage gravy. Upstairs are three lovely bedrooms, each with a whirlpool. A hot tub is available for overnight guests. Prices: $85 to $125. Opens at 7:00 A.M. Monday through Saturday and 9:30 A.M. Sunday; closes at 8:00 P.M. Tuesday through Thursday, 9:00 P.M. Friday and Saturday, and 2:00 P.M. Sunday and Monday.

Louisiana Guest House Bed & Breakfast, 1311 Georgia Street; (573) 754–6366. A two-story Cape Cod house with two large rooms furnished with family antiques. Also large baths with claw-foot tubs. Breakfast of eggs Benedict, fruit, homemade muffins, homemade apple butter. Children over twelve welcome. No pets. Smoking permitted outside. www.bbon line.com/mo/la. Rates: $75 to $85. Packages available.

Rivers' Edge Motel, 201 Mansion; (573) 754–4522. Perched on a bluff before the Mississippi River Bridge, this thirty-two-unit motel has two suites overlooking the river. Rooms include TVs, coffeemaker, and microwave. Children welcome. Rates: $42 to $59.

Two Rivers Marina, Highway 54, Rockport, Illinois; (217) 437–2321. Right across the bridge from Louisiana, the marina has camper hookups, cable TV, showers, laundry facilities, a camp store, and picnic areas with barbecue grills. Behind the campground lie 242 wooded acres for hiking. The Lighthouse Inn serves burgers and other sandwiches, plus a daily lunch special. Dinner includes prime rib, steaks, seafood, and pasta for reasonable prices. Camper hookups are $17.

For More Information

Clarksville Visitor Center, Highway 79 North, P.O. Box 560, Clarksville, MO 63336; (573) 242–3132; www.clarksville.mo.com.

Hannibal Convention & Visitors Bureau, 505 North Third, Hannibal, MO 63401; (573) 221–2477; www.visithannibal.com.

Louisiana Chamber of Commerce, 202 South Third Street, Suite 210, Louisiana, MO 63353; (573) 754-5921; www.louisianamo.com or www.pikecountytourism.com.

NORTHERN ESCAPE FOUR

Rural Northern Missouri: Moberly/Macon/Kirksville/Unionville

Small-Town Life / 2 Nights

This escape will take you off the interstates and onto the blue highways—those roads less traveled that connect small towns with smaller towns, some still thriving and some struggling. The four towns visited here represent rural Missouri life. They have not rolled over and given up their residents to the more populated areas of the state. Enough young residents stay or return after college to make these areas work.

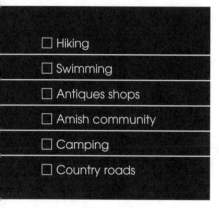

☐ Hiking

☐ Swimming

☐ Antiques shops

☐ Amish community

☐ Camping

☐ Country roads

While this escape won't offer you crowded amusement parks, overpriced retail shops, or equally overpriced restaurants, it will offer you a chance to explore a different way of life, a chance to peek into what life might have been like fifty or more years ago. At the very least, you won't have traffic jams.

Given life as a railroad town in the 1880s, Moberly relied heavily on the railroad to keep the town going. As a halfway point between St. Louis and Kansas City, Moberly enjoyed a lively reputation as a meeting place for famous and infamous denizens of those cities. Railroad consolidation in the 1980s caused some industry to depart, leaving Moberly with an uncertain future. The residents, however, committed themselves to preventing their town from fading back into the prairie from which it came, and the town is now finding a new identity.

Macon, 25 miles to the north, was settled in the early 1800s by pioneers from Kentucky and North Carolina. An old trail called the Bee Trace ran in almost the same line as present Highway 63, and it passed through Macon. Each fall, the farmers followed this trail to get honey, which was the only sweetener available then.

Now at the junction of two national highways, 36 and 63, Macon is a thriving community boasting a 1,830-acre park with a 2,400-acre lake. It

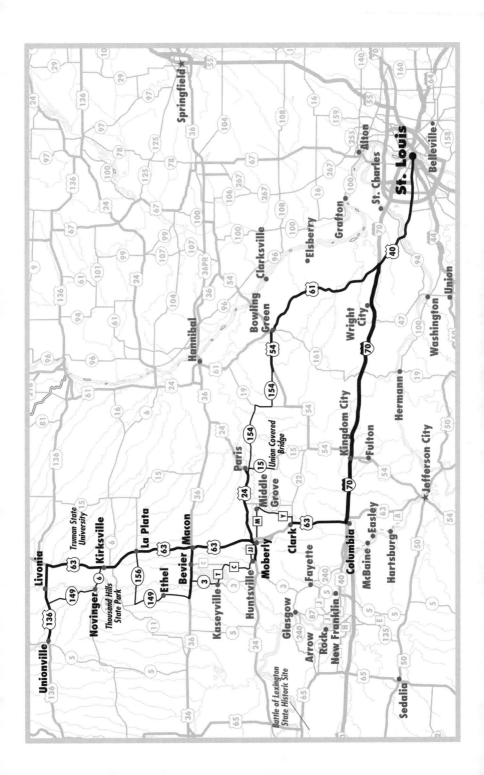

also has the reputation of being the "antiques center" of Missouri, and supports a live theater group.

Kirksville, whose name means "village of churches," is the birthplace of osteopathic medicine. In 1892, Andrew Taylor Still established the first school devoted to osteopathic medicine. Today the Kirksville College of Osteopathic Surgeons draws students from all over the United States and abroad.

Unionville, at one time a vital farm community, is situated about 20 miles south of the Iowa state line amid rolling hills of lush farmlands. The courthouse, built in 1924, occupies the town square in the town's center.

These are the largest towns you will see. On this escape you will pass through Huntsville, Bevier, Ethel, and La Plata, each holding onto its piece of Missouri history.

Two of these towns have colleges: Kirksville is home to Truman State University, a school known nationally for its high academic standards; Moberly Area Community College draws students statewide.

Day 1 / Morning

While you don't need an early start, 9:00 A.M. would be a good time to leave. If you have a rack, take your bikes along. You will see a lot of good places to ride on this trip. Go west on US–40/I–64 for 25 miles until this road intersects with I–70; then take the Kansas City exit and head west on I–70.

In about 80 miles, you'll reach Columbia and the junction of I–70 and US–63. You're probably ready to stretch your legs, and **The Pinnacles** is the perfect place. Go north on 63 approximately 12 miles to Pinnacles Road—a sign for the Silver Meadows Girl Scout Camp is a good marker to look for. Follow the gravel road about ¼ mile to the park. With natural hiking trails and picnic areas, The Pinnacles' main attraction is a 1,000-foot-wide rock wall formed by retreating glaciers after the last ice age. Don't hike on The Pinnacles, though, because this erodes the limestone; instead, use the trail along the top. Hiking information is available at the park. Call (573) 445–9792 for information.

Return to US–63, turn right, and drive approximately 12 miles to the US–63/Highway 22 junction. Turn right on 22 and drive 2 miles to Route Y, then turn left and drive through the **Amish Community,** a side trip that will take you back in time before electricity and gas became mainstays. You will find many little shops offering handmade quilts, candies, sorghum, and other home-crafted products along this road. Follow Y until you reach Route M, then turn left. Go straight on Route M into **Moberly.**

You will cross US–63, but keep going straight. After crossing 63, the first major stop sign you come to will be Business Route 63, also known as Morley Street. Turn right for your lunch stop.

LUNCH: The **Americana Grill** at 1403 South Morley Street (660–263–4747) offers a good menu with a good selection at equally good prices. The chicken salad on wheat is especially tasty, as is the Cajun cheddar burger or the three-cheese bacon-chicken sandwich. Be sure to try the onion rings—unique seasoning! The lemonade hits the spot on a warm day. If you have a hungry child, they even have a six-ounce prime rib—or peanut butter and jelly.

Afternoon

General Omar N. Bradley, the last five-star general in the United States and known as "The G.I.'s General," made Moberly his hometown, although he was born in Clark, Missouri. The **Randolph County Historical Society,** 223 North Clark Street (660–263–9396), has a genealogical library and General Bradley memorabilia, plus other interesting artifacts and documents about Moberly's history. Open Monday 10:00 A.M. to noon, Thursday 1:00 to 3:00 P.M., and Saturday 9:00 A.M. to noon.

The **Randolph County Railroad Museum,** 101 North Sturgeon Street, focuses on Moberly's railroad history with displays of a caboose, a switchman's shanty, and a 7½-inch gauge scale model of a steam engine. Inquire at the Randolph County Historical Society about museum hours or call (660) 263–9396 or (660) 263–6070. A statue in the general's honor stands at the entrance to **Rothwell Park,** on Holman Road at the west end of town.

After looking at the statue and other memorials, you might want to take advantage of the walking trails through the park and by the lake.

A short drive through the park and by the lake will put you on Highway 24. Go west for 5 miles until you reach Huntsville, Missouri, and turn right on Route JJ. In approximately 10 miles, turn left on Route T toward Kaseyville, Missouri. You will go across **Thomas Hill Reservoir and Conservation Area,** a 4,950-acre man-made lake offering fishing, boating, and waterskiing. Get out, stretch your legs, and take in the quiet country air before continuing your journey.

In a couple of miles, you'll dead-end into Route 3. Turn right and drive 10 miles to US–36. Go right, and in 5 miles you'll be in **Macon, Missouri.** At the intersection of 36 and 63, turn right. In about a mile you'll see Jackson Street on your right. At 502 Jackson is your bed-and-breakfast for the night—**St. Agnes Hall.** Before dinner tonight you can check in, and then take some time to unwind on the B&B's rear deck sheltered by locust trees and elephant ears and surrounded by lush perennials. There's also a hot tub that awaits for the ultimate relaxation.

When you're ready for dinner, head back to US–36, which will take you to your dinner destination.

DINNER: No visit to central Missouri would be complete without dinner at **The Pear Tree.** Located in **Bevier, Missouri,** a 4-mile trip west of Macon on US–36 and Route C, this New York–style eatery attracts patrons from all over the state and beyond. Reservations are imperative (660–773–6666), and you should call well in advance of your trip.

Anyone who's eaten at The Pear Tree will recommend that you start your meal with a stack of freshly fried onion rings, a well-known favorite. Steaks are done to perfection, and, if you want to splurge, order the tempura-batter fried lobster served on a bed of French fries. Salads are served in ice-cold bowls with hot garlic croutons. Desserts include New York cheesecake, ice cream that is freshly churned daily, and Raspberry Royale ice cream with brandy sauce. Prices are on the upper side of moderate.

While waiting for your table, you may want to stroll through Bevier, formerly a thriving coal-mining town that boasted 7,000 residents. When the mines closed, the population shrank to 665.

LODGING: After dinner, retrace your route to St. Agnes Hall. Built in the late 1840s and rumored to have once been a "safe house" for the Underground Railroad, the B&B had also been converted to a boarding and day school for girls in 1884.

Scott and Carol Phillips have refurbished the two-and-a-half-story house—a B&B since 1986—into a relaxing respite from a day's drive. Call (660) 385–2774 for reservations. Rates: $68 to $98 a night. www.bbim.org/saintagneshall.

Day 2 / Morning

BREAKFAST: At St. Agnes Hall. Awake to the sounds of a quiet small-town morning and enjoy an outstanding breakfast. You might get a plate of fruit, topped with flavored yogurt and granola, and cinnamon twists and apple bread or fresh sourdough bread with Carol's homemade plum jelly. Or try Scott's homemade biscuits and scrambled eggs, with cheese, onions, and mushrooms, and a big slice of ham steak—referred to by one guest as "Jurassic Pork."

Macon is home to many antiques stores, and Carol will gladly provide you with a list. Settle your breakfast with a stroll down Vine Street, one of Macon's two main streets (the other is Rollins Street). Pop in to the **Carousel Antique Mall,** 125 Vine Street. Although not technically open until 10:00 A.M., the proprietor is usually there early. You can browse among antique lamps, plates, old magazines, dinnerware, and some things valuable only to the person who finds them special.

Next stop is **Miller Rexall Drug,** 115 Vine Street, where you can sip an original fountain Coke or eat "for real" ice cream at the counter. At the **Ben Franklin Store,** 103 North Rollins, you'll find everything from Beanie Babies to stuffed bears and cake pans to candles, fine gifts, and craft needs.

Continue your trip west on Highway 36 for about 3 miles and turn off to **Long Branch Lake,** an 1,800-acre park with campsites, boating facilities, fishing, and a great beach for swimming. A trail follows the lake shoreline, and in the 160-acre native prairie, you can see such native grasses as Indian grass and wild indigo.

Back on Highway 36 go 7 miles west to Highway 149 and turn right. You'll be heading north toward **Ethel, Missouri,** about 9 miles away. A mile before you reach the little town, look on the left for **White Oak Farms and Gift House.** Dean and Barbara Rauer have designed a number of theme herb and perennial gardens such as a hummingbird/butterfly garden, biblical garden, culinary garden, medicinal garden, waterfall garden, and Missouri prairie-plant garden. In the Gift House are racks of dried flowers and herbs, beeswax candles, birdhouses, herbal vinegars, and many other collectibles. The Rauers host a "Spring Fling" in May and an Open House in October for all their Christmas items, including Barbara's hand-painted Christmas gourds.

Continue north on 149 for 21 miles to Highway 156. This beautiful drive through the Chariton River Valley takes you up rolling ridges for spectacular views of Missouri farmland. Turn right and drive 16 miles to **La Plata.** Be careful driving on these roads. You're in Amish Country again, and you will probably encounter a buggy or two.

Once in La Plata, drive past the **Gilbreath-McLorn House,** 225 North Ownby Street, built for $6,000 in 1846, and an example of the Queen Anne exposed-frame architecture favored by monied Missourians. For tours call (660) 332-6144.

The old **Santa Fe Depot,** built in 1888 and now leased by Amtrak, is the only train stop in Missouri north of Kansas City. It also features a **Naturescape Living Classroom** of native grasses, wildflowers, and perennials. To reach the depot, go north on Ownby from the Gilbreath-McLorn House, cross the railroad tracks, and the depot will be right there.

Leave La Plata on 156 East and go to US–63. Turn left and drive 15 miles to **Kirksville, Missouri.**

LUNCH: Driving into Kirksville, turn left at the intersection of US–63 and Route 6. This keeps you on Business 63. Look on the right for the Best Western Shamrock Inn, where you will find **Ailerons,** 2523 Business Highway 63 South; (660) 665–6700. You might start with bruschetta—grilled French bread with chopped tomato, red onion, garlic, cilantro, basil, and olive oil. Their number-one sandwich is The Aviator, two slices of sourdough with smoked turkey breast, bacon, tomato, cheese, and honey mustard, and grilled in Parmesan butter. Or try the veggie grill, also a good choice. Inexpensive.

Afternoon

Drive back to US–63 and turn left to go north. Go about 18 miles to US–136 and turn left. No large towns here. You are in the remote northern Missouri hills now. Keep your eyes peeled for local wildlife—you might see a large group of wild turkeys running across the road, for example. After about 8 miles you'll come to **Livonia, Missouri,** and Route N. Turn right, and in 5 miles is **Rebel's Cove,** a 4,100-acre park with access to one of the few unchanged areas of the Chariton River. Along with a heavy forest, this area contains wetlands, croplands, haylands, and ponds. The river makes a 2.5-mile loop, doubling back and coming to within a few hundred feet of itself. This meandering river has created

An old stone building on Highway 156

several oxbow lakes and marshes where you might spot a river otter flipping along the riverbank or a great blue heron or bald eagle soaring overhead.

Return to US–136 for the 12-mile drive to **Unionville,** a small farming community centered around the town square. (Note the imposing three-story courthouse on the square.) **The Unionville Flower Shop,** 2722 West Main (also Highway 136), has more than fresh flowers: Dried flowers, potpourris, candles, bath oils, and soaps are also sold here. Driving back east to the town square, turn right, park the car, and browse around **Creative Expressions.** Here you'll find a big selection of Missouri crafts by local craftspersons, and antiques and collectibles.

Leaving Unionville, drive east on 136 for 10 miles and turn right on Highway 149. This road contains two straight sections, and while it curves and bends, it also provides some of the prettiest scenery you will see on this trip. Skimming the tops of ridges, then dropping into valleys, you will see old barns and farmhouses, country churches and cemeteries, and ghosts of old general stores and gas stations.

After 21 miles of hills and dales, you arrive at **Novinger,** an old coal-mining town that at one time boasted a population of 5,000. Residents now commemorate its history with the **Coal Miner Museum and Library** (660–488–6818), open from 2:00 to 4:00 P.M. on the first and third Sunday of the month from May through August; and the **Novinger Log Homestead** (660–488–5280), a restored two-story log cabin built in 1848, open Monday, Wednesday, and Friday from 1:00 to 3:00 P.M., plus Saturday and Sunday from 1:00 to 4:00 P.M. between Memorial Day and Labor Day.

Turn left onto Highway 6 for the 8-mile drive back to Kirksville.

DINNER: Walk around Kirksville's town square to build your appetite and to get to **Minn's Cuisine,** 216 North Franklin Street, for dinner; (660) 665-2842. The fillet with peppercorn sauce and the salmon Wellington with white-wine sauce are both wonderful. A homemade sweet vegetable bread complements the meal. Moderate prices.

If you haven't had dessert, stop at the **Washington Street Java Company,** 107 West Washington Street, and enjoy a cappuccino or double raspberry mocha. The Milky Way, an iced chocolate milk with espresso, hazelnuts, and caramel, wouldn't be a bad choice on a hot summer's night! Desserts such as brownies and cheesecake are also available. You can either enjoy your treat at the little coffeehouse and listen to live music, if it's the right night, or you can take your goodies with you to your hotel.

LODGING: Check into historic **Travelers Inn Christian Bed & Breakfast** (800–320–5191), 1 block west of the town square at the corner of Washington and Main Streets. An elegant hotel built in 1923, the Covenant Life Fellowship Church saved the Travelers from destruction. It offers large, comfortable rooms and is conveniently located right off the town square. It also has a front porch, where you can relax or chat with the other guests. Rates range from $59.95 to $79.95.

Day 3 / Morning

BREAKFAST: Feast downstairs at **Felicity's** the next morning. You can order a wide variety of omelets and other breakfast fare that includes delicious cornbread biscuits, or you can have oatmeal and raisins, something not often seen on a menu. Felicity's also serves dinner and is known for its barbecued ribs.

After breakfast, peek into **Savannah Sweets and Chocolates** and **Main Street Books and Gifts,** located off the main hotel lobby.

A stroll through **Truman State University** will take you to one of the prettiest campuses in the state. The **E.M. Violette Museum** (660–785–4532) hosts many unusual exhibits and is open Monday through Thursday, 9:00 A.M. to 1:00 P.M. **The Kohlenberg Lyceum Series** brings such well-known artists as the St. Louis Symphony and performances such as *The Nutcracker,* as well as plays including *Death of a Salesman.* For information call (660) 785–4000. Events run from August to April.

Osteopathic medicine was born in Kirksville in 1892, when Andrew Taylor Still established the first school of osteopathic medicine. You can view the cabin where Still was born and the one-room schoolhouse enclosed in the **Still National Osteopathic Museum,** 800 West Jefferson Street; (660) 626–2359. Photographs, documents, and artifacts ranging from bloodletting instruments to a completely dissected human nervous system are also on display. Admission is free, and hours are 10:00 A.M. to 4:00 P.M. Monday through Friday (open until 7:00 P.M. on Thursday) and noon to 4:00 P.M. on Saturday.

Located 3 miles from Kirksville off of Highway 6 is **Thousand Hills State Park.** Besides a 573-acre lake where you can fish, boat, or swim, the park features an enclosed petroglyph site. Figures such as crosses, arrows, and snakes are thought to have been carved by tribes native to this area between A.D. 400 and 900.

LUNCH: Return to Highway 6 and drive to the 6/63 junction. Turn right, go through town, and start your trip home. When you reach the junction of Highways 63 and 24 at Moberly, make a lunch stop at **The El Vaquero Mexican Restaurant;** (660) 263–6336. Located at the intersection of these highways in the Ramada Inn, this restaurant offers traditional Mexican food with a good vegetarian selection.

Afternoon

You're now on your last leg—of the journey, that is. Turn right, out of the restaurant lot, and go 17 miles to Route C. Turn right, and in approximately 2 miles (follow the signs), you'll arrive at the **Union Covered Bridge,** one of the four remaining covered bridges in Missouri. Built in 1871, this bridge spans the Elk Fork of the Salt River and is closed to traffic, but it presents wonderful opportunities for taking pictures. Covered bridges have been labeled "Kissing Bridges" because young couples often looked forward to a Saturday-night buggy ride through the bridges, where they could steal a kiss.

Backtrack to Highway 24 and drive until you come to Paris, Missouri. Turn right on Highway 154 and follow it to Bowling Green, Missouri, approximately 50 miles away.

You're about an hour away from St. Louis driving south on Highway 61. And so ends your trip through rural Missouri.

There's More

Columbia

Rudolph Bennitt Wildlife Area. Located off Route F off Highway 63, 1 mile south of Highway 122 north of Columbia. Areas of Native American life are still seen in this forested area. Also a wonderful camping and hiking place. For information call the Missouri Department of Conservation at (573) 884–6861.

Kirksville

Thousand Hills State Park. If you feel like camping, this is the place to go. Pitch your tent and hike the many trails that cut through the woods. There's also a swimming beach, playground, and picnic facilities. A marina and beautiful lakeside restaurant are also available. Located 3 miles from Kirksville on Highway 6. (660) 665–6995. Restaurant hours are seasonal, so call ahead; (660) 665–7119.

Macon

Atlanta/Long Branch Conservation Area. Located 8 miles north of Macon off Highway 63; take State Road J and then go south on State Road RA to this 4,470-acre park. Camping and hiking give you an opportunity to see bald eagles and Canada geese. Quail, deer, and turkey hunting in season. For information call the Missouri Department of Conservation at (660) 785–2420.

Special Events

April. The Lolli Brothers Alternative Livestock Sale. Macon. See camels, llamas, emus, and many more exotic animals for sale and display. For information contact the Macon Chamber of Commerce at (660) 385–2811.

May. Coal Miner Days. Novinger. Arts, crafts, tours. (660) 665–3766.

Livonia Fox Hunt. Livonia. (660) 933–4773.

June. El Kadir Shrine Rodeo. Kirksville. NEMO Fairgrounds. One of the oldest and largest rodeos in the state. (660) 665-3766.

Livonia Bluegrass Festival. Livonia. (660) 933-4773.

July. Northeast Missouri State Fair. Kirksville. Fairgrounds. Rides, arts and crafts, food, and livestock shows.

The Randolph County Fair, held in Rothwell Park, Moberly. Livestock shows, demonstrations, arts and crafts, and a midway. Call (660) 263–6070 for information.

September. Annual Native American Pow-Wow. Moberly. Native Americans from across the country perform ceremonial dancing and drumming. There are also many traditional crafts and foods. Held in Rothwell Park. Call (660) 263–6070 for information.

Putnam County Fair. Unionville. Country-western artists; crafts and needlework including quilts, local art, and, of course, lots and lots of livestock.

October. The Red Barn Arts and Crafts Festival. Kirksville. Features many local artists and craftspersons. Held at the Courthouse Square.

Bluegrass Festival. Kirksville. NEMO Fairgrounds.

Unionville Fall Festival. Unionville. Craft exhibits, farmers market, entertainment with contests and games all day. (660) 947–2080.

Other Recommended Restaurants and Lodgings

Ethel

The Cottage Restaurant, 106 North Walnut Street; (660) 486–3274. Enjoy homemade bread, apple dumplings, smoked pork chops, and a German-chocolate brownie sundae to name a few of their delicious menu items. Inexpensive.

The Hunter's Inn, 120 Ralph Street; (660) 486–3403. This bed-and-breakfast is a 1913 Montgomery Ward home that was delivered by way of the Santa Fe Railroad and hauled up the hill by horse and wagon for construction. Two rooms. Rate: $50 per night.

The Recess Inn, 203 East Main Street; (660) 486–3328. A great bed-and-breakfast in a renovated historic schoolhouse that was built in 1910. Three rooms with private bath. Rates start from $60.

Kirksville

The Dukum Inn, 111 South Elson; (660) 665–9764. Local tavern with a sixty-year history serving imported beers and good bar food. Inexpensive.

Thousand Hills Dining Room, Thousand Hills State Park; (660) 665–7119. Steaks, fish, chicken, pasta, and sandwiches. Hours are 4:00 to 9:00 P.M. Monday through Friday and 8:00 A.M. to 9:00 P.M. Saturday and Sunday. Moderate.

The Wooden Nickel, 114 South Elson; (660) 665–2760. Local cafe with such specialties as blackened fettuccine and smoked barbecue brisket, kielbasa, and chicken. Inexpensive.

Macon

The Apple Basket, 105 North Rubey; (660) 385–7015. The place for hand-breaded tenderloins. Inexpensive.

Apple Basket Inn Bed & Breakfast, 903 East Briggs Road; (660) 385–4913. A Southern plantation offering Southern hospitality. Moderately priced restaurant serves steaks, salads, and sandwiches. Breakfast for guests only. Rates: $65 to $70.

The Gaslight Room, 203 North Rollins; (660) 385–4013. An area institution serving steaks, chicken, chops, and wonderful cinnamon rolls. High moderate to expensive.

The Stagecoach Inn, 309 Vine Street (corner of Vine and Jackson); (660) 385–2774. Macon's oldest standing structure, first post office, and stagecoach station. Scott and Carol Phillips, who own St. Agnes Hall bed-and-breakfast, own this B&B. Fully equipped kitchen available to guests. Breakfast served at St. Agnes Hall, 2 blocks away. Rates: $68 to $88.

Moberly

Magic City Dining, 107 North Williams; (660) 263–1810. Open for breakfast and lunch only, 6:00 A.M. to 2:00 P.M. Tasty country breakfasts. Lunch features salad bar, sandwiches, and daily specials. Moderate prices.

Richard's Steakhouse, 1633 South Morley Street; (660) 263–2221. Steaks, chicken, chops, and pastas at moderate prices.

Unionville

Tony's, 2121 Washington Street; (660) 947–3193. Enjoy the best and largest tenderloin you've had in years. They also serve "Iowa Chops," thick pork chops with mashed potatoes and gravy. Tony's is the local hangout, with overalls as the dress code. Inexpensive.

For More Information

Kirksville Area Chamber of Commerce, 304 South Franklin, Kirksville, MO 63501; (660) 665–3766; kvacoc@kvmo.net; www.kirksville chamber.com.

Macon Area Chamber of Commerce, 218 North Rollins, Macon, MO 63552; (660) 385–2811; macc@missvalley.com.

Moberly Area Chamber of Commerce, P.O. Box 602, Moberly, MO 65270; (660) 263–6070; chamber@moberly.com; www.moberlymo.com.

Putnam County Foundation, P.O. Box 2000, Unionville, MO 63565; (660) 947–2080.

NORTHERN ESCAPE FIVE

Lexington/Excelsior Springs/Weston/ St. Joseph, Missouri

A Trip Back in Time / 3 Nights

History buffs will particularly enjoy this trip. Spend one day amid ante-bellum mansions and touring a Civil War battle site. The next day will find you in a historic river town with charming antiques shops, a winery, and a gourmet restaurant. In St. Joseph, relive the exciting days of the Pony Express, see where Jesse James met his demise (in his home!), and investigate a fascinating museum that will take you through "the streets of Old St. Jo."

☐ Civil War sites

☐ Pony Express history

☐ Historical towns

☐ Shopping

☐ Spa

☐ Mineral springs

You will make an exact square on this trip and cover a lot of ground since St. Joseph is almost 400 miles from St. Louis. Your return will be by Highway 36, which runs east-west through the northern half of the state.

Day 1 / Morning

Get an early start because you have a 175-mile drive to Lexington and lunch. Go west on I–70 for about three hours to Route 13. This is your Lexington exit. If you're not ready for lunch, however, in another 6 miles look for Route AA to **Higginsville** and the **Confederate Memorial State Historic Site.** Built in 1891, this site honors those Missourians who fought for the Confederacy. The cemetery includes the graves of 803 Confederate veterans and their families. Admission is free; (660) 584–2853. Drive back on Route AA to Route 13, turn right, and proceed to Lexington.

LUNCH: In **Lexington** at the **Victorian Peddlers Tea Room,** 900 Main Street (660–259–4533), you can eat and browse around the many antique and craft items in the store. In fact, the very table where you eat will probably be for sale, as well as the dishes. The California Wrap with

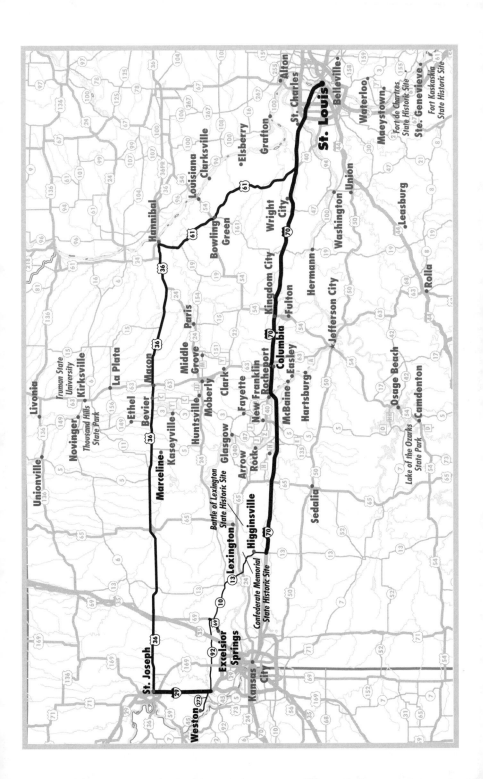

turkey, bacon, avocado, and ranch dressing in a spinach tortilla will take care of the heartiest appetite. The Reubens and quiches sell fast. Save room for dessert—the bread pudding is the star, but don't overlook the Cherry, Chip, or Earthquake cakes. Prices range from $3.95 to $7.50. Hours are 11:00 A.M. to 2:00 P.M.; closed Monday.

Afternoon

Drive through this small town with its tree-lined streets and antebellum homes and return to the days of horse-drawn carriages and wagon trains. Tour the **Battle of Lexington State Historic Site** and the **Oliver Anderson House,** where a three-day battle raged in September 1861 between Union and Confederate troops. Bullet holes remain in the wall, plus one hole made by a cannonball. After listening to the story of the house, take the battlefield walking tour; then go through the museum and watch the video. Admission to the house is $2.50 for ages thirteen and over, $1.50 for ages six through twelve; under six, free. The self-guided walking tour, video, and museum are free. Open Monday through Saturday 9:00 A.M. to 4:20 P.M. and Sunday 11:30 A.M. to 4:20 P.M.; (660) 259–4654.

After the tour, drive around and see some of the historic antebellum homes. Tours of these homes can be arranged by phone with the **Lexington Tourism Bureau;** (660) 259–4711. Other points of interest are the **Lexington Historical Museum,** with exhibits from the Santa Fe Trail and Pony Express, and the **Lafayette County Courthouse,** built in 1847, the oldest courthouse in constant use west of the Mississippi. A Civil War cannonball from the Battle of Lexington remains lodged in the east column. From June through September the museum is open Monday through Friday 1:00 to 4:30 P.M., Saturday 10:00 A.M. to 4:30 P.M., and Sunday 1:00 to 4:00 P.M. Open on weekends in May and October. Open by appointment (660–259–4711) October through April. Admission: $2.00 for adults, $1.00 for children.

Leaving Lexington on Route 13, you will pass the **Madonna of the Trail,** which honors those women who helped settle the West. This monument is one of twelve in every state crossed by the National Old Trails Road. After crossing the Missouri River, drive 8 miles to Highway 10. Turn left for the 10-mile drive to **Excelsior Springs,** the next stop on your escape.

DINNER: The **Wabash BBQ Restaurant** (646 South Kansas City Avenue) has a tantalizing variety of smoked meats. Housed in an old

Wabash train depot, the restaurant has won awards for its barbecue, including fourth place in the American Royal for Best BBQ Chicken. Try The Smokey Stack—choose two kinds of meat (brisket, ham, turkey, or pork) with two sides for $8.25—or rib dinners starting at $9.95. On Saturday night, listen to jazz under the stars in the Wabash Blues Garden. Free admission. Open Sunday through Thursday 11:00 A.M. to 9:00 P.M. and Friday and Saturday 11:00 A.M. to 10:00 P.M.; (816) 630–7700; www.wabashbbq.com.

LODGING: The historic **Elms Resort and Spa,** 401 Regent (800–THE–ELMS), with its massive limestone exterior and huge rooftop sign THE ELMS, will be your stop tonight. It is about a half block north of the restaurant. Not only does the hotel offer luxurious rooms, but it also has a spa and wellness center, which offers such services as massage, body wraps, yoga, meditation, and hydrotherapy, to mention just a few. You should make reservations in advance if you plan to use these services. Room rates start at $119 a night; package plans are also available, which start at $225 per night. The hotel's wooded sixteen acres include a pool and hiking and biking trails. www.elmsresort.com.

The hotel has hosted several famous guests in its history, including Franklin Roosevelt, Marilyn Monroe, and Al Capone (Capone would gamble in what is now the hotel conference room while his henchman kept a watch out for an ambush). Harry Truman stayed in the hotel the night of his famous presidential victory in 1948. www.elmsresort.com.

Day 2 / Morning

BREAKFAST: Enjoy a relaxing breakfast in the **Elms Hotel Dining Room** before checking out. Delicious French toast, perfect egg dishes, and a beautiful fruit plate are but a few choices to enjoy.

Your trip to Excelsior Springs would not be complete without a stop at the **Hall of Waters,** 201 East Broadway. Built in 1937 through the Works Progress Administration, this Art Deco building, with its terrazzo floors and Mayan decor, was built to be the best and most complete health resort in the country by using the water from the springs throughout the town. People came from all over the country to relax and heal in the waters. Now you can get a variety of spa packages and spend the day being pampered and cleansed. The hall also houses the World's Longest Water Bar, where you can choose from dozens of exotic waters such as "Glacier," "AME," or "Elderflower," and other mineral waters from around the

The Hall of Waters, Excelsior Springs

world, or you can buy beautiful soaps and other spa goodies. Open Monday through Friday 9:00 A.M. to 5:00 P.M., Saturday and Sunday 10:00 A.M. to 5:00 P.M.; (816) 630–0753.

The **Olde Towne District** features many unique antiques and specialty shops, such as the **Enchanted Frog** and the **Olde English Garden Shop.** Don't miss visiting the **Excelsior Springs Historical Museum,** located in the former Clay County Bank Building (101 East Broadway), for a look at many early-twentieth-century household items, such as clothes and dishes, and business offices that include a reconstructed dentist's office. Open Monday through Friday 10:00 A.M. to 4:00 P.M. Tours by appointment. (816) 630–0101.

LUNCH: Before leaving town, grab a burger at **Ray's Lunch,** 231 East Broadway (816–637–3432), an Art Deco–styled diner from the 1920s complete with black-and-white tile floor. The menu is good, but observe the locals. They know about items not listed, such as the breakfast Garbage Sandwich—your choice of ham, bacon, or sausage with crispy hash browns, eggs, and cheese on a grilled hamburger bun—or the bacon double cheeseburger. Breakfast, Monday through Friday 6:00 to 11:00 A.M.;

lunch, 11:00 A.M. to 2:00 P.M. Open at 7:00 A.M. Saturday. Closed Sunday. Under $10.

Afternoon

Leave Excelsior Springs by way of Highway 92 and follow it for about 35 miles until it intersects with Highway 273. Turn north and drive 5 miles to **Weston,** another historic river town that thrived until a flood in 1881 changed the course of the Missouri River. Early-twentieth-century homes and businesses now dot the hills above the floodplain.

For serious antiquing, Weston is the place for both primitive and imported antiques. Such stores as **D.B.s Antiques, Currant Cottage, Doppler's Mercantile,** or many others along Main Street will keep you occupied for hours. Want to look at some unusual clothing or footwear? Try **Missouri Bluffs Boutique and Gallery.** For primitive country-folk art, look into **Stitches and Stems** for locally made items such as herb racks, wreaths, and dolls.

For a bit of Weston History, tour the **Weston Historical Museum,** 601 Main Street (816–386–2977), founded in 1960. Exhibits cover periods including slavery, the Civil War, and westward expansion. Open from 1:00 to 4:00 P.M. Monday through Saturday and 1:30 to 5:00 P.M. Sunday. Closed Monday, holidays, and during January and February. No admission.

If you've worked up a thirst walking up and down Main Street, check out **Pirtle's Winery,** 502 Spring Street. Located in a historic church, Pirtle's has a wide variety of delicious wines you can sample while eating bits of tasty French bread to "cleanse the palate." If something sweet sounds better, pop into the **Sweet Suite,** 511 Main Street, for ice cream, soft drinks, homemade fudge, and other candies and specialties.

DINNER: It may be an 1847 antebellum house, but the decor at **The Avalon,** 608 Main Street (816–640–2835), belies its heritage. A glossy hardwood floor, a few eclectic art pieces on the walls, and crisp white tablecloths on the tables give you a hint of the unusual menu. Applewood grilled meats, fresh seafood, and pasta—plus such dishes as wild boar, ostrich, and elk—make this an interesting experience. Moderate to expensive. Open Tuesday through Saturday 11:00 A.M. to 3:00 P.M.; dinner seatings 5:30 to 9:00 P.M.; Sunday lunch, noon to 4:00 P.M.; dinner, 4:00 to 7:00 P.M. Reservations recommended for dinner.

LODGING: You may have to backtrack about twenty minutes, but a night at the **Dome Ridge Bed and Breakfast** is worth it. Drive out of Weston following Highway 92 about 15 miles to Highway C. Turn right on C, follow to Martin Road, and turn on Martin. Martin Road will become Northwest Walker Road. Turn left to 14360 Walker Road. This B&B is a geodesic dome nestled in seventeen acres of woods. If you're lucky, you can sit on the deck and see all manner of wildlife such as raccoons, possum, and deer up close. Amenities include a gazebo with a barbecue grill, a hot tub, a pool table, and a movie library with more than 200 titles. Four bedrooms with private baths. Rates: $70 to $95. No smoking or children. (816) 532–4074; www.bbim.org/domeridge.html.

Day 3 / Morning

BREAKFAST: At the Dome Ridge B&B. Owners Roberta and Bill Faust don't scrimp on breakfast, so bring your appetites to the table. Sausages, frozen fruit (a whipped, frozen strawberry fruit mold with chunks of fresh fruit), and their special Belgian waffles—with a secret ingredient that makes them the lightest ever—will hold you for more than a few hours.

Check out by 10:00 A.M. for the trip to St. Joseph. To get to St. Joseph, go back to Highway C. At Highway 92 turn left to I–29, then go north 30 miles to St. Joseph. The first stop is the **Stetson Factory Outlet Store,** 3601 South Leonard; (816) 233–3286. Since 1865 Stetson has been making hats that have been worn by celebrities from Hopalong Cassidy and Roy Rogers to Harrison Ford and John Wayne. Watch the video depicting the entire process; then browse among the hundreds of hats for sale.

The Glore Psychiatric Museum, 3406 Frederick Avenue (816–387–2310), assures a tour out of the ordinary. Occupying the grounds of the original 1872 State Lunatic Asylum No. 2, which is now a prison, the museum chronicles, through displays and dioramas, such early forms of treatment as dunking, bleeding, blistering, and other bizarre notions of psychiatric care, as well as present-day therapies. See the surgical instruments used for lobotomies and lobectomies as well as electric-shock equipment. Open Monday through Saturday 9:00 A.M. to 5:00 P.M. and Sunday 1:00 to 5:00 P.M. Free admission.

LUNCH: The Belt Brewery, 2317 North Belt (816–676–2739), offers burgers and sandwiches, along with meat loaf with garlic mashed potatoes, barbecued pulled pork, and steaks and chops. The hot wheat bread and honey butter brought to every table is especially nice. Brewery tours are also an option. Under $10.

Afternoon

This will be an afternoon of museum hopping. At the **Pony Express Museum,** 914 Penn Street (816–279–5059), see a film of how the Pony Express began and then track the riders' journey from St. Joseph to Sacramento, California, through deserts and mountains. See the dangers that awaited them and a relay station where they changed horses. Open Monday through Saturday 9:00 A.M. to 5:00 P.M., Sunday 1:00 to 5:00 P.M. Admission: adults, $4.00; seniors, $3.00; students seven to eighteen, $1.50; children six and under, free.

Next, stop at the **Jesse James Home Museum,** Twelfth and Penn Streets (816–232–8206), where Jesse met his demise. Walk through the little cabin, see the alleged bullet hole in the wall from Jesse's death, and his death picture. Open June through August, Monday through Saturday 10:00 A.M. to 5:00 P.M. and Sunday 1:00 to 5:00 P.M.; September through May, Monday through Saturday 10:00 A.M. to 4:00 P.M. and Sunday 1:00 to 4:00 P.M. Admission: adults, $2.00; students eighteen and under, $1.00; and seniors, $1.50.

Plan to spend at least an hour and a half to two hours in the remarkable **Patee House Museum,** Twelfth and Penn Streets; (816) 232–8206. The actual headquarters of the Pony Express, it was originally the Hotel Patee House. Two floors feature such exhibits as "The Streets of Old St. Jo," including a dental office, a general store, a jail (complete with artifacts of murder and mayhem), a barber shop, horse-drawn carriages, old Model Ts, a locomotive, and antique fire trucks. Have some sarsaparilla in the 1854 Buffalo Saloon. April to October: Monday through Saturday 10:00 A.M. to 5:00 P.M. and Sunday 1:00 to 5:00 P.M.; weekends only November and January through March; closed December. Admission: adults, $3.00; seniors, $2.50; students eighteen and under, $1.50.

Housed in an 1879 Gothic mansion, the **St. Joseph Museum,** 1100 St. Charles Street (816–232–8471), offers an internationally famous Native American collection along with St. Joseph and Midwest natural history. Children will enjoy the many hands-on exhibits and a Touch and Go Room, where they can climb into a fort and play in a tepee. The museum has three floors of exhibits guaranteed to make you linger. Open Monday through Saturday 9:00 A.M. to 5:00 P.M. and Sunday 1:00 to 5:00 P.M.

Admission: adults, $2.00; students seven through eighteen, $1.00; children six and under, free.

DINNER: For a touch of Cajun food in northwest Missouri, **Boudreaux's,** 224 North Fourth Street (816-387-8183), featuring authentic Louisiana cuisine in the heart of downtown in historic Warehouse Row, is the place to go. Start your dinner with fried alligator in a cream-style gravy (Yum! $6.95) or crab bisque ($4.95 for a bowl). Boudin, crawfish boulettes, gumbo, red beans and rice, shrimp étoufée, oysters Boudreaux—what to choose? Dinners range from $8.95 to $17.95, with most in between.

LODGING: A showcase of the Midwest, the **Shakespeare Château Bed & Breakfast,** 809 Hall Street (888–414–4944), will make you feel like royalty. The 1885 Victorian mansion features forty stained-glass windows, Zuber murals, and classic antiques. Wine and hors d'oeuvres await you on your arrival, and Jacuzzis are available for those sore legs. Seven uniquely furnished rooms with private baths. Smoking permitted outside. Children welcome in specified rooms. No pets. Rates: $110 to $175. www.shakespearechateau.com.

Day 4 / Morning

BREAKFAST: At the Shakespeare Château. In a house such as this, would you expect less than an above-average breakfast? Yours could include Fanciful French Toast, fruit, juice, and muffins served in the large dining room with soft music playing in the background. The perfect place to visit and make new friends.

Before checking out, tour the rest of the **Hall Street Historic District** between Sixth and Ninth Streets. The Hall Street area became the city's first Historic District in 1974 and is listed on the National Register of Historic Places. Commanding a majestic view of the city and the Missouri River, the Hall Street homes symbolize the prosperity and optimism of St. Joseph's golden age.

Nearby is the **Robidoux Row Museum,** Third and Poulin; (816) 232–5861. Built in 1843 by Joseph Robidoux, the founder of St. Joseph, to help meet the needs for temporary housing during the pioneer period, the building now includes exhibits featuring Robidoux family history and early St. Joseph history, as well as several rooms restored to illustrate their original purpose. Rates: adults, $2.00; children twelve to eighteen, 50 cents; children twelve and under, free. Call for hours.

If you have time, another interesting attraction is the **Albrecht-Kemper Museum,** 2818 Frederick Boulevard; (816) 233–7003. This museum houses one of the finest collections of eighteenth-, nineteenth-, and twentieth-century American art in the Midwest, with more than 1,300 works. It hosts traveling exhibitions of local, regional, and national significance throughout the year. Rates: adults, $3.00; students thirteen to eighteen, $1.00. Hours: 10:00 A.M. to 4:00 P.M. Tuesday to Friday; 1:00 to 4:00 P.M. Saturday and Sunday. Closed Monday and federal holidays.

After your sight-seeing, head east on Frederick Street. You have a two-hour drive until lunch, so you might want a mid-morning snack. Stop at the **Golden 'n' Glaze Donut Shop,** 1825 Frederick; (816) 232–3568. This shop has been in St. Joseph for many, many years and offers only five or six varieties of doughnuts—but oh, so good. A sack will hold you in good stead on your drive to Macon for lunch.

Stay on Frederick Street, until I–29. Go south to US–36 and then go west.

Marceline, the hometown of **Walt Disney,** is about 120 miles from St. Joseph. Disney's boyhood home is privately owned, and any tours need to be arranged with the family. For more information call Tour Marceline at (660) 376–2332.

LUNCH: The **Long Branch Restaurant** is just off US–36 before you get into Macon. Any place with oilskin tablecloths is usually good, and this one is no different. The Sunday buffet included roast beef, ham, turkey, and fried chicken with all the trimmings. Also hot tenderloin and roast-beef sandwiches. Nothing more than $10 and well worth a stop. (660) 385–4600.

Hannibal is 65 miles from Macon on US–36. Once there, turn south on US–61 for the 115-mile drive home. There are many places along the way for rest stops.

There's More

Excelsior Springs

Excelsior Springs Golf Course, 1201 East Golf Hill Drive; (816) 630–3731. An eighteen-hole golf course featuring two lakes and natural hazards. Designed with the help of a Scottish pro who believed in hitting over lakes and woods, the course is a challenge. A bonus is the Log Cabin. Built in 1835, the golf clubhouse was just built around it, and the room looks exactly as it was left, complete with snowshoes over the fireplace. The Battle of Fredericksburg was fought during the Civil War in 1864 on the fourteenth green (before the golf course was built). Greens fees: weekdays before 3:00 P.M., $19; after 3:00 P.M., $14; weekends before 5:00 P.M., $23; after 5:00 P.M., $14.

The Paradise Playhouse Dinner Theatre, 101 Spring Street; (816) 630–3333. Decorated in a Polynesian theme, this dinner playhouse is situated right in the heart of downtown Excelsior Springs—3 blocks from the Elms Resort & Spa. Cabaret-style tables in four-tiered levels. Dinner includes an ever-changing buffet with a full-service bar. Shows on Friday and Saturday nights and Sunday afternoons. An occasional "Just Desserts" Thursday-evening performance is also available. Tickets range from $23 to $25 per person.

Watkins Mill State Park and State Historic Site, Watkins Woolen Mill; (816) 296–3357. The mill is the country's only nineteenth-century textile factory with the original machinery, including a gristmill. The village origi-nally included the Watkins home, a school, and a church, most of which have been restored. Open Monday to Saturday 10:00 A.M. to 4:00 P.M. and Sunday 11:00 A.M. to 5:00 P.M. Tours are $2.50 for adults, $1.50 for chil-dren ages six through twelve; children under six are free.

St. Joseph

Antiquing. St. Joseph has a plethora of antiques shops. Some of the stores are close to one another, such as the 15th and Penn Antique Center, 1505 Penn Street (816–232–0045), open Monday through Friday 10:00 A.M. to 4:00 P.M., most Saturdays, and by appointment; Penn Street Square, 1122 Penn Street (816–232–4626), open Monday through Saturday 9:00 A.M. to 5:00 P.M. and Sunday, 1:00 to 5:00 P.M.; and The Corner Shoppe, 1503 Penn Street (816–232–0045), open Monday through Friday 10:00 A.M. to 4:00 P.M.

Cool Crest Garden Golf, 1400 North Belt; (816) 232–2663. Play minia-ture golf in tranquil flower gardens amid sculptures, waterfalls, and nostal-gic music to create a relaxing experience for the family. Rate: $3.50 per person. Open Monday through Saturday 10:00 A.M. to 10:00 P.M. and Sunday noon to 10:00 P.M.

Historic Home Tour. Call the St. Joseph Convention and Visitors Bureau; (816) 233–6688.

Twin Spires Museum, 501 South Tenth Street; (816) 233–2988. The twin-spired building contains beautiful stained-glass windows from Austria that are embedded 18 inches into the walls. The partially burned Jewish Torah on display was found by Allied Forces in a warehouse at the end of World War II. Open 9:00 A.M. to 1:00 P.M. Monday through Friday and Sunday noon to 4:00 P.M. Admission: adults, $2.00; $2.50 for guided tour.

Weston

Red Barn Farm, 16300 Wilkerson Road; (816) 386–KIDS. Children love this working farm with all the required animals such as chickens and cows. Strawberries to pick in summer, apples and pumpkins in fall. Open spring through fall.

Snow Creek Ski Area, 1 Snow Creek Drive (off Highway 45); (816) 640–2200. Snowboarders and skiers alike will enjoy the twelve trails for all ability levels. Midnight skiing on Friday and Saturday.

Vaughn's Orchard & Country Store, 23200 Highway 273; (816) 386–2900. Have a picnic, take a wagon ride, and enjoy the apples and pumpkins. Gift store with apple-related items among other specialties for all ages.

Special Events

March. Annual Antique Show and Sale. Weston. A variety of antiques along with vintage clothing, dolls, quilts, glassware, books, and more. This show has a reputation of being one of the premier shows in Missouri. Dealers from other states bring their finest items to Weston with select primitives and other fine antiques. Contact (888) 635–7457.

Missouri State Championship Chili Challenge. St. Joseph. Held in St. Joseph Civic Arena, downtown; (816) 364–3836. Sample chili made by professional and amateur cooks from all over the region. Also flea markets and live music.

May. The Gatsby Festival. Excelsior Springs. Hot jazz, cool blues, and flappers. Vintage movies, a style show, and an art show are only part of this annual festival. Includes a "Fly-in" at the Excelsior Springs airport with a pancake breakfast; blues at the Wabash BBQ; dance at The Elms; booths, vendors, and art at the water bar and on the street. Car show and kids games as well as other music and entertainment. Call (888) 811–0753.

June. Sacred Hills Encampment. St. Joseph. Visit the rugged days of yes-teryear and learn about the region's Native American heritage at this encampment with living history, storytelling, and music. Krug Park. (816) 271–5500.

July. Fourth of July Festival. Excelsior Springs. The second-largest fireworks display north of the Missouri River. All-day town picnic with games, food, and music. Held at the Excelsior Springs High School, 612 Tiger Drive; (816) 630–6161.

August. St. Patrick's Fiesta. St. Joseph. St. Patrick's Catholic Church, downtown; (816) 279–2594. A queen coronation dance starts off this weekend of fun, which includes a midway and booths with American and Mexican food.

Trails West. St. Joseph. Civic Center Park, downtown; (800) 216–7080. St. Joseph's biggest art festival celebrating the city's cultural heritage. Fine art, folk art, stage performances, and historical reenactments, plus music and food.

September. Southside Fall Festival Roundup, Hyde Park and Alabama Streets, St. Joseph; (816) 238–3515. This festival includes a rodeo, food booths, crafts, entertainment, and a grand parade with more than 2,000 people taking part.

Waterfest. Excelsior Springs. Fall festival held downtown and featuring a Watershed program geared toward water education. A healthy-living edu-cational program will also be featured. Entertainment, music, arts, crafts, and more. Contact the chamber of commerce, (816) 630–6161 or (866) 730–6161.

October. Applefest. Weston. The traditional old-fashioned celebration of the harvest and lost arts. Folk artists demonstrate and sell their wares on Main Street. Artists display their handcrafted woven baskets, willow and barn-wood furniture, pottery, dried-flower arrangements, quilts, and more. There's also a garden market and special demonstrations by apple-butter and cider makers, blacksmiths, and hay balers. Food, drinks and, of course, apple dumplings, are offered, as well as entertainment. Contact (888) 635–7457.

Pony Express Pumpkinfest. St. Joseph. The free fall family arts festival includes live entertainment, children's costume parade, festival rides, pumpkin games, and food. Don't miss the lighting of the "Great Pumpkin

Mountain." Hundreds of carved and electrically lit pumpkins will magically come to life on the Friday night of the fest. Pony Express Museum, (816) 279–5059 or (800) 530–5930; www.ponyexpress.org.

November through December. Month-long Christmas celebration. Excelsior Springs. The festivities start with the mayor's tree-lighting ceremony the Thursday before Thanksgiving. Christmas trees decorated by area businesses fill the Hall of Waters.

December. Mineral Water Bowl. Excelsior Springs. A football game between two regional teams held the first Saturday in December. Festivities start the day before, then a parade the morning of the game with the game in the afternoon. Roosevelt Field, 101 Richmond Avenue; (888) 630–6161.

Other Recommended Restaurants and Lodgings

Excelsior Springs

The Broadway Creamery & Deli, 115 West Broadway; (816) 630–0322. Stop in for a deli sandwich and a scoop of handmade ice cream. We recommend the meatball sandwich on homemade bread with cheese cooked into the bread ($3.59). Make it a combo with chips for $5.39. Open Tuesday to Saturday 11:00 A.M. to 5:00 P.M.

The Inn on Crescent Lake, 1261 St. Louis Avenue; (816) 630–6745. Owned by two graduates of the French Culinary Institute in New York, this 1915 renovated Georgian colonial mansion gives the appearance of being on a peninsula since it is surrounded by two lakes. Swimming pool, exercise room, and paddle boats. Evening meals are available if specified when making reservations. Six rooms, two suites, all with private baths. Rates: $115 to $250 per night. Children over sixteen welcome. No pets. Smoking outside only. www.crescentinn.com.

Lakeview Country Inn Bed & Breakfast, 15940 Y Highway, 3 miles northeast of Excelsior Springs; (816) 630-0565. Situated in an Ozark setting on forty acres, this inn includes a fully stocked five-acre pond, paddle boats, horse stables, a reception area for weddings, a Jacuzzi, an in-ground pool, abundant wildlife, and two private rooms with indoor and outdoor entrances. Rates: $125 and $165, with a Hall of Waters Spa Package available for an additional $95.

The Mill Inn, 415 St. Louis; (816) 637–8008. A local standby serving family-style food with daily specials such as ham and beans. Famous for their cinnamon rolls (get there quick!), bread pudding, and mile-high pies. Under $10.

The Monterey Motel, Highway 10 and Concourse; (816) 637–3171. Kitchenettes and one-bedroom suites starting at $55.

Lexington

Graystone Bed & Breakfast, 324 South Twenty-fifth Street; (660) 259–7775. Built from 1833 to 1836, this lovely old antebellum home is one of the oldest in Lexington. Furnished in period antiques and reproductions, this five-room home will make you feel a part of another time. Rates are $75 per night and an additional $25 for children.

The Parsonage Bed & Breakfast, 1601 South Street; (660) 259–2344. A cafe area where you can sit and socialize over cappuccino or tea and a hot tub make this three-bedroom home a comfortable place to rest your head. Rates: $75 to $85. Children welcome. No smoking or pets.

St. Joseph

Fredrick Inn Steakhouse, 1627 Frederick; (816) 364–5151. Casual family atmosphere with chicken, steaks, chops, and exceptional prime rib with twice-baked potato. Prices under $20.

Jerre Anne Cafeteria & Bakery, 2640 Mitchell; (816) 232–6585. A St. Joseph institution since 1930, Jerre Anne's reputation has spread far beyond the Missouri state line. Famous for home-cooked pies, pastries, breads, and cakes made fresh daily. Open Tuesday through Saturday 11:00 A.M. to 7:00 P.M. Under $10.

River Towne Resort, 4012 River Road; (816) 364–6500. A romantic getaway on the Missouri River. Cottages include kitchenettes, massive stone fireplaces, Jacuzzi tubs for two. Furniture made from native logs by local craftspeople. No pets. Rates: $90 to $145. Sunset Grille Restaurant on premises; (816) 364–6500. Famous for River Towne catfish and prime rib. Also, lunch with soups, salads, and sandwiches. Moderate prices.

Weston

American Bowman Restaurant, 500 Welt Street; (816) 640–5235. Weston's oldest restaurant offers mid-nineteenth-century atmosphere and classic food such as an Irish Carvery, where you choose an entree such as ham, turkey, or corned beef. You get six vegetables, a salad, and bread. Prices range from $7.25 to $14.95. If you're not that hungry, sandwiches and soups are available. Open for lunch Tuesday through Friday 11:30 A.M. to 3:00 P.M. and for dinner 5:00 to 9:00 P.M.; open Saturday 11:30 A.M. to 9:00 P.M. and Sunday 11:30 A.M. to 6:00 P.M.; closed Monday. Moderate.

Benner House, 645 Main Street; (816) 640-2616. Get lost in the past in this "steamboat gothic" B&B with a wraparound porch from which guests can view bluffs on the Kansas side of the Missouri River. Get acquainted with other guests in the parlor, then stroll Weston's historic streets. Four guest rooms with private baths. No smoking, children, or pets. Rates: Friday, Saturday, and holidays, $120; Sunday, $90.

The Hatchery House, 618 Short Street; (816) 640–5700. Built in the 1850s, this house was converted into a boardinghouse in the 1930s. With its inexpensive prices, it was popular with newlyweds and young couples. The name came from the many children who were conceived (or hatched) in the house! Enjoy a glass of wine and hors d'oeuvres before dinner. In the morning the two-course breakfast includes Hatchery House Coffee with home-baked breads. Four bedrooms, one suite. Rates: $100 to $140. No pets. Smoking outside only. Inquire about policy on children.

The Lemon Tree Bed & Breakfast, 407 Washington Street; (816) 386–5367. Located across the old millstream from the historic district, this cheerful and bright bed-and-breakfast provides a hot tub, swimming pool, and spa in a three-story antebellum home connected by multilevel decks. Guests are welcomed with a meat, cheese, and fruit platter and a bottle of wine. Sample from the evening dessert bar with goodies like cream puffs, cheesecake, and fudge. Fresh coffee and homemade muffins are delivered to your door in the morning; a bountiful breakfast, such as pork chops and eggs or ham and egg strata, is served in the dining room. Three bedrooms with private baths. No pets. Children over thirteen welcome. Smoking permitted outside. Rate: $160.

The Vineyards, 505 Spring Street; (816) 640–5588. Located across the street from Pirtle's Winery, this restaurant offers an eclectic menu at moderate prices, such as garden green salad with almonds and blue cheese, rosemary potatoes, open-face Cajun pork tenderloin or linguini with chicken, artichokes, and sun-dried tomatoes. Open for lunch Wednesday to Saturday 11:00 A.M. to 2:00 P.M.; dinner from 6:00 to 8:30 P.M. Open on Sunday for brunch 11:00 A.M. to 4:00 P.M. and early dinner from 4:00 to 7:00 P.M. Reservations recommended.

Weston Cafe, 405 Main Street; (816) 640–5558. A typical small town cafe offering home-style cooking at good prices. Open Monday to Thursday 6:00 A.M. to 9:00 P.M., Friday and Saturday 11:00 A.M. to 10:00 P.M., and Sunday 2:00 to 6:00 P.M.

For More Information

Excelsior Springs Chamber of Commerce, 101 East Broadway, Excelsior Springs, MO 64024; (816) 630–6161 or (800) 730–6161; escoc@epsi.net; www.exsmo.com.

Lexington Heritage Tours; (660) 259–2094.

Lexington Tourism Bureau, 1029 Franklin Avenue, Lexington, MO 64067; (660) 259–4711; www.historiclexington.com.

St. Joseph Convention and Visitors Bureau, 109 South Fourth Street, St. Joseph, MO 64502; (800) 785–0360; www.stjomo.com.

Weston Development Company, 502 Main Street, Weston, MO 64098; (888) 635–7457; http://ci.weston.mo.us.

WESTERN
ESCAPES

WESTERN ESCAPE ONE

St. Charles, Missouri

The Little Hills / 1 Night

St. Charles is a charming city on the Missouri River that has been welcoming visitors since 1769. The city was founded by French Canadian fur trader Louis Blanchette and was named Les Petites Côtes ("The Little Hills").

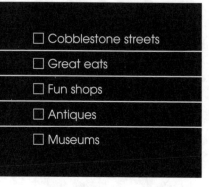

- ☐ Cobblestone streets
- ☐ Great eats
- ☐ Fun shops
- ☐ Antiques
- ☐ Museums

The town grew into an important trading center for countless pioneers because of its strategic location on the Missouri River and its entrance to the western territory known as the Louisiana Purchase. In 1804 William Clark and Meriwether Lewis departed up the Missouri River seeking the way to the Pacific Ocean. They would return to St. Charles two years later on their way to their journey's end in St. Louis. St. Charles is filled to the brim with rich history that also includes being Missouri's first state capital, the origin of the Boone's Lick Trail, as well as home to Daniel Boone. Many people who call St. Charles home have worked diligently to preserve its past while welcoming the present. They now welcome you as their guests.

Day 1 / Morning

Getting to St. Charles is easy. Head west on Highway 70 to the Fifth Street exit and go north, which will be a right turn. Take a right on Boone's Lick and go a few blocks until you reach Main Street. If you're closer to Highway 40, you can get to St. Charles and Main Street by heading west on Highway 40 and exiting onto Highway 94 going north, which will be a right turn. Continue on Highway 94 all the way until you cross over Highway 70. After you've crossed over Highway 70, take a right onto Boone's Lick, which will lead you directly to Main Street. You can either make a left on Main Street and find street parking or continue on Boone's Lick, which curves around to the back side of the shops, parallel to the

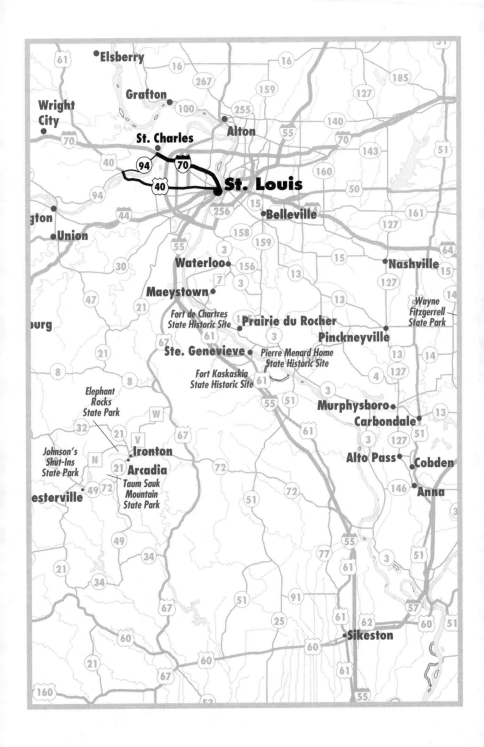

river, where you'll find a number of parking lots. From downtown St. Louis the trip should take about twenty-five minutes. You'll want to arrive in St. Charles around 10:00 A.M. since that's when most shops along Main Street open.

The first thing most people want to do when they come to Old St. Charles is browse and shop. Main Street, which is divided into South Main Street and North Main Street, is chock full of fun little shops specializing in a whole range of things, including crafts and gift items, jewelry, specialty foods, garden accessories, and everything in between. Starting at the southern end of Main Street, there are many shops worth seeing. **Laura's LaPetite,** 709 South Main Street (636–724–4207), is filled with country gifts and primitives from bears to wooden boxes, as well as some jewelry. Need a little pick-me-up? Try a sample of the delicious dips and spreads found at **Main Street Marketplace,** 708 South Main Street; (636) 940–8626. Craving a veggie dip, flavored cream cheese, muffin, or cookie mix? How about kitchen tools and home accessories? If so, you'll find it here. It's almost impossible not to run across something great tasting that you absolutely need to take home. Perhaps your tastes lean toward the more refined. If you're missing your proper British tea or just can't find those great little biscuits you had when you were in London, there's a good chance **The English Shop** has it; it's located at 703 South Main Street; (636) 946–2245.

Next, meander down to **The Flower Petaler,** 620 South Main Street; (636) 946–3048. With more than a dozen rooms filled with silk floral arrangements, home accessories, and art, this place has nearly everything floral you could imagine. And if you don't find exactly what you want, the shop's designers will custom-make whatever it is you need. Stop at **String Along with Me** if jewelry is your thing. This store has the best selection of sterling silver charms you've ever seen, as well as beads, accessories, and fashion and designer jewelry. They also do repair work and custom designs. String Along with Me is located at 523 South Main Street; (636) 947–7740.

Next, treat yourself to something truly beautiful. **The Haviland Museum,** 625 South Main Street (636–925–0745), is home to the largest museum (and the only museum in the United States) of Haviland china from Limoges, France. For more than 150 years, Haviland has been making stunningly beautiful china place settings and accessories including some specially commissioned for United States presidents. Here's your chance to view some of the most exquisite pieces from a private collection that numbers more than 8,000. Donna Hafer, owner of the collection and an expert on Haviland china, gives a wonderful educational tour that includes a look at a set of Haviland china that once belonged to Judy Garland, a commemorative Veiled Prophet plaque, and an extremely rare tea set that dates from the 1850s. Tours, which cost $2.00, are conducted Tuesdays and Thursdays at 11:30 A.M., 12:30 P.M., and 1:30 P.M. Donna encourages people to come visit the museum, located in a Victorian-era home, and is more than happy to show her collection at other times or days by appointment. Please note: Due to the delicate nature of the china and because none of the pieces is in a display case, the museum is generally not suited for small children.

LUNCH: Magpie's, 903 South Main Street; (636) 947–3883. Swing back down the street to this little cafe that's known for its outstanding potato soup. A nice selection of sandwiches and salads rounds out the cafe's offerings. Open daily 11:00 A.M. to 3:00 P.M., until 9:00 P.M. on Friday and Saturday. Inexpensive.

Afternoon

Farther down South Main Street is **The Homestead,** 407 South Main Street (636–946–2700), and its companion store, **The Homestead Too,** 401 South Main Street. The Homestead offers colonial, country, and primitive accessories, crafts, and some furniture. The Homestead Too is where you'll find kitchen gadgets, gourmet foods, and kitchen decor.

Continue down South Main Street to **Patches Quilt & Shoppe,** 339 South Main Street; (636) 946–6004. Stop in to browse the wonderful selection of quilt fabrics and patterns. The handiwork of these talented quilters is outstanding—so much so, you may decide to sign up for a quilting class yourself. **Holiday House,** 329 South Main Street (636–946–0007), is the place for any and all types of Christmas ornaments year-round. They have a wonderful collection of old German-style glass ornaments as well as a variety of collectibles. **Pop's General Store,** 322 South Main Street (636–723–6040), has an old-fashioned general-store atmosphere and specializes in antiques, old and reproduction signs, gifts, and candy. **The Glass Workbench,** 318 South Main Street (636–946–2002), has a beautiful collection of handcrafted stained-glass items and offers classes, along with supplies, if you're interested in making stained-glass items yourself. Next door is **Tiffany Garden,** 314 South Main Street; (636) 946–4539. The shop is filled with Victorian garden accessories, charming gifts, and practical gardening items. The seasonal outdoor flower market always has something unusual worth adding to your garden. If you or someone you know likes bears, **The Bear Factory,** 307 South Main Street (636–940–0047), is where you'll find an outstanding collection of bears, bear accessories, and other collectibles.

Take a break from shopping for a tour of the **First State Capitol of Missouri,** 200–216 South Main Street; (636) 940–3322. Tours are given Monday through Saturday 9:00 A.M. to 4:00 P.M. and Sunday 11:00 A.M. to 5:00 P.M. From 1821 to 1826 the state legislature met in St. Charles. These two legislative buildings have been restored and furnished to that time period for visitors to get a first-hand look at life in St. Charles at the turn of the nineteenth century. The cost of the tour is $2.50 for adults, $1.50 for kids six through twelve, and free for kids under six.

After the tour, stop in the **Visitor's Center** at 230 South Main Street (636–946–7776) and pick up a brochure of the walking tour of Frenchtown for use tomorrow. The Visitor's Center is open Monday through Friday 8:00 A.M. to 5:00 P.M., Saturday 10:00 A.M. to 5:00 P.M., and Sunday noon to 5:00 P.M.

DINNER: Bonaparte's Brasserie, 140 North Main Street; (636) 940–WINE. Start with a basis of Country French cooking, jazz it up with a Spanish influence. Add a relaxed atmosphere in a charming historic building and a glass or two of wine from an inventive wine list. The result? No doubt, one of the best meals you've had in a long time. Start with an appetizer of garlic shrimp or mushrooms Bonaparte (mushrooms stuffed with sun-dried tomatoes, artichokes, and green peppercorns, and topped with a roasted-garlic cream sauce). Excellent salad choices include a spinach salad with warm bacon dressing or goat cheese salad topped with breaded goat cheese, pine nuts, and walnut vinaigrette. Entrees include a wonderfully flavorful salmon lasagna with spinach, tomato, and a lemon-butter sauce; filet mignon with blue cheese; oven-roasted quail; and chicken breast with a raspberry-mustard cream sauce. The waiters are friendly and knowledgeable and don't rush you out the door. Plan on taking your time and enjoying the food and atmosphere. Moderate to expensive.

Evening

After dinner, walk a few blocks toward the First State Capitol, where you'll often find **horse-drawn carriages.** A twenty-minute ride around Main Street is $25 and a forty-minute ride about $35. The clomp-clomping of the horses' hooves on the cobblestone pavement can't help but make you slow down and think of what life was like on this historic street many years ago.

LODGING: The Old Elm Tree Inn, 1717 Elm Street; (636) 947–4843; www. oldelmtreeinn.com. Located in a historic district within a few blocks from Lindenwood University, and just a five-minute drive from Main Street, The Old Elm Tree Inn is a restored 1904 Victorian home with three bedroom suites, each with private bath. Nestled among shade trees and a delightful garden complete with gazebo, the inn is a welcome retreat after a long day of sightseeing. Owner Martha Kooyumjian, a native of St. Charles, welcomes you with light refreshments and a tour of the inn. Suites include the Rose Suite, the Bridal Suite, and the World's Fair Suite, in honor of the 1904 World's Fair held in St. Louis. The home is decorated in the traditional Victorian style but has been completely updated to include modern conveniences such as cable TV and in-room phones as well as minirefrigerators with complimentary refreshments. Rates range from $95 to $130.

Day 2 / Morning

BREAKFAST: The Old Elm Tree Inn. A typical breakfast includes fresh fruit, eggs Benedict, pan-fried candied bacon, warm lemon bread, fresh-squeezed orange juice, coffee, and tea. Breakfast is served in the dining room on wonderful flowery china with linen napkins and sterling silver. Everything is deliciously prepared, and Martha makes sure no one goes away hungry.

After breakfast, linger around the inn and relax on the porch swing or take a stroll in the garden. Head up toward Lindenwood University, one of the oldest schools west of the Mississippi, for a walk around the grounds. The entrance is just 2 blocks from the inn. If you prefer, you can start your **walking or driving tour of historic Frenchtown,** which is primarily clustered at the north end of Main and Second Streets. Exit the inn onto Kingshighway and go right. Go left on First Capitol. At Second Street go left. The first French colonial home is located at 619 North Second Street, and the majority are clustered within a 3-block area. For detailed information about the homes, pick up the *French Colonial Architecture Historic Tour* brochure at the Visitor's Center located at 230 South Main Street. According to the Visitor's Center's brochure, "the vernacular French colonial style house design so unique to the Frenchtown area of St. Charles is defined by a front or rear gallery (porch), a raised basement, a laterally lined floor plan, and a double-pitched hip room. The original village had no business district, since the French used their private homes for business affairs. The architecture of Frenchtown is distinguished by its German-built (later immigrants) brick renditions of the French colonial style."

Plan on spending extra time on North Second Street. This area of Frenchtown is the hub of the antiques district and includes such shops as **French Connection Antiques,** 826 North Second Street (636–947–7044), which offers quality antique and semiantique furniture. They also offer reupholstering and refinishing of your existing furniture. There are half a dozen blocks' worth of interesting shops to browse. Most open at 10:00 A.M. Monday through Saturday and noon on Sunday. Closing time for most shops is 5:00 P.M. Some shops are closed Tuesday and Wednesday.

LUNCH: Little Hills Winery, 501 South Main Street; (636) 946–6637 or (877) LT–HILLS. Rest your weary feet and have a glass of Missouri wine at this delightful restaurant. The Winery serves a variety of salads and sandwiches along with some great appetizers worth trying. Start your meal with the baked Brie with almonds. This wedge of delectable melting cheese is served with a loaf of French bread and is absolutely mouthwatering. The Missouri sausage and imported cheese platter is also a nice complement to a glass of wine. For your entree try the chicken-and-Brie sandwich with homemade apple-onion marmalade or the grilled chicken wrap. Both are very tasty. The wait for your meal can be long at times, but if you're not in a hurry, this is a great people-watching place. Make sure you sit outside on the terrace for the best view. Inexpensive.

Afternoon

If you enjoyed the wine from lunch, stop in at **Little Hills Wine Shop** next store to the restaurant (427 South Main Street; 636–724–3565). Pick up a bottle of Missouri wine to go, as well as other wine-related souvenirs. The shop can also ship bottles of wine if you prefer.

After lunch, spend some time browsing the shops of North Main Street. **The Worthington Stove and Hearth Hardware Store,** 222 North Main Street (636–947–3165), is a perfect example of what a hardware store would have looked like years ago. They've added a few new items like kids play gyms, but you'll get the idea once you step inside. **Belle Fleur,** 315 North Main Street (636–949–9953), is a charming little shop offering vintage and reproduction furniture, floral design, home accents, and gifts.

Lewis & Clark Center, St. Charles

Head down toward South Main Street and make a left on Riverside Drive to the **Lewis & Clark Center,** 701 Riverside Drive; (636) 947–3199. Real-life exhibits show the Lewis and Clark expedition, which was very important to the St. Charles area. Detailed information from their journals is included. The museum is open daily from 10:30 A.M. to 4:30 P.M.; admission is $1.00 for adults, 50 cents for kids.

DINNER: Pio's Restaurant & Lounge, 401 First State Capitol Drive; (636) 724–5919. Pio's has been a mainstay in St. Charles for many, many years. And for good reason. They make the absolute best pizza I've ever had. It has a thin (but not cardboardlike) crust with a special sauce unlike any other. The hamburger pizza, with grilled, crumbled beef and special seasonings generously sprinkled on top, is especially wonderful. Although Pio's serves steaks, pastas, and the like, it's the pizza that has kept me coming back for nearly twenty-five years. You'll find an eclectic mix of folks at the restaurant—from kids dressed up for their prom to older folks who've had a standing reservation for as long as they can remember. The dark-paneled decor hasn't changed much over the years, the waitresses call you "babe" and "hon," and the rest rooms could stand to be a little larger, but that's all part of Pio's charm. Did I mention the pizza was great?! Inexpensive.

When you're ready to head home, just continue up First Capitol heading west (away from the historic Main Street area) to Highway 70 East toward St. Louis, or continue down First Capitol, which now becomes Highway 94, about fifteen minutes to Highway 40 East toward St. Louis.

There's More

Historic South Main Street Walking Tour. Pick up a detailed information sheet at the visitor center to know more about the history of the buildings along South Main. (636) 946–7776.

Special Events

May. Lewis and Clark Heritage Days. Authentic reenactment of the Lewis and Clark encampment. Parade, demonstrations, crafts, and food. (636) 946–7776.

July. Fourth of July Festival. Traditional Independence Day celebration. Crafts, fireworks, entertainment, children's area. (636) 946–7776.

August. Festival of the Little Hills. The largest festival of the year. More than 300 craft booths, plus food and entertainment. (636) 946–7776.

November and December. Christmas Traditions. Santa parade each weekend, candlelight shopping, and dining. (636) 946–7776.

Other Recommended Restaurants and Lodgings

Baymont Inn & Suites, 1425 South Fifth Street; (636) 946–6936. Five blocks from Historic Main Street. Indoor pool, lounge, free continental breakfast. Rate is $80 per room (double occupancy).

Boone's Lick Trail Inn Bed and Breakfast, 1000 South Main Street; (636) 947–7000; www.booneslick.com. This six-room B&B inn in a historic building is decorated in early American and primitive antiques and reproductions and framed by a wonderful rose garden. Rates from $115 to $165.

Eckert's Tavern, 515 South Main Street; (636) 947–3000. Creative twists on appetizers, salads, and sandwiches. Outdoor dining. Inexpensive.

Miss Aimee B's, 837 First Capitol Drive; (636) 946–4202. This is a wonderful tearoom restaurant serving quiche, soups, sandwiches, and incredible desserts. Browse the quaint shops on the second floor of this historic building. Inexpensive.

Trailhead Brewing Company, 921 South Riverside Drive; (636) 946–2739. Located at the corner of Boone's Lick and South Main Street, this is a great place for good pub food and beer. Try the raspberry beer; even non–beer drinkers like it. Inexpensive.

For More Information

Greater St. Charles Convention and Visitors Bureau, 230 South Main Street, St. Charles, MO 63301; (636) 946–7776 or (800) 366–2427; www.historicstcharles.com.

WESTERN ESCAPE TWO

The Weinstrasse: Augusta/ Washington/Hermann, Missouri

Missouri Wine Country / 1 Night

Just across the Missouri River is an area that will make you think you have arrived in another country. The Missouri Weinstrasse, or "Wine Road," borders the eastern bank of the Missouri River and winds through lush valleys and wooded hills that produce some of the great Missouri wines.

- ☐ Wineries
- ☐ Shopping
- ☐ Antiques stores
- ☐ Fruit and vegetable farms
- ☐ Arts and crafts
- ☐ Historic areas
- ☐ Cycling

Settled in the mid-1800s by German and French immigrants who thought the terrain most resembled their homeland, this area proved to be perfect for wine making. Fortified by the glacial soil lying just below the surface, the grapes grew easily on the gently rolling hillsides.

Missouri ranked second to California in wine growing until Prohibition, which wiped out most vineyards and caused farmers to seek other means of support. But then, in the mid-1960s, the vineyards started blooming once more, and now this area draws people from all over the country.

Fall maintains its hold as the most popular season for visitors because of the spectacular fall-foliage display along the Weinstrasse. During this time the wineries feature bands and foods, while the little towns hold festivals of all types and arts-and-crafts fairs.

All the wineries described have won awards, so be prepared to sample some outstanding Missouri wines. B&Bs proliferate along the road, as well as quaint little eateries, four-star restaurants, and many antiques and specialty shops.

One word of caution: Although the wineries are open year-round, their hours do vary according to season, so if you're planning a visit, be sure to call the wineries and the shops in advance.

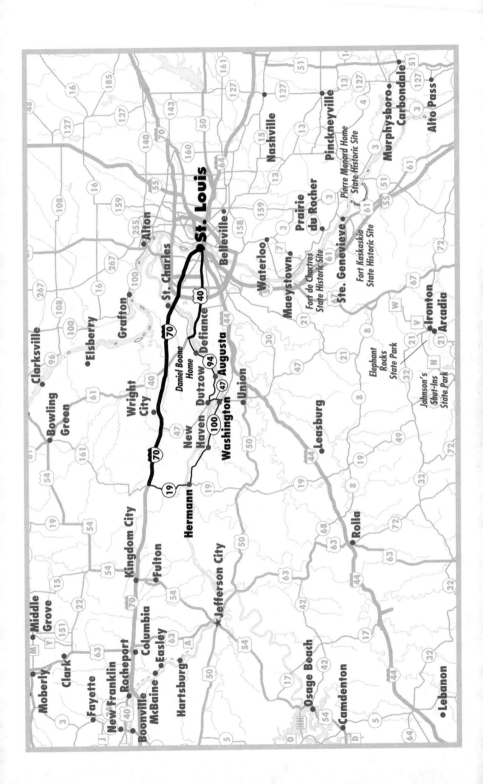

Day 1 / *Morning*

You can make your own schedule for this trip. If you don't care to visit all the wineries, you can spend more time in the shops or exploring. Either way, you should get an early start, perhaps 9:00 A.M.

Begin your day by heading west out of St. Louis on U.S. Highway 40. Since you're heading into country that begs for picnicking, you could bring a cooler and stop at **Annie Gunn's Smoke House,** 16806 Chesterfield Airport Road; (636) 532–7684. Go into the grocery by the restaurant and pick up some of their delicious smoked meats. Grab some bread, cheese, a couple of choice mustards or other spreads, and a dessert—cheesecake, perhaps?

If you don't want to stop so soon, all the wineries offer a variety of meats, cheeses, and crackers to complement their wines. Besides food, you can buy all types of specialty items, from cork pullers to glasses to T-shirts.

Cross the Missouri River and 1 mile later, you'll turn west on Highway 94 toward Augusta, Missouri. Drive 7 miles to Highway F and turn right. Drive 5 more miles to **The Historic Daniel Boone Home and Boonesfield Village.** Completed in 1810, the Georgian-style home housed Daniel—along with his wife Rebecca, their son Nathan, his wife, and fourteen children—until Daniel's death in 1820. The village currently has five buildings saved from demolition, including a one-room school-house from 1832, an 1837 cabinetmaker's shop, and the 1838 Old Peace Chapel, containing original cylinder-glass windowpanes. Admission: adults, $12.00; seniors fifty-five and over, $10.00; children four to eleven, $4.00. The museum is open from March 1 through the day before Thanksgiving from 9:00 A.M. to 6:00 P.M. The Boone home and village also hosts candlelight tours the first two weekends (Friday and Saturday night) of December from 6:00 to 10:00 P.M. Visitors are encouraged to arrive by 8:30 P.M. to see the entire village. Admission: adults, $12.00; children four to eleven, $8.00 (before December 1); adults $15.00; children, $10.00 (after December 1). (636) 798–2005; www.geocities.com/Athens/Parthenon/7109/.

Driving back to Highway 94, turn right; in 2 miles you will arrive in **Defiance,** officially recognized as a town in 1893. Stop in **Seasons & Memories** and look at the Willow Art furniture and dulcimers made by proprietors Faithe and Art Reed. Relax on their porch with a cold drink, and you might hear some live music.

After you pass Defiance, 2 miles on the right will be **Sugar Creek Winery,** perched on a hillside overlooking the Missouri River Valley. In the tasting room you might want to sample Birdlegs Blush. If you want to know about the name, just ask! (314) 987-2400; www.sugarcreekwines.com.

Leaving Sugar Creek, drive 2 miles to **Montelle Winery.** Situated 400 feet atop Osage Ridge, this winery offers one of the more spectacu-lar views of the valley and river. It also has the distinction of being located in the first American wine district, which includes Augusta, Missouri. Don't leave without trying the Chambourcin. (636) 228–4464; www.montelle.com.

Located just a mile and a half west of Montelle is the charming town of Augusta, founded in 1836. At that time the town was on the Missouri River, but flooding in the 1870s caused the river to cut a new channel, leaving the town high and dry but also leaving fertile farmland, which has sustained the town and people around it. You can spend hours walking through this little town filled with shops of all types. Peek into **The Augusta Emporium Antique Store** for great finds. Or stop in **The Bread Shed,** 270 Jackson Street, for delicious breads such as cinnamon, cherry wine, or Parmesan.

Centennial Farms, 199 Jackson Street (636–228–4338), is a must-see. Established in 1821, the farm has been in the Knoernschild family since 1855 and is listed on the National Register of Historic Places. They raise a variety of vegetables and fruits including fourteen kinds of apples, seven kinds of peaches, and yellow-fleshed watermelons called "yellow dolls." In May, customers can pick strawberries; in June they can pick black raspberries, and in July, blackberries. Besides growing a wide variety of perennials and herbs, the Knoernschilds make their own apple butter and honey. Inside the barn is a hive with glass sides so that children can see the bees make honey.

Augusta is also home to two wineries, **Augusta Winery** and **Mt. Pleasant Winery.** The Augusta Winery is located in the center of town at the corner of High and Jackson Streets, whereas Mt. Pleasant (5634 High Street) sits on a vineyard-covered bluff on the western edge of town. The Augusta Winery number is (636) 228–4301; www.augustawinery.com. To reach Mt. Pleasant, call (800) 467–WINE.

If microbrews are more to your taste, the **Augusta Brewing Company** (636–482–BEER), located off the Katy Trail, has a selection of beers (even root beer!) plus munchies, soups, and sandwiches sure to please the palate.

LUNCH: A good place for lunch is **Ashley's Rose Restaurant and Inn,** 5501 Locust Street (636–482–4108). You can eat either inside or on the enclosed patio outside. Try the Wiener schnitzel with potato pancakes, or spicy barbecue pork. An outstanding turkey club with fruit is also a good choice, or you can build your own burger. Inexpensive.

Strolling around this quaint village will entertain you for hours. Local artisans and craftspeople sell their wares in the little shops. Antiques, gifts, furniture, books, clothing, baked goods—all found within a good walk.

After eating, peek next door to **Eloquent Expressions,** 5501A Locust Street, a charming shop featuring many embroidered items including polo/golf shirts, sweatshirts, fleece, towels, jackets, and caps. If the selection doesn't suit you, you can choose from more than 15,000 in-stock designs, ranging from sports to animals to children's to special orders that can be done, in most cases, while you wait.

Afternoon

After you leave Augusta, turn left on Highway 94, and more wineries await. **Louis P. Balducci Vineyards** (636–482–8466) sits among rolling hills—a beautiful setting in which to sample wines such as a fruity vignole. Three more miles down 94 is the town of **Dutzow** and the **Blumenhof Winery** (800–419–2245). Sit in the wine garden, feel the sun shining down on you, and listen to the sounds of the country.

Driving through the little town of Dutzow, you will follow Highway 94 West until you see signs for Highway 100. Turn left, and this will take you back across the Missouri River to **Washington, Missouri,** a historic river town with lots of Lewis and Clark history. This drive takes about twenty minutes.

If you're a history buff, start with the **Washington Historical Museum,** Fourth and Market Streets (636–239–0280), open Tuesday to Saturday 10:00 A.M. to 4:00 P.M. and Sunday 1:00 to 4:00 P.M.; closed December 24 to March 1. Administrator Marc Houseman will gladly give you some background on the historical offerings of the museum, which also houses an extensive genealogical library. Admission is free.

While you probably don't smoke corncob pipes, you might be interested in visiting the **Missouri Meerschaum Company,** 400 West Front Street (636–239–2109), the world's only corncob-pipe factory, started in 1869. This tour shows the evolution of the corncob pipe and the different styles. Some of them are quite elegant!

Browse the **Gary R. Lucy Gallery,** Main and Elm Streets (636–239–6337), to see beautiful prints from the nationally known local artist. His prints depicting life on the Missouri and Mississippi Rivers will give you a flavor of life in the days when steamboats played a major role in passenger and freight travel.

Enjoy a delicious cappuccino at **Not Just Cut & Dried,** 227 Elm Street, while you look at unusual soaps and other home-and-garden items. From May to October local farmers sell their produce and other wares at the **Farmers Market,** City Park. For Missouri products visit **I.B. Nuts and Fruit, Too,** in a historic riverfront building at 120 West Front Street.

After looking through the restored **Amtrak Station** and viewing the **Daniel Boone History Exhibit,** walk down to **Riverfront Park,** have a seat on a bench, and just watch the river roll by. A wonderful way to wind down after your day.

DINNER: Have dinner on the riverfront at the **American Bounty Restaurant,** 430 West Front Street; (636) 390–2150. Housed in an 1858 home, this award-winning restaurant serves contemporary American cuisine from an ever-changing menu that makes sure you never tire of visiting. Start with vegetable cigars or dilled Havarti with crostini. Entrees range from fresh Atlantic salmon with herbed honey Dijon to potato-and-fresh-herb–encrusted chicken breasts. Be sure to save room for their signature green-apple cobbler with maple batter. Moderate.

LODGING: After dinner, walk next door and check into the **Schwegmann House Bed and Breakfast Inn,** 438 West Front Street; (800) 949–2262. You'll want to explore this three-story, 130-year-old mansion with its nine bedrooms, dining room, and parlor. Each room has its own bath and phone, and front rooms look out over the Missouri River. The inn also has its own gift shop with specially made soaps from Karen's Garden, cocoas, teas, prints, and CDs and tapes. Rates range from $110 to $150 per night. This wonderful house stands rather close to the railroad tracks, so, for those who prefer not to be lulled to sleep by the rhythm of the rails, earplugs are provided. Children allowed Sunday through Thursday. No smoking or pets.

Day 2 / Morning

BREAKFAST: At the Schwegmann House. You don't have to dash from your bed—relax and enjoy the morning. Sit in the parlor and read from one of the many books on Washington's fascinating history. Make sure your stomach is sufficiently empty to eat a wonderful breakfast of, perhaps, baked pecan French toast, chocolate-banana muffins, ham, and fruit. You will not soon be hungry for lunch.

You might not want to leave Washington yet. If that's the case, look into the **Hudson House,** 119 East Main Street, where many local Missouri craftspeople sell such items as clocks, quilts, pictures, candles, and much more. **Loaves and Fishes,** a general store located in the old Depot at 325 West Front Street, has bulk foods such as grains, spices, jellies, pasta, and organic and Amish products.

Washington abounds in antiques shops, and, if you're not careful, you could spend the whole day here. A few in the historic downtown area are **Attic Treasures,** 100 West Front Street; **Tamm Haus Antiques and Gifts,** 110 Main Street; **Teacup Antiques,** 110 Main Street; and **Waterworks Antiques,** 1 Elbert Drive.

Leave Washington on Highway 100 going west toward Hermann, Missouri, a peaceful drive through lush farmland and gently rolling hills. In 13 miles, just before you reach **New Haven, Missouri,** you'll come to **Robller Vineyard Winery**, a lovely little winery that has a wonderful dry red Norton wine. You can also find many delicious items such as chocolate, pasta, meats, and cheeses to make a basket—or just to eat.

After leaving Robller, take a little side trip through **New Haven's Historical Downtown** by the river. In 1 block you'll find a restored Art Deco theater, antiques shops, and two good restaurants, **The Front Street Grille** and **Raymond's.** Since you may not be ready to eat, keep these in mind for another trip. But you might want to pop in to **B.J.'s Ice Cream Shop.**

About 13 more miles and you arrive in **Hermann,** a storybook German village with brick homes hugging the street, much like those in Germany, and it has kept the same charm since its founding in 1836.

Before Prohibition, Hermann was the nation's second-largest wine-producing region. Drive up the hill to **Stone Hill Winery** (800–909–WINE), Hermann's first and largest winery, run by the Held family. They grew mushrooms during Prohibition, but thirty years ago they began producing award-winning wine that is now making its mark nationally. A tour of the winery is a must. Walking through the cool caverns and smelling the kegs makes you feel as though you're in another world. You will emerge from the cellars into the historic main house, where you can sample the wines and browse through the large gift shop.

Stone Hill Winery, Hermann

LUNCH: Now you're ready for the **Vintage Restaurant at Stone Hill,** the winery's original stable and carriage house, complete with hay chutes and feeder troughs. Have a seat at one of the shiny oak tables, set with glittering crystal, and be ready to try such delicious German fare as Wiener schnitzel, sauerbraten, and sausage.

Afternoon

After lunch, visit the **Deutschheim State Historic Site Museum and Gift Shop,** 109 West Second Street. Tours are held daily from 10:00 A.M. to 3:00 P.M. **The German School Museum,** Fourth and Schiller Streets (573–486–2017), houses the town museum, and you can check out the clock-tower mechanism, running since 1890. Open April 1 through October 31, 10:00 A.M. to 4:00 P.M. Monday through Wednesday, Friday, and Saturday, Sunday noon to 4:00 P.M.; closed on Thursday.

You can amuse yourself for hours in Hermann. Coffee shops, candy and gourmet shops, and antiques and craft shops will entice you to spend your time and money in this charming town.

If you're a train enthusiast, stop by **The Train Haus,** 215 Schiller Street (573–486–0117), a must for the collector and hobbyist. **Damhorst**

Toys, 311 Market Street (573–486–9090), features handmade wooden puzzles and toys by local artist Carol Damhorst, and a miniature village of Hermann historic buildings.

If you're ready to leave, get on Highway 19 and go north across the Missouri River. In 15 miles you will see I–70. Go east for the 70-mile trip back home.

There's More

Oak Glenn Vineyards and Winery, Highway 100, 2⁷⁄₁₀ miles east of the Missouri River Bridge; (877) 486–5057. A beautiful place to stop, sip wine, and view the gorgeous Missouri River Valley. Open daily noon to 6:00 P.M. March through October; noon to 5:00 P.M. November through February.

Shopping. Hermann has many antiques shops in the downtown area that can keep you occupied for many more hours.

Washington, Missouri. Fort Charrette, 4515 Old Highway 100 East; (636) 239–4202. Tour the La Charrette Fur Trading Post museum and village on the Missouri River Bluff. Fort Charrette was situated south of the Missouri River when visited by Lewis and Clark in 1804, and it was reconstructed at this site along with a 1790–1815 trading post and village houses containing period furnishings. This site offers one of the most beautiful views of the Missouri River on this trip. Shown by appointment only.

Wineries. If you haven't had enough, there are more wineries close to Hermann:

Adam Puchta Winery, Highway 100, 2 miles east of Hermann on Frene Creek Road; (573) 486–5596. Open daily 10:00 A.M. to 6:00 P.M., open at 11:00 A.M. on Sunday.

Bias Vineyards & Winery, Berger, Missouri, west of New Haven; (573) 834–5475. Open daily 10:00 A.M. to 6:00 P.M., open at 11:00 A.M. on Sunday; winter hours close at 5:00 P.M.

Hermannhof Winery, Highway 100, east of Hermann; (800) 393–0100. Open daily 10:00 A.M. to 5:00 P.M., open at 11:00 A.M. on Sunday.

Special Events

March. Annual Wurstfest. Hermann. Features a wurst competition and an exhibition of Missouri's finest sausage at the Jaycee Hall in the City Park. Other events include a sausage-making contest, gourmet sausage sampling, and live German music and folk dancers at the Stone Hill Winery Pavilion. (800) 932–8687; www.hermannmo.com.

May. Art Fair and Winefest. Washington. Held at Rennick Riverfront Park on Front Street. Taste wines from ten Missouri wineries. Also an art show featuring original works by Missouri artists and a food area with all types of cuisine. Held on the third weekend in May. (636) 239–7575 or (888) 7WASHMO.

Maifest, a traditional German celebration of spring at all Hermann-area wineries, including Bias Winery in Berger, Stone Hill Winery in Hermann, and Robller Vineyard in New Haven. (800) 932–8687; www. hermannmo.com.

June. Augusta Blue Grass Festival Afternoon. Centennial Farms. Bring your blankets and lawn chairs. Homemade blackberry pies, homemade root beer, and "brats." Adults, $5.00; children eight to twelve, $2.50; children seven and under, free.

July. The Cajun Concert on the Hill. Stone Hill Winery, Hermann. Features a Cajun band and dancers from the Louisiana bayous, who perform toe-tapping Cajun music. And, of course, you get to eat wonderful Cajun delicacies. (800) 932–8687; www.hermannmo.com.

August. Fair. Washington. The state's third-largest fair. Features livestock competitions, big-name entertainment, motor sports, and rides. Some past performers include the Beach Boys, Deana Carter, REO Speedwagon, and Kenny Chesney. Held at the Washington Fair Grounds starting the first Wednesday in August. (888) 7–WASHMO.

September. Fall Festival of the Arts and Crafts. Washington. One of the area's biggest attractions, held on the last weekend in September. Downtown streets are lined with the works of many artists and craftspeople selling their wares. A children's area gives the little ones some hands-on activities. A food court featuring pork steaks, tenderloins, kettle corn, and more varieties of food and drink ensures you won't leave hungry. (888) 7–WASHMO.

October. Octoberfest. Hermann. Citywide celebration offers German food, music, arts, and crafts. Stores and restaurants feature special foods promoting the German tradition. Check with the various wineries for their own events during this time.

Pumpkinfest. Augusta. Every weekend in October, Centennial Farms celebrates the harvest with pumpkin figures (look out for Dorothy, Toto, and the Wicked Witch of the West!), wagon rides to the pumpkin fields, and a country store loaded with fall goodies such as cider, apples, and pies. All done to the smell of bratwurst cooking on an open grill. (636) 228–4338.

December. Annual Candlelight Christmas Walk. Augusta. Held the first two Fridays in December. Visit Santa Claus at the library, enjoy roasted chestnuts on a street corner, and visit local shops offering refreshments, holiday gifts, and works of local artists. (636) 228–4005.

Other Recommended Restaurants and Lodgings

Augusta

H.S. Clay House Bed and Breakfast, 219 Public Street; (888) 309–7334. Shaded woods and perennial gardens surround this charming B&B. Guests are greeted with seasonal drinks and sweets, and appetizers and "welcome punch" are served before the dinner hour. Pool and spa available. Rates: $135 to $185. www.hsclayhouse.com.

Lindenhoff Bed and Breakfast, Walnut and Jackson Streets; (636) 228–4617. Located in the heart of Augusta, within walking distance of wineries, shops, and restaurants, this vintage Victorian B&B features a secluded garden and Jacuzzi. Homemade breakfasts include sweet Belgian waffles or German-style peach pancakes with hickory-smoked bacon or ham, and fruit. Rates: $120 to $135 per night. Call for other packages. www.lindenhof-augusta.com.

Dutzow

The Dutzow Deli & Grill, Highway 94; (636) 433–5118. Delicious hamburgers, cheeseburgers, and deli sandwiches include the Route 94 (roast beef, ham, turkey, and cheddar with mustard) or the Trailblazer (turkey, ham, cheddar, with champagne mustard). Inexpensive.

Hermann

In case you want to spend another night in Hermann, there are nearly fifty B&Bs to entice you to extend your visit.

Hermann Hill Vineyard & Inn, 711 Wein Street (573–486-4455), offers five rooms with private balconies and spectacular views. Rates: $125 to $250 per night. No smoking, children, or pets.

My Mother's Garden Cottage (573–486–3596) is a charming brick cottage and gift shop located on Schiller Street in the heart of the historic district. Rates: $85 per night weekends, $65 weekdays.

Marthasville

The Little House, 403 Depot Street; (888) 483–2587. A cozy, early-twentieth-century, two-bedroom cottage where you can truly get away and make it your house. Located on the Katy Trail, with bike rentals nearby. Party of two, $110, plus $20 for each additional person; children under seven are free. No smoking indoors and no pets.

Washington

Richard's on the Riverfront, 116 West Front Street; (636) 239–2111. Housed in a sixty-year-old brick warehouse, this restaurant—formerly Char Tony's—is a Washington staple. Customers enjoy fine dining in an upscale Italian atmosphere with entrees to match. The signature dish is Pasta Tuttamare, but there are also Angus fillets, strip steaks, and prime ribs. Moderate.

Cowan's Restaurant, 114 Elm Street; (636) 239–3213. Open six days a week; closed Tuesday. Wonderful breakfasts, great dinners, especially the breaded boneless pork cutlet. Famous for unbelievable mile-high pies—and they are! Inexpensive.

La Dolce Vita Bed & Breakfast Vineyard & Boutique Winery, 72 Forest Hills Drive; (636) 239–0399. Gourmet breakfasts and afternoon snacks. Rate: $90 per night. No smoking, pets, or children.

Washington House, 100 Front Street; (636) 239–2417. A historic inn built around 1837 for trappers and traders on the river. A beautiful Missouri River view from all rooms. Rate: $85 per night. No smoking.

For More Information

Augusta Chamber of Commerce, P.O. Box 31, Augusta, MO 63332; (636) 228–4005; www.augusta-missouri.com.

The Hermann Welcome Center, 312 Market Street, Hermann, MO 65041; (800) 932–8687; www.hermannmo.com.

The Missouri Weinstrasse, P.O. Box 147, Augusta, MO 63332; www.moweinstrasse.com.

The Washington Visitors Center, 301 West Front Street, Washington, MO 63090; (636) 239–7575; www.washmo.org.

WESTERN ESCAPE THREE

Fulton/Jefferson City, Missouri

A Taste of History in Mid-Missouri / 1 Night

Sure, you may vaguely know Fulton because it's on the way to The Lake of the Ozarks. And you may think you know Jefferson City because you once went there on a school field trip. But have you ever really taken the time to get to know these two towns in their own right? Now's your chance.

□ Winston Churchill Memorial

□ Charming shops

□ Our state's capital

Although it's a cliché, life does seem to move at a slower pace in these mid-Missouri bergs, which is part of the reason they're worth visiting. Getting out of the city, slowing down, and enjoying the simpler things in life is what these towns have to offer. Fulton, which is home to Westminster College and William Woods University, the famed Winston Churchill Memorial, and a section of the Berlin Wall, prides itself on its restored neighborhoods and its quaint downtown. Jefferson City, the hub of state government, is really more of a quaint, approachable community with a plethora of history worth exploring.

Day 1 / Morning

The quickest way to get to Fulton is to hop on Highway 70 West to Kingdom City (exit 148). Turn left and head toward Fulton on Highway 54. You'll want to stay left at the fork in the highway and head toward Business 54. You'll go about 7 miles once you get off Highway 70 before entering the town of Fulton. Take a right on Tenth Street, then a left on Court Street, and then a right on Seventh Street. The Winston Churchill Memorial is at the corner of Seventh and Westminster. The entire trip should take about one and a half to two hours.

Your first stop is the **Winston Churchill Memorial and Library,** 501 Westminster Avenue (573–642–5369; www.wcmo.edu), on the campus of Westminster College. It was here that Churchill gave his famed "Iron Curtain" speech. The memorial is open 10:00 A.M. to 4:30 P.M. daily

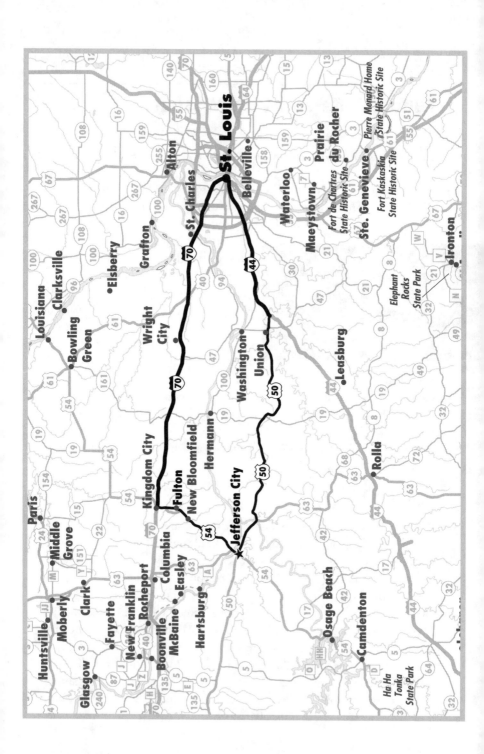

except Thankgiving, Christmas, and New Year's Day; admission is $3.50 for adults, $2.50 for seniors, and free for children twelve and under.

Start off by entering the museum for a tour, which includes original letters from Harry S Truman and Churchill, a life-size replica of Churchill's hand cast in bronze, and other facinating pieces of history related to Churchill. Don't miss the slide show, which is a minilesson in world history and well worth the fifteen minutes.

At the end of the museum, climb the stairs to visit the historic **St. Mary the Virgin Aldermanbury Church.** Upon hearing of its demise and scheduled demolition, the British transported this twelfth-century church stone by stone from London to Fulton as a tribute to Churchill. Although not used on a weekly basis, the church does host occasional weddings and baptisms. Note the intricately stitched kneeling cushions hung along each pew. Next, step outside and enjoy the Isabelle Witmarsh garden tucked alongside the church. It's easy to miss this quiet little retreat in the traditional English garden style. Finally, gaze at a piece of modern history in an authentic section of the Berlin Wall, which was transported to Fulton after its fall. Artist Edwina Sandys, granddaughter of Churchill, carved silhouettes of people out of the wall, and it stands in tribute to freedom.

LUNCH: Exit the Memorial on Seventh Street and go east 5 blocks. Make a right onto Court Street and travel 2 blocks to **Court Street Coffee,** 529 Court Street, Fulton; (573) 592–0606. Relax in this cafe tucked in the back of specialty shops. Enjoy your choice of sandwiches, soups, salads, coffees, and teas. The reasonably priced combination meal of a warm chicken Caesar sandwich and the mandarin salad is delicious. Enjoy artwork by local artists, all for sale, while you sip a warm cup of coffee. Court Street Coffee is open Monday through Friday 7:00 A.M. to 6:00 P.M. and Saturday 8:30 A.M. to 6:00 P.M. Inexpensive.

Afternoon

Of course, after a great meal it's on to shopping. Downtown Fulton has some delightful specialty shops. Court Street Coffee shares a building with **The Classic Touch,** 529 Court Street (573–624–9420), which specializes in home accessories and gifts. Across the hallway is the **Bunny Patch,** 529 Court Street (573–642–8036), which sells infants' and children's clothing, toys, and accessories.

Next door is **The Picket Fence,** 531 Court Street (573–642–2029), which offers gifts, decorations, garden items, and kitchen specialties. Lots

St. Mary the Virgin Aldermanbury Church, Westminster College, Fulton

of candles, potpourri, decorative plates, garden sculpture, and dishes fill the charming shop. Tena Jasper, the shop's owner, also makes and sells collectible "Folklore Dolls."

Directly across the street is **Blattner Home Furnishings,** 528 Court Street (573–642–2600). If you're at all interested in furniture, you'll find something you like on one of three floors of displays at this family-owned store. The selection is stylish yet functional, and the company regularly delivers to St. Louis and Lake of the Ozarks. The prices are very reasonable, and the staff is pleasant and well informed without being pushy.

Back across the street is the **Kingdom of Callaway Historical Society**, 513 Court Street (573–642–0570), open Tuesday through Friday 10:00 A.M. to 4:00 P.M. and some Saturdays during special community events. If you want to know why the county is called the Kingdom of Callaway, the historical society volunteers can tell you. Think you might have relatives that come from these parts? The historical society has a considerable amount of genealogy information and is eager to help.

Rest your weary feet and pick up any essentials you may have forgotten at **Saults Drug Store,** 505 Court Street; (573) 642–4186. Saults is a charming small-town drugstore complete with an old-fashioned soda fountain. Pull up a stool at the counter for an authentic experience and order a strawberry phosphate (yes, someone still makes phosphates) or a milk shake. The prices are reasonable, and conversation with the fountain workers is delightful. They'll make just about any ice-cream creation you want; just tell them how if they're not familiar with your personal favorite and they're happy to oblige. Saults also has a nice little gift shop within the store that's fun to browse.

When you've had your fill of shopping, get in the car and head north on Business 54 (Bluff Street) toward Highway 70 about 2 miles to the **Auto World Museum,** 1920 North Bluff Street; (573) 642–5344. Here you'll find the Midwest's largest private collection of rare and antique cars. The museum is home to the oldest and rarest car, an 1895 Haynes. The only other car like it in existence is located in the Smithsonian in Washington, D.C. The museum also houses a DeLorean (of *Back to the Future* movie fame), two solar-powered cars created by students from the University of Missouri at Columbia, and other older cars guaranteed to bring back memories. In addition to the cars, fire trucks, and tractors, there's a minimuseum of eclectic collections including more than 400 doll's head vases, Kennedy memorabilia, and farm tools. The museum is open daily 10:00 A.M. to 4:00 P.M. Admission is $5.50 for adults, $4.50 for seniors and active military personnel, and $2.00 for children twelve and under.

DINNER: Sir Winston's Restaurant and Pub, 1205 South Business 54; (573) 642–7733. From downtown Fulton go south on Court Street until it ends, and make a left onto Second Street, then a quick right onto South Business 54. Drive about 1½ miles to the restaurant on the right-hand side of the road. Sir Winston's is open Monday through Friday 11:00 A.M. until 1:00 A.M. and Saturday 4:30 P.M. until 1:30 A.M. With a clubby, relaxed atmosphere, everyone is sure to find something they'll enjoy at Sir Winston's. The varied menu ranges from burgers and fries to prime rib, with prices ranging from $6.00 for sandwiches and burgers to $17.00 for steaks and specialties. The restaurant is known for its Hickory Smoked Prime Rib, which is available on Friday and Saturday only. Other delicious options include the catfish, which can be prepared a variety of ways, and the spinach, cheese, and artichoke-hearts appetizer. The house salad of iceberg lettuce, apples, walnuts, blue cheese, and raspberry vinaigrette dressing is quite yummy. Wine, beer, and mixed drinks are available. Kids are welcome and can choose from an assortment of typical kids' fare for about $5.00. Inexpensive to moderate.

LODGING: For a relaxing end to your evening, drive back north on Business 54, make a left at the stoplight onto Tenth Street, and then go 3 blocks and make a left onto Court Street. Go about 1½ blocks to your bed-and-breakfast, **Romancing the Past Bed and Breakfast,** 830 Court Street (573–592–1996; www.romancingthepast.com), for drinks by the parlor fireplace or on the front porch. This historical Queen Anne home, built around 1868, is owned by Renee and Jim Yeager. The Yeagers have done a marvelous job transforming the home into a Victorian jewel complete with period furnishings, a beautiful parlor with gas-burning fireplace, and soft music wafting throughout the house. Three private rooms await you, ranging in price from $135 to $150 on weekends, with a discount for weekday guests. For extra-special occasions like wedding nights and anniversaries, guests may want to consider the Renaissance Suite, which includes a bedroom and sitting room. All rooms have private baths, including one with a whirlpool tub for two and another with an oversized shower. One room, overlooking historic Court Street, has a private deck and swing for relaxing. Renee is eager to make each guest's stay memorable and will work with you on special requests you may have. Credit cards are accepted. Children are not allowed. (Please see "Other Recommended Restaurants and Lodgings" for alternate lodging if traveling with kids.)

End the evening with a dip in the outdoor hot tub while you soak up the quiet of this small town. Feel the tensions melting away?

Day 2 / Morning

BREAKFAST: Romancing the Past Bed and Breakfast. Wake up to the aroma of fresh-baked goods for breakfast. The food is anything but typical breakfast fare here, but, generally speaking, guests can expect to be served some type of bread entree, a breakfast meat, fresh fruit, juice, tea, and coffee. The passion-fruit tea was a welcome addition, and the cream cheese–filled French toast sprinkled with almonds was heavenly. Fill up while you can because you'll want a boost of energy for the second leg of your trip.

After breakfast check out of the B&B and take a **walking tour** of Court Street, home to beautiful, large houses set far from the street in even bigger front yards. You can easily imagine what life was like more than a hundred years ago by just strolling up and down this grand boulevard. A copy of the walking tour is available from the Kingdom of Callaway

Chamber of Commerce, 409 Court Street; (573) 642–3055 or (800) 257–3554. Have them fax or mail you a copy before you leave home. The bed-and-breakfast may also have a copy available.

Once back at your car, you're ready to head to **Jefferson City.** Head toward Highway 54 by getting on West Fourth Street and traveling about a mile, which will lead you to the highway entrance. You'll want to take Highway 54 west (which is really going south to Jefferson City) for the twenty-minute drive to the state's capital.

As you cross over the Missouri River Bridge, stay to the right. Exit onto Main Street and go left. Follow the signs for the state capitol building and park in designated metered spots around the building, or, if crowded, at one of the surrounding garages or lots. (*Tip:* Park on the side closest to the Governor's Mansion, and it'll be less of a trek to the other sites you'll see.) Jefferson City's a very easy city to navigate, and you can see the capitol from virtually every direction, so it's unlikely you'll get lost. If you do, the people are friendly and will point you in the right direction.

Your first stop is the **Capitol Building.** Completed in 1918, this Renaissance-style building sits high on a bluff and spans three acres in the heart of Jefferson City. Your first stop is the Missouri Museum, located on the first floor. The museum features Missouri-related exhibits of historical significance as well as contemporary offerings. Make sure you see the Thomas Hart Benton murals on the third floor. Guided tours of the building are given each day every hour on the hour beginning at 8:00 A.M., with the last tour at 4:00 P.M.; there is no tour at noon. For more information call (573) 751–2854. (Note: If you're at the capitol on a Tuesday, Wednesday, or Thursday from January through mid-May, you can see legislators in action from the visitor gallery. Talk about seeing your tax dollars at work!)

LUNCH: Madison's Cafe, 216 Madison; (573) 634–2988. You can walk to Madison's from where you're parked, which is probably your best bet, or you can try to find a spot on the street. From the capitol head 2 blocks east (toward the Governor's Mansion) and make a right on Madison, where you'll find the restaurant, which has been a Jefferson City mainstay for many years. Their house salad, with provolone cheese, red onion, and artichoke hearts, is excellent, as are their pizzas, pasta, and sandwiches. Lunch will be in the $8.00 range. Hours are Monday through Friday 11:00 A.M. to 10:00 P.M. (11:00 P.M. on Friday) and Saturday 4:30 to 11:00 P.M.; closed Sunday. Inexpensive to moderate.

Afternoon

After lunch and if the weather is nice, head toward the Governor's Mansion, 1 block from the capitol on Madison. Just behind the mansion is the **Governor's Garden,** which is open to the public. Built in the late 1930s, the garden is filled with a wonderful display of flowers as well as pools and walkways, which makes for a wonderful break before continuing on your trip.

Next, head toward the train tracks to **Jefferson Landing** for a visit to some of the oldest buildings in the area. **The Lohman Building,** which dates from the mid-1830s, is believed to be the oldest structure in Jefferson City. The building has a small museum depicting the history of the area and is open daily from 10:00 A.M. to 4:00 P.M. Next door is the **Union Hotel,** which now houses the **Elizabeth Rozier Gallery** for art exhibits. It is open Tuesday to Sunday from 10:00 A.M. to 4:00 P.M. For more information call (573) 751–2854.

Now it's time to head home, but instead of taking Highway 70, we'll take the back roads of Highway 50, a very scenic and easy-to-drive two-lane highway that'll bring you face to face with Missouri country and eventually connect to Highway 44 in Union. From Jefferson Street take Jefferson up the hill, cross over High Street, head down the hill a few blocks, and make a left onto Highway 50, also called Whitton Expressway, and you're headed out of town. Noted stops along the way home include Rosebud, which is home to a handful of antiques shops. The drive home from Jefferson City should take you about two and a half to three hours, depending on your stops.

There's More

Fulton

Fulton Area Walking Trail. Starting at the end of Court Street in Memorial Park, the 3½-mile walking trail connects all three city parks and meanders along the scenic William Woods College. Pack a picnic lunch for eating under the new covered bridge. Renee Yeager at Romancing the Past can provide a picnic lunch or you can stop at one of the local grocery stores before heading out.

Gladys Woods Kemper Center for the Arts on the Campus of William Woods, 200 West Twelfth Street (573–642–2251); open 8:00 A.M. to 4:30 P.M. The gallery is primarily a teaching center for students of the college but is open to the public free of charge. The gallery showcases local, regional, and international artists, and much of the work is for sale. The center features an outdoor sculpture gallery.

Jefferson City

Runge Nature Center on Commerce Drive in Jefferson City. (Mailing address: 2901 West Truman Boulevard, Jefferson City, MO 65109.) Hands-on experiences focusing on the wildlife habitats in Missouri, large fish aquarium, wildlife-viewing area, and hiking trails. (573) 526–5544.

Special Events

July. July 4th Celebration and Sky Concert. Jefferson City. Fireworks, hot-air balloons, music, and arts and crafts in the downtown area. (573) 634–3616.

Show-Me State Games. Jefferson City. Athletes of all ages from around the state compete. (573) 882–2101.

August. Callaway County Fair. Fulton. (800) 257–3554.

September. Callaway Community Festivals. Fulton. Enjoy a juried art show, live jazz, and heritage crafts demonstrations held throughout town. Plenty of activities for the kids, crafts for sale, various entertainment, and food vendors. (800) 257–3554.

October. Hatton Craft Festival. Hatton. The small town of Hatton literally hosts this annual pre-Christmas craft fair. All the townspeople help by parking cars, baking pies, directing traffic, and cooking up some of the best homemade doughnuts, ham and beans, and corn bread. (800) 257–3554.

December. Christmas in the Capital. Jefferson City. An old-fashioned Christmas celebration in downtown Jefferson City featuring living window displays, music, carriage rides, and tours of historic buildings. (800) 769–4183.

Other Recommended Restaurants and Lodgings

Fulton

Amerihost Inn, Highway F and Highway 54, 556 Amerihost Drive; (800) 434–5800. This new facility is great for traveling families and boasts suites, including some with whirlpools. Features an indoor pool area and exercise room and free continental breakfast.

The Loganberry Inn, 310 West Seventh; (573) 642–9229; www.logan berryinn.com. Prime Minister Margaret Thatcher and Polish President Lech Walesa both stayed here and no doubt savored the scrumptious secret-recipe chocolate chip cookies. The upstairs room, with window-ledge seating, is especially quaint. Hosts Cathy and Carl McGeorge are charming and have quite a knack for cooking. Weekend rates $95–$160; weekday discounts.

Jefferson City

There are a number of hotels, bed-and-breakfasts, and restaurants in the Jefferson City area. Contact the Jefferson City Convention and Visitors Bureau for a complete listing. (800) 769–4183 or www.visitjefferson city.com.

For More Information

Jefferson City Convention and Visitors Bureau, P.O. Box 776, Jefferson City, MO 65101; (573) 632–2820 or (800) 769–4183; www.visitjefferson city.com.

Kingdom of Callaway Chamber of Commerce, 409 Court Street, Fulton, MO 65251; (573) 642–3055 or (800) 257–3554; www.callaway chamber.com.

WESTERN ESCAPE FOUR

The Katy Trail: Hartsburg/McBaine/ Rocheport, Missouri

A Journey by Bike / 1 or 2 Nights

Sometimes it's just nice to get out of the car and really take to the open trail by way of bicycle. One of Missouri's jewels, the Katy Trail, offers bicyclists, hikers, and even cross-country skiers, the opportunity to not only get some great exercise but also to see some of the prettiest country our state has to offer.

- ☐ Biking
- ☐ Hiking
- ☐ Cross-country ski trail
- ☐ Antiques shops
- ☐ Arts and crafts shops
- ☐ Country restaurants

Known as the Katy Trail State Park, the trail lies in the bed of the Missouri-Kansas-Texas Railroad (KATY) and runs 225 miles between St. Charles and Clinton through the heart of Missouri. It is the longest Rails-to-Trails project in America, encompassing twenty-six trailheads and forty trail communities.

The trail is dotted with charming little towns. Each has its own special quality as well as a watering hole of some sort. Most have restaurants and/or B&Bs; some of the larger towns have wineries and antiques shops.

Travelers also capture a bit of Missouri history as the trail slices through the wine country known as "Missouri's Rhineland," founded by German immigrants in the late 1800s. Heading westward, the trail passes through Rocheport, with some houses predating the Civil War. Keep going west and you will find the end of the trail at Clinton, Missouri, with its town square featuring a drugstore and soda fountain from the 1880s.

Much of the time the trail follows the Missouri River, affording travelers an up-close and personal look at "Big Muddy." But the best part is no steep hills! The trail has only minor grades, which is one reason riding the Katy is one of the state's most popular activities. Although you can plan trips of any length, this particular trip will take you from Hartsburg, Missouri, to Rocheport, Missouri, a distance of about 25 miles.

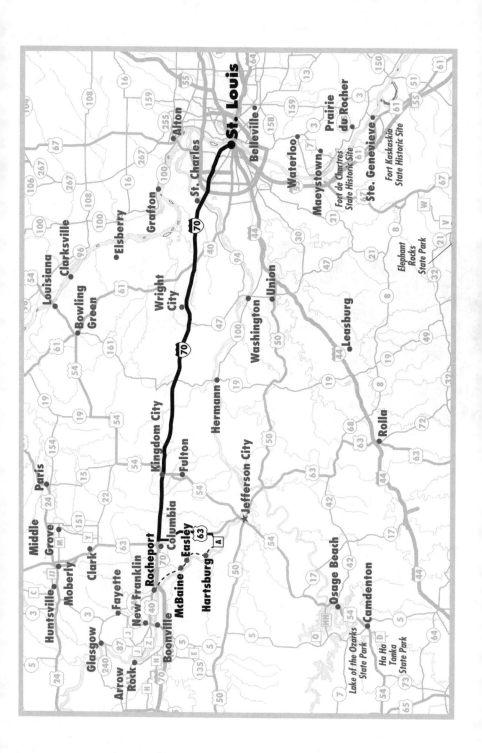

A good thing to remember is that many of the places listed here are seasonal. Be sure to call before making your trip. Even during the cycling season, which runs from April through October, some businesses along the trail close for a day or two during the week since they are open every weekend.

This trip is only one sample of many trips that you could plan on the Katy Trail. By accessing the Web site www.katytrail.showmestate.com, you can plan a trip of any length. If you have children, plan your trip according to their age and ability. The trip described here took about six hours, with many sight-seeing stops included. It could be done a lot quicker by experienced cyclists who don't get sidetracked.

Day 1 / Morning

Grab your bike, munchies, and a minimum change of clothes and get on the road by 8:00 A.M. You will head west out of St. Louis on I–70 and drive 125 miles to Columbia, Missouri. Just as you reach the eastern edge, you will come to the I–70/US–63 junction. Turn south on Highway 63 toward Jefferson City and go 13 miles to Route A; turn right, and the road will dead-end 5 miles later in Hartsburg.

If you don't have a bike, the **Hartsburg Cycle Depot,** 30 South Second Street (573–657–9599), will fix you up with one suited to your needs. The shop also has such bike accessories as pants, shirts, sunglasses, water bottles, and other needs. If you don't have a backpack for your change of clothes, you will need to rent a pannier, a saddlebag-type piece of equipment that fits over the rear of the bike and holds enough gear for two people. Rates are $6.00 an hour or $20.00 a day for a mountain bike, $8.00 an hour or $25.00 a day for a specialty bike such as a tandem or recumbent bicycle. And don't forget your helmet! Knowing that a well-fed cyclist is a happy cyclist, the Depot offers blue plate specials such as turkey and cheese sandwiches, Boca burgers, or cheddar cheese quesadillas for $6.00. This includes chips and a drink. Other snacks are also available.

So, you're started on your big adventure. You take off pedaling and, before you know it, to your left lies "Big Muddy," its current going in the opposite direction you are. Watch the skies and you're apt to see Canada geese, blue herons, and other migratory birds. Skittering out of your way and into the underbrush go squirrels, foxes, and a shrew or two—and snakes. Yes, snakes like to crawl across the trail, and they look like sticks, so try to steer around them (this does not happen often).

The Katy Trail at Hartsburg

After 3 miles, you'll see tepees on your right as you pedal into Wilton. Take a break and visit the **Riverview Traders General Store** (573–657–1095), right off the trail. Owners Robert and Maggie Riesenmy share their Native American heritage with visitors by way of original crafts, artwork, and the handmade tepees. Snacks, drinks, and sandwiches are also available.

Back on the bikes and on the trail. The sweet country air drives city thoughts out of your brain, and all that's on your mind is that flat, smooth trail ahead.

LUNCH: You have a couple of options for lunch. You can either bring your own and buy drinks at **Cooper's Landing** (573–657-2544), then have a picnic, or you can lunch at the Cooper's Landing about 9 miles from Hartsburg. This place is seasonal, so be sure to call ahead. Lunch is "by appointment" during the week, but it is open Friday, Saturday, and Sunday year-round. Deli sandwiches, chips, dips, and microwave food, along with drinks, are available.

Afternoon

After lunch, cycle 7 miles to McBaine, turn left on the paved road, and cycle over the levee for 1⅒ miles. There you will find the **Great Burr Oak Tree** of mid-Missouri. More than 350 years old, this giant oak has survived plague, pestilence, and the Great Flood of 1993.

Backtrack to McBaine and turn left back onto the trail. You will pass through the 3,635-acre **Eagle Bluffs Conservation Area,** a restored river wetland and the largest wetland in the country using municipal wastewater to support it. Again, another good place to spot wildlife, on the ground as well as in the sky.

Now you start the longest part of your trip, an 8-mile jaunt to Rocheport. But this section is also one of the prettiest of the trail. Soon after leaving the fields of McBaine, you'll start traveling in the shade of trees and magnificent bluffs along the trail. These bluffs were held sacred by local Native Americans, and among the sites you will see are a Native American petroglyph high on the bluffs, a cave said to be used by Lewis and Clark, and a fresh spring bubbling up from the bluffs.

Soon you pass under the I–70 bridge. You see people walking along, some pushing strollers or walking dogs, and you realize you're almost at Rocheport. If you have pedaled at a leisurely pace, this trip will take anywhere from four to six hours, depending on how many times you stop and for how long.

DINNER: 2nd and Central (yes, that *is* the address); (573) 698–2221. Cozy one-room restaurant with wonderful food selections such as salmon Wellington (salmon, mushrooms, onions, and spinach wrapped in a puff pastry) with lemon caper cream sauce and grilled asparagus for $17.50, or hand-cut beef tenderloin fillet with merlot mushroom sauce, horseradish mashed potatoes, and crab-stuffed portobello mushrooms ($25.00). Dinners are all-inclusive with homemade soup or salad and homemade bread. Desserts are homemade, too. Be sure to make reservations ahead of time since the room holds only forty-five people. Oh, you can walk to the restaurant from the B&B.

LODGING: Before eating dinner, check in at **Katy O'Neil Bed and Bikefest,** 101 Lewis Street, located right on the Katy Trail; (573) 698-BIKE. Try to reserve the restored boxcar in the backyard of the main house. Owner Rodney O'Neil is a veteran cyclist who has made many cross-country bike trips. He will entertain you with stories of his journeys, and he also plays a mean piano for entertainment. A big plus is his hot tub, just the thing for those challenged (not aching!) muscles. He also has a DVD player and cable for those who might be suffering withdrawal. The main house includes a family suite with private bath, queen-size bed, and futon. He also has a bunkhouse that will sleep six. Prices range from $40 for the bunkhouse to $105 for the boxcar and suite, depending on day of the week and number of people.

Day 2 / Morning

BREAKFAST: At Katy O'Neil Bed and Bikefest. Rodney serves a substantial breakfast of bacon, eggs, and pecan waffles in his kitchen filled with railroad memorabilia. His home has a comfortable feel, and it's always fun exchanging stories with other guests while you wait for breakfast, either in the parlor or walking around the grounds.

Point your bike east in the direction of the old **MKT Tunnel** and cycle through, feeling the history of the past in the darkness. Built in 1893, the 243-foot-long tunnel's ceiling remains black from the smokestacks of long-past engines.

Ride back through the tunnel and head to downtown **Rocheport.** Most shops are open during the week, and a walk through the local museum will give you a look at Rocheport's history. French for "Port of Rocks," Rocheport was placed on the National Register of Historic Places in 1976. If you happen to be there from April to October, you can take a historic walking tour sponsored by the Friends of Rocheport (573–698–2041).

Park your bike in Rocheport's charming downtown and look at some of the shops, such as **Flavors of the Heartland** and **Rocheport Gallery,** both housed at 204 Second Street. Flavors of the Heartland is a gourmet and specialty food shop specializing in Missouri-made products. The gallery features paintings, pottery, and sculpture, mostly by Missouri artists. Hours are 11:00 A.M. to 5:00 P.M. Monday through Saturday and noon to 5:00 P.M. on Sunday; however, if you plan to visit on Monday or Tuesday, it would be best to call (573) 698–2063 before you go.

Across from Abigail's Restaurant is Rocheport's latest addition, the closest thing to Barnes & Noble you will find here. **Pebble Publishing,** a publisher of regional-interest books, such as the *Katy Trail Guidebook* and *Exploring Missouri Wine Country,* has opened its "world headquarters" and bookstore at 205 Central Street. The historic brick building makes a perfect backdrop to browse more than 500 Missouri-related books, videos, CDs, and more. If you are a Lewis and Clark buff, you will enjoy the interesting displays, maps, and photographs. Hours are 9:00 A.M. to 5:00 P.M. Monday through Friday, 10:00 A.M. to 3:00 P.M. Saturday, April through November. (573) 698-3903. www.pebblepublishing.com.

Another stop should be **Rose Marie Muno Calligraphy,** at the corner of Third and Clark Streets. Rose Marie creates things from scratch, which start with calligraphy; then she expands it to maps and frames, banners, and dolls. She also decorates old chairs with a theme. She lives at her store, which is open when she's home, so you should call her ahead of time at (573) 698-5250. Hours are usually 10:00 A.M. to 5:00 P.M.

You can stop and grab a bite to eat and a drink at Cooper's Landing (573-657-2544), which is 12 miles from Hartsburg. The place is seasonal, so be sure to call. From April through October you could also stop at Chim's Thai Kitchen for fresh Thai food. Chim operates out of a small trailer and makes everything to order.

Afternoon

Back on the bike and 15 miles to Hartsburg. It may seem long, but the sound of the tires on the gravel and the wind whipping past your ears make a lovely song by which to ride.

Once back in Hartsburg, you have two options. You can either go home, or if you just can't give up the rural scene yet, you can spend the night.

DINNER AND LODGING: The **Globe Hotel Bed & Breakfast** (573-657-4529) is an old hotel first opened in 1893. The rate is $70 a night. If you've rented your bike, turn it in at the Cycle Depot, then check in at the Globe, wash up, and walk over to the **Thorn Hill Winery,** 15 East Main Street (573-657-4295). Sit on the patio, sip a glass of wine and enjoy the sunset while you kibitz with other cyclists about the "huge" buck you saw or the snake (it was how long?) stretched across the trail. After a drink at the winery, slip over to **The Soggy River Bottom Saloon and Eatery** (573-657-2221) for great bar food, appetizers, dinners, and a wide selection of beers. Live entertainment on weekends. Inexpensive.

There's More

The beauty of the Katy Trail, besides the obvious, is that you can schedule trips for as long or as short as you want. The twenty-six trailheads are spaced about 10 to 12 miles apart, and most have lodging and food, in addition to snacks, bike repair, and other trail necessities. The trail is also accessible for motorized wheelchairs and alternative cycles for the physically challenged. Call (660) 882–8196 for information or check out www.katytrail.showmestate.com.

Marthasville, Missouri. Although this is located closer to St. Louis, Scenic Cycles will not only rent bicycles but will provide shuttle service to six major trailheads: Clinton, Sedalia, Boonville, New Franklin, Jefferson City, Marthasville, and St. Charles. They will also pick you up at Lambert Field in St. Louis and get you ready for your adventure. (314) 433–2909.

The MK&T Fitness Trail. If you choose, you can bike from McBaine to Columbia, Missouri, on the 9-mile MK&T fitness trail. This takes about an hour and takes you close to downtown Columbia. Contact the Columbia Convention and Visitors Bureau (800–652–0987) for information.

Rocheport, Missouri. Friends of Rocheport Historical Museum, 101 Moniteau Street; (573) 698–3701. Open mid-April through October, Saturday and Sunday 1:00 to 4:00 P.M.

Special Events

June. Lewis & Clark Rendezvous/Missouri River Celebration. Rocheport. Commemorates Lewis and Clark's visit and subsequent journal entry relating their visit to the Rocheport area. Includes appearances by Lewis and Clark living-history buffs, their replica boats, arts and crafts, displays pertaining to the Missouri River, and a day of live music. People of all ages will enjoy this event. Visit www.rocheport.com.

Lions Club Picnic. Hartsburg. (573) 657–2729 or (573) 657–2396.

July. American Legion Post 424 Fish Fry. Hartsburg. Fish fry plus chicken and ham dinner. (573) 657–2729 or (573) 657–2396.

October. Pumpkin Festival. Hartsburg. One of the most popular festivals in the state. Musicians, craftspeople, and artists all show their wares, plus a plethora of pumpkin things. (573) 657–2729 or (573) 657–2396.

Planned Progress Chili Supper and Halloween Costume Contest. Hartsburg. (573) 657–2729 or (573) 657–2396.

November. American Legion Auxiliary Post Holiday Crafts and Bake Sale. Hartsburg. (573) 657–2729 or (573) 657–2396.

December. Christmas Tree Lighting Festival. Hartsburg. Caroling. (573) 657–2729 or (573) 657–2396.

Other Recommended Restaurants and Lodgings

Hartsburg

Volunteer Park is available for camping. For more information contact Carl Thomas at (573) 657–2729.

Rocheport

Abigail's, 206 Central Street; (573) 698–3000. Menu features such eclectic selections as pasta with Gorgonzola and spinach or grilled rib eye with stuffed mushrooms. All desserts are homemade and range from pies and cakes to biscotti and tarts. Reservations recommended. Moderate.

Les Bourgeois Winery & Bistro, Highway BB and I–70. Seated on the bluffs overlooking the Missouri River, this view is worth the 1-mile uphill walk from Rocheport. Sample the meat-and-cheese plate at the outdoor wine garden at the A-Frame Winery (573–698–3401), or dine on full-course gourmet fare, indoors or outdoors, at the restaurant (573–698–2300). The A-Frame is open noon until sunset March through October. The wine garden and bistro are open Tuesday through Saturday 11:00 A.M. to 9:00 P.M., with Sunday brunch from 11:00 A.M. until 3:00 P.M.

The School House Bed & Breakfast, Third and Clark Streets; (573) 698–2022. An old schoolhouse built around 1914 is now the site of a unique ten-room B&B. Each room has a private bath, and two rooms feature Jacuzzis. Innkeepers John and Vicki Ott and Penny Province provide such delicious breakfasts as eggs Florentine, chocolate chip muffins, strawberries and cream, and other seasonal fruit. Children ages ten and up welcome. Rates: $95 to $215.

Trailside Cafe, First and Pike Streets; (573) 698–2702. Sandwiches and burgers served inside or outside along the Katy Trail. Also, bike sales, rental, repair, and equipment and accessories.

Yates House Bed & Breakfast, 305 Second Street; (573) 698–2129. Two lovely homes with six bedrooms, each with private bath. Lodgers can dine outside in season on brick patios surrounded by lush perennial gardens. Conrad and Dixie Yates serve such fare as tomato-cheese pie with oven-roasted potatoes topped with Gruyère cheese, chocolate-banana muffins, and ham with praline-mustard sauce. Rates from $115 to $225 for the garden-house suite. No pets or children.

For More Information

For information on Rocheport, Missouri: Columbia Convention and Visitors Bureau, 300 South Providence Road, Columbia, MO 65270; (800) 652–0987; www.visitcolumbiamo.com or www.rocheport.com.

The Complete Katy Trail Guidebook by Brett Dufur, Pebble Publishing, P.O. Box 2, Rocheport, MO 65279; www.pebblepublishing.com.

Hartsburg Tourism Group, c/o Hartsburg Cycle Depot, 30 South Second Street, Hartsburg, MO 65039; (573) 657–9599.

Missouri Department of Natural Resources, Division of State Parks, P.O. Box 176, Jefferson City, MO 65102; (800) 334–6946; www.mostate parks.com.

Columbia/Boonville/Glasgow/Fayette/ New Franklin, Missouri

Exploring Boone's Lick Country / 2 Nights

A two-hour drive west on I–70 will put you in the town of Columbia, the home of the University of Missouri, Columbia College, and Stephens College. It goes without saying that a college town offers a lot of diversity as far as entertainment, sports, or any type of leisure-time activity.

☐ College town

☐ Museums

☐ Hiking

☐ Shopping

☐ Art galleries

☐ Small-town sights

☐ State parks

The university (within walking distance of downtown) has many attractions, including museums and a concert series that has included a variety of artists such as Kenny Rogers and Bill Cosby, plus productions of *Showboat, Chicago,* and *Carmen.*

Columbia boasts an active downtown with attractive covered walkways and unique restaurants, specialty shops, and galleries. For the more energetic visitor, there's a state park with a hiking trail and a biking-and-hiking trail that connects to the Katy Trail. Columbia Parks and Recreation also hosts a number of activities such as the new skateboard park, golf, swimming, and tennis.

Boonville, the oldest town in central Missouri, is west of Columbia. Named for Daniel Boone, Boonville has the oldest theater still in use west of the Allegheny Mountains, and was the center of Boone's Lick Country, near the start of the Santa Fe Trail.

Across the Missouri River lie New Franklin, Glasgow, and Fayette, all small towns with their own hold on a particular piece of Missouri history, from the Civil War to the Santa Fe Trail.

Day 1 / Morning

The drive to Columbia from the I–70/US–40 junction is about 85 miles. If you leave around 9:00 A.M., you'll have a chance to stop at the

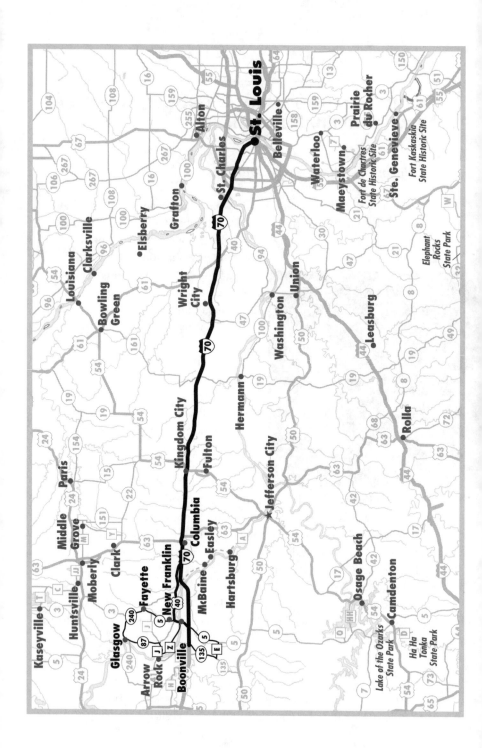

Warrenton Outlet Mall, which is about forty-five minutes away. With such stores as Bass Co., Bad Dog Sportswear, the Gap Outlet, and Levi's Outlet, maybe you can find more stuff to wear for your trip.

LUNCH: With the stop in Warrenton, plan to arrive in Columbia at noon so that you can have lunch and begin your afternoon activities. Exit at the intersection of I–70 and US–63 and go south. Turn right at the Broadway exit. This will be Columbia's main street, and you'll hit the downtown area in about a mile. Go to Ninth Street, turn left, and look for **Shakespeare's Pizza,** 225 South Ninth; (573) 449–2454. Served with a dash of humor (the servers holler your name over a loudspeaker), this pizza stands among the finest in the state. Located across from the Mizzou campus, it gets crowded for any occasion. Three rooms with concrete floors and walls decorated with fun pictures and posters give this place an "A" for atmosphere.

Afternoon

While you're downtown, look in at some of the galleries, boutiques, and other specialty stores. University towns are known for having unique shops, and Columbia is no exception, with such places as **Cool Stuff,** 808 East Broadway, offering merchandise from around the world plus the largest selection of beads and sterling silver rings in Missouri; **Bluestem Missouri Crafts,** 13 South Ninth, a treasure trove of art—jewelry, glass, and paintings by local and regional artists and craftspeople; and **Latin World,** 812 East Broadway, where you can find Brazilian tables with inlaid gemstones, alpaca sweaters, and Peruvian wall hangings. Not only a gallery, but a gift shop, **Poppy,** 914 East Broadway, is where you'll find things that you didn't know you needed, from wine decanters and pottery pitchers to funky jewelry. **Village Wine & Cheese,** 929 East Broadway, features delicious wines, cheeses, deli items, and desserts. Also gourmet kitchen items from pasta to pottery, oils to olives, baskets to biscotti.

At **The Candy Factory,** Seventh and Cherry Streets, you'll find a huge assortment of goodies including Gummi bears, truffles, and fudge. Follow the painted clouds up the stairs to see candy making in action. You'll also find gift items such as pottery and candles.

If art galleries are more to your liking, check out **Illumia,** by artist Paul Jackson, a talented water colorist, 916 East Walnut Street, (573) 875–2846; **Legacy Art and BookWorks,** 1010 East Broadway, open seven days a week and weeknights until 8:00 P.M.; and the **Missouri Art Gallery,** 9 North Tenth Street, open 10:00 A.M. to 5:00 P.M. Monday through Friday.

Shopping can make a person hungry, so take a break and head to **Peggy Jean's Pies,** 1605 Chapel Hill Road (573–447–1119). The pies by Peggy and Jean are nothing short of fantastic, from German chocolate meringue to lemon to strawberry/rhubarb. They come in little single-serving pans as well as regular size. And you can watch the art of pie making through a big glass window. Go to Providence Road, turn right, and go to Forum Boulevard, then left 1 block to Chapel Hill. Peggy Jean's is on the right.

After you've run out of money, drive out Providence Road 4 miles to **Rock Bridge Memorial Park,** a free attraction open all year from dawn to dusk. This park features natural rock formations and many different hiking trails, with the **Devil's Icebox Trail** having the most impressive rock formations. A boardwalk trail goes up 63 feet to the Rock Bridge and then loops around through a natural tunnel. (This trail is not suitable for little ones ages one to three.)

DINNER: Columbia is home to many excellent restaurants—you can pick your menu and ambience. **Addison's,** 709 Cherry Street (573–256–1995), offers first-class food at moderate prices in an upbeat atmosphere. The turkey club wrap in a spinach tortilla is a filler for $6.25. If your appetite wants more, try Jeremy's strip steak. You can choose an eight- or twelve-ounce steak for $12.95 or $15.95 respectively. Side items include rosemary new potatoes, sweet-potato chips, smashed garlic potatoes, and the best French fries you'll find anywhere.

Evening

If you're looking for evening entertainment, look no farther than downtown. The **Missouri Theater,** 203 South Ninth Street, which dates from before the Depression, houses the Missouri Symphony Society. For information on upcoming events, call (573) 875–0600. For the latest in popular music, **The Blue Note,** 17 North Ninth Street, hosts well-known artists from all over the country as well as local talent. You can hear everything from reggae to folk to rock at this restored vaudeville theater. Call (573) 874–1944 for a calendar of events.

The Hearnes Center, 660 Stadium Boulevard (573–882–2056), is the home of the Mizzou Tiger basketball team and also the main venue for nationally known artists such as Sheryl Crow, The Chieftains, and Ray Charles. **Deja Vu,** 405 Cherry Street, not only has dance music but is Columbia's only comedy club and features some of the best comedians on the circuit. (573) 443–3216.

LODGING: For a place within walking distance of downtown and the university, the **University Avenue Bed and Breakfast** offers a comfortable, homey atmosphere at reasonable prices. You can burrow in one of the rooms, each with private bath and television, mingle with other guests in the living room, or just sit and read from the multitude of material offered. Founded by three nurses, the B&B is decorated with interesting medical memorabilia. Children over ten welcome. No smoking. Rates are $80 to $90, with discounts for seniors, AAA, and alumni. (800) 499–1920; www.bbim.org/universityave/.

Day 2 / Morning

BREAKFAST: At the University Avenue Bed and Breakfast. Your hearty breakfast might include fruit, coffee cakes, and a delicious egg dish—more than enough to hold you until lunch.

Start your day with a walk to the Mizzou campus and stroll around the famous columns that stand in the quadrangle of the campus. There you will find, believe it or not, Thomas Jefferson's original tombstone. After his death in 1826, Jefferson was buried at Monticello in Virginia, but his gravesite fell into a deplorable condition because of the estate's bankruptcy. In 1882 Congress funded the repair of the gravesite and erected a new monument. Since the University of Missouri was the first state university in the Louisiana Purchase, it requested the original, and on July 4, 1885, this monument was unveiled. The marble plaque has since been moved for safekeeping inside a vault in Jesse Hall and is shown once a year on Jefferson's birthday, April 2.

On the east side of the campus are two museums. The **Museum of Art and Archaeology,** located in Pickard Hall, features art and artifacts from six continents from the Paleolithic period to the present, along with special exhibitions, talks, seminars, and programs. The museum is open Tuesday through Friday from 9:00 A.M. to 5:00 P.M., Thursday evenings from 6:00 to 9:00 P.M., and Saturday and Sunday from noon to 5:00 P.M. Admission is free. (573) 882–3591; www.research.missouri.edu/museum. The **Museum of Anthropology,** 100 Swallow Hall, is a permanent exhibition gallery with an extensive Native American collection. Admission is free. Hours are 9:00 A.M. to 4:00 P.M. Monday through Friday.

At the **Boone County Historical Society/Walters-Boone Historical Museum,** 3801 Ponderosa Street, you can see exhibits on the settling and history of Boone County. Inside the museum is the **Montminy Gallery,** with changing exhibitions. Hours April through October are

1:00 to 5:00 P.M. Tuesday through Sunday; November through March, 1:00 to 4:00 P.M. Wednesday, Saturday, and Sunday. Suggested donation $2.00 for adults and $1.00 for children under twelve. (573) 443–8936.

If you have an hour before lunch, try to visit the **Shelter Gardens,** 1817 West Broadway; (573) 445–8441. Stroll through this five-acre garden that contains more than 300 varieties of trees and shrubs and more than 1,500 kinds of perennials and annuals. Take a peek at the replica of the one-room schoolhouse and the fern grotto. A special feature here is a garden for the visually impaired. Free concerts are held here every Sunday evening throughout the summer. The gardens are open every day throughout the year except for Christmas.

LUNCH: Before setting out on the rest of your journey, step back in time and have lunch at **The 63 Diner,** 5801 Highway 763 South; (573) 443–2331. You can't miss it—the back end of a Cadillac is sticking out of the building. Waitresses in poodle skirts serve such fare as "The Blue Moon" burger ($4.60) and "The Cadillac" (a prime-rib sandwich at $6.75). Look at all the fifties memorabilia while you sip a cherry, vanilla, or chocolate Coke.

Afternoon

Drive back to I–70 and go west. In about 30 miles you'll reach Boonville and Highway 5. Exit right and go left (south). In 11 miles you'll reach **Ravenswood,** a thirty-room mansion built in 1880. Although the mansion has fallen into some disrepair, you can imagine the original grandeur. The massive dining-room table is set with exquisite china and crystal. Your tour ($5.00) will take you up two stories and into the attic, where you can walk around the widow's walk. (660) 882–7143. Reservations are welcome.

After touring Ravenswood, turn left out of the driveway and in 3 miles you'll come to Highway E. Turn right and go 5 miles to Highway A. Turn left and in approximately 2 miles on the right, you'll see **Crestmead,** a magnificent Italianate mansion. The house has sixteen rooms with 8-foot windows extending to the floor. Tours are $3.00. Call (660) 834–4140 for times.

Leaving Crestmead, turn left onto Highway A and drive to the junction of Highways E and 135. Turn left on 135 and, in about 5 miles on your left, you will see **Pleasant Green Plantation,** which had its beginnings in 1818. For your return turn right onto Highway 135 and drive about 17 miles to I–70. Turn right and drive 5 miles to Highway 5 at **Boonville.** Exit right and turn left on Highway 5 to go into town.

Although the outskirts are populated with chain restaurants and stores, the main street seems to have not changed in fifty years. This picturesque town on the Missouri River has more than 400 buildings listed on the National Register of Historic Places. If you go to the **Chamber of Commerce,** 320 First Street (660–882–2721), you can get a map of self-guided tours. You can also call the **Friends of Historic Boonville** for information on tours; (660) 882–7977. While you are at the Chamber of Commerce, be sure to pick up a map of the South Howard County Trail Crossroads. This will help you on your journey tomorrow.

The **Old Jail & Jail Barn,** 614 East Morgan Street, was built in 1848 by slaves with stone quarried on the riverbank and is the site of Missouri's last public hanging in 1930. The **Hain House,** 412 Fourth Street, was built in 1836 by Swiss immigrant George Hain and stayed in the Hain family until the last Hain descendant died in 1959. It is now owned by the **Friends of Historic Boonville** and is open for tours. **Thespian Hall,** 522 Main Street, was built from 1855 to 1857 by a group of sixty men who formed The Thespian Society and decided they should have a place to perform. It is now the oldest theater still in use west of the Alleghenies.

Continue your stroll down Main Street and peek into such stores as **Your Money's Worth** (at 305), full of antiques, crafts, and collectibles. Here, you'll also find Louise's Tea Room for soup, sandwiches, and desserts. For coffees or a light lunch, stop at Cafe Au Lait (at 315).

DINNER: The Stein House, 421 Main Street (660–882–6832), a local hangout for many years, serves up steaks, seafood, sandwiches, and wonderful pasta dishes like chicken tarragon fettuccini. Moderate prices in a comfortable atmosphere.

LODGING: Staying on Main Street (Highway 5), drive north across the Missouri River Bridge and turn right on the first road, Country Road 463. You can't miss **Rivercene,** a three-story mansion with six Italian marble fireplaces built in 1844 by riverboat baron Joseph Kinney for his wife. Eight large bedrooms all have queen-size beds, sitting areas, and private baths. Rates are $90 to $150. No smoking or pets. (800) 531–0862.

Day 3 / Morning

BREAKFAST: At Rivercene. Proprietor Ron Lenz knows how to fix a substantial breakfast, and you will be more than satisfied with your morning repast. He can also tell you some tales about the "flood of '93," when Rivercene came dangerously close to being swept away.

As you leave Rivercene, the concrete marker signifying the actual start of the **Santa Fe Trail** will be on the left, almost hidden in the weeds. At this point, use the map from the Chamber of Commerce and you can actually follow some of the Santa Fe Trail. Cross over Highway 5 from Rivercene to Highway 187. You will see markers for the town of Franklin, Missouri, one of the largest towns west of St. Louis until a flood in 1826 washed the town away, causing residents to move north and form the town of New Franklin. A stone marker on the left represents the long-gone town square. There is also a monument marking the *Missouri Intelligencer,* the first newspaper west of St. Louis.

In 4 miles turn left on Route Z. You will pass by **Cedar Grove, Benjamin Cooper Cemetery,** and **Joseph Cooper Cemetery.** At the intersection of Z and Route J, you can turn left down a gravel road and see the site of **Cooper's Fort,** where Captain Sashel Cooper was killed by Native Americans.

Backtrack to Route J and drive to Highway 87. Along here you can turn onto 187 to the **Boonslick Historical Site.** You are in the heart of **Boone's Lick Country,** which takes its name from the large salt lick worked by Daniel Boone's sons beginning in 1805. Salt was an essential commodity in this area and attracted large numbers of settlers.

Driving back to Route 87, you'll find **Glasgow, Missouri,** a river town founded in 1836 that features fifty buildings more than one hundred years old, many predating the Civil War. It is also the home of the **world's first all-steel bridge,** built in 1879 across the Missouri River, and America's oldest family-owned drugstore, **Henderson's** (on First Street), where you can still get homemade malts, milk shakes, and phosphates. A bloody Civil War battle was also fought here in 1864.

Take Highway 240 South out of Glasgow 12 miles to **Fayette, Missouri,** home of **Central Methodist College,** founded in 1854 and on the National Register of Historic Places. On Methodist's campus, **Brannock Hall** was occupied by Federal troops during the Civil War. A town square with a beautiful old courthouse invites you to stroll around the square and peek in the shops. You can really spend some time in **Dawn's Heavenly Herbs,** with unusual treasures and a good collection of books on herbs and cooking. Also on the square is the **Fountain Cafe,** with wonderful breakfasts and good home cookin'.

Before leaving, be sure to visit the 120-year-old **Morrison Observatory** and look through the telescope. Public viewings are held every Tuesday at 7:30 P.M. www.system.missouri.edu/cmaa.htm.

Town square in Fayette, Missouri

Leave Fayette on Highway 5, and in 11 miles you'll reach **New Franklin, Missouri.** In the middle of town is a marker erected in 1913 commemorating the start of the Santa Fe Trail. Stop by the **South Howard County Historical Information Center,** 101 East Broadway (660–848–2102), and get information on a walking tour of historical homes in New Franklin. Weekends, 2:00 to 4:00 P.M., weekdays by chance.

The **Horticulture and Agroforestry Research Center** of the University of Missouri is located in New Franklin. This center provides a place for students and faculty to do many horticultural research projects. Also on the grounds is the **Hickman House,** a Georgian cottage-design home, one of the oldest brick houses in Missouri. A small-scale reconstruction of Missouri's first botanical garden, built in 1820, ties the center to the local cultural heritage. (660) 848–2268; www.missouri.edu/~agwww/AES/horticulture.

LUNCH: From New Franklin follow US–40 for 8 miles to Highway 240. Turn right, drive through Rocheport, and in 1 mile, on the right, you'll see rolling hills covered with grapevines. Take the second turn to the right into **Les Bourgeois Winegarden & Bistro.** The view from this restaurant is nothing short of spectacular from a point high on a bluff overlooking the Missouri River Valley.

Your appetite should be in fine form. Menu notables are the smoked pork shoulder with a raspberry barbecue sauce and caramelized onions and pepperjack cheese on a baguette, or grilled portobello mushrooms on focaccia bread with roasted red-pepper goat cheese, your choice for $8.00. Open Tuesday through Saturday 11:00 A.M. to 9:00 P.M., Sunday 11:00 A.M. to 3:00 P.M. (573) 698–3060.

If this lunch seems too lavish, before you reach the Bistro, turn right and drive through the vineyards to the original wine garden and A-Frame, where you can purchase a picnic lunch of fruit, sausage, cheese, and crackers. Enjoy a picnic on the terraced grounds overlooking the Missouri River.

Return to Highway 240, go right, and in 2 miles you will come to I–70. Go east on I–70 and head back to St. Louis.

There's More

Columbia

Columbia Skate Park, a skateboard park located in the Cosmopolitan Recreation Area on Business Loop 70 West, off I–70. A first-rate facility for those inline skaters traveling with you. No charge. (573) 874–7460.

Devil's Icebox Wild Cave Tour. Spend three to eight hours in one of the longest caves in Missouri. Includes a water passage, which entails canoeing and portaging; $25 per person. Call the park office at least two weeks ahead of time. Rock Bridge Memorial Park. (573) 449–7402.

First Thursday Gallery Walks are held at the numerous downtown galleries on the first Thursday of every month. For more information call the Office of Cultural Affairs at (573) 874–6387.

Lake of the Woods Golf Course, 6700 St. Charles Road; (573) 474–7011. An eighteen-hole golf course, plus swimming pool, carts; open year-round. Fees and hours same as LA Nickell.

LA Nickell Golf Course, 1900 Park Side Drive; (573) 445–4213. An eighteen-hole course with carts. Open Memorial Day through Labor Day 7:00 A.M. to dusk and 8:00 A.M. to dusk remainder of year. Monday to Thursday, $14; Friday, weekends, and holidays, $18; special twilight fees.

Martin Luther King Memorial Gardens, 800 South Stadium Boulevard; (573) 874–7460. Landscaped gardens with walkways and benches where you can see Dr. King's writings as part of a sculptured amphitheater. Located next to the MK&T Trail.

MK&T Fitness Trail. Walk, jog, or bike on an 8-mile trail from Fourth and Broadway at Flatbranch Park (downtown) to the Katy Trail at McBaine, Missouri. Parking at Forum, Stadium, and Scott Boulevards accesses. An urban pathway through dense woods and open fields where you can see foxes, birds, and other wildlife.

The Perche Creek Golf Club, 5 miles west of Columbia on I–70 at the Midway exit, features miniature golf, batting cages, a driving range, and an eighteen-hole, par-three course. (573) 445–7546.

Sports. Spend a weekend afternoon or evening watching the Mizzou Tigers play Big 12 basketball or Big 12 football. For tickets, call (800) CAT–PAWS.

Twin Lakes Recreation Area, 2500 Chapel Hill Road; (573) 874–7460. Swimming, boating, fishing, and sand volleyball. A six-acre swimming lake with deck, diving platform, and water slides. Sand beach slopes into water—perfect for kids. **Little Mates' Cove,** a water playground apart from the lake for children under age eleven, features slides, water cannons, and fountains.

University Concert Series is held from October until May. Past performances have included Bill Cosby, the St. Petersburg State Ice Ballet, and London City Opera's *Merry Widow.* Call (573) 882–3781 for ticket information.

Special Events

April. Earth Day in Columbia. A community celebration and downtown festival with street fair, children's activities, entertainment, and environmental education exhibits. (573) 874–7460.

Big Muddy Folk Festival. Boonville. Held at Thespian Hall. (660) 882–7977.

May. Memorial Day Weekend celebration. Columbia. An outstanding air show to honor all veterans, with more than fifty military aircraft from World War I to the present. Parachute team, military-aircraft demonstration team, and patriotic music performances. Held at Columbia Regional Airport with a downtown parade. (573) 443–2651.

June. Art in the Park, Stephens College Campus. Columbia. Family-oriented fine-arts festival for all ages. Local and out-state artists with fine arts and crafts. Entertainment stage, hands-on art activities, and food. (573) 443–8838.

Downtown Twilight Festivals Every Thursday. Columbia. Fun and entertainment for children of all ages. Musical performances, demonstrations by local artists, horse-drawn carriage rides, petting zoos, clowns, and magicians. (573) 442–6816.

Heritage Days. Boonville. Four days of fun and food including a parade, arts and crafts, an antique carnival, wine and beer gardens, and historic tours. Call the chamber of commerce for details at (660) 882–2721.

July. Boone County Fair and Horse Show. Boonville. Includes a carnival midway, horse and livestock exhibitions, entertainment, and food, food, and more food. (573) 474–9435.

August. Boonville Festival of the Arts, held in Thespian Hall. A week of ballet, symphony, and chamber music. (660) 882–7977.

September. Columbia Festival of the Arts, Courthouse Square. Downtown Columbia. Annual celebration of the arts with live performances of music, dance, theater, and literature readings, and visual artists displaying and selling their works. Children's art area, food vendors. (573) 874–6386.

Heritage Festival, Historic Maplewood Farm, Nifong Park. Columbia. Reflects the spirit of mid-Missouri in the late nineteenth and early twentieth centuries. Artisans and tradespeople demonstrate their trades and sell their wares. Music, entertainment, contemporary crafts, children's activities, storytelling, kettle corn, hayrides, pony rides, and more. (573) 874–7460.

Santa Fe Trail Day. New Franklin. Parade, baby show, barbecue, and dance and other contests. (660) 848–2102.

December. Downtown Holiday Festival, first Friday. Columbia. Celebrates season traditions with live window displays, strolling carolers, a visit from Santa Claus, holiday treats, and hayrides. (573) 442–6816.

First Night in downtown Columbia on New Year's Eve. A nonalcoholic event with food, fun, entertainment, and prizes.

Other Recommended Restaurants and Lodgings

Boonville

Lady Goldenrod Inn, 629 Spring Street; (660) 882–5764. Another historic home close to Main Street, with comfortable accommodations. The hosts will serve you dinner if you request it when you make your reservations. Rate: $52.35 per night. Inquire about children. No smoking inside the house.

Main Street Cafe, 402 Main Street; (660) 882–9934. Meeting place for the morning "regulars." Good home cookin' with better-than-average breakfasts and burgers. Inexpensive.

Morgan Street Repose, 611 Morgan Street, is a charming B&B in a home on the National Register of Historic Places. Rates: $75 to $110 per night. No children under twelve. (800) 248–5061.

Columbia

Booche's, 811 South Ninth, a legend for hamburgers served on napkins with a side of chips. Many pool tables with many regulars at this place. Recognized by *USA Today* as one of the best college-town hamburger places in the United States. (573) 874–9519. Very inexpensive.

Boone Tavern, 811 East Walnut Street, is a Columbia landmark, located next to the Boone County Courthouse. Prime rib, seafood, and steaks are served amid Boone County history. Open seven days a week, 11:00 A.M. to late night, with Sunday brunch 10:00 A.M. to 2:00 P.M. (573) 442–5123. Inexpensive to moderate.

Days Inn Conference Center, 1900 I–70 Drive Southwest. Near malls, restaurants, entertainment. Full cable and a pool. (800) DAYS INN; http://members. aol.com/daysinncol. Rates start at $79.99.

The Drury Inn, 1000 Knipp Street; (573) 445–1800. Located next to Columbia Mall, which has stores such as Dillards, Eddie Bauer, Gap, and Target. Includes continental breakfast, TV, indoor pool, Jacuzzi, and free access to Gold's Gym. www.drury-inn.com. Rates start at $69 to $95.

Flat Branch Pub & Brewing, 115 South Fifth, is mid-Missouri's only microbrewery and restaurant. Many good menu items, including hot artichoke dip with fresh veggies, Caesar salads, unusual sandwiches, homemade bread, and many beer selections. Open daily for lunch, dinner, and late-night. (573) 499–0400. Inexpensive.

The Gathering Place, 606 South College; (573) 815–0606. Antique walnut, cherry, and tiger maple furniture enhance this elegant, yet comfortable, B&B. All rooms include private bath, cable TV, and data-port telephones. No smoking or pets. Rates are $85 to $145.

Murry's, 3107 Green Meadows Way. Great food and great jazz. Don't miss their green-pepper rings, fried and dusted with powdered sugar! Good salads, pasta, sandwiches, and desserts like chocolate-malt cake and ice cream. (573) 442–4969. Inexpensive.

Taylor House Bed and Breakfast, 716 West Broadway, (573) 256–5567. Grand 1908 Queen Anne home on the national and local historic registries. Six rooms with private baths and Internet access. Children welcome; no pets. Smoking outside in designated areas. Rates: $125 to $150.

New Franklin

Katy Roundhouse, 1893 Katy Drive; (800) 477–6605. A one-hundred-year-old building with the look and feel of the Missouri-Kansas-Texas Railroad "glory days." Only open on weekends, the restaurant serves steaks cut fresh daily by a local market and cooked over an open flame. All homemade foods from breads to soups. Also offers tent camping and RV hookups.

For More Information

Boonville Chamber of Commerce, "The Restored Katy Depot," 320 First Street, Boonville, MO 65233; (660) 882–2721; www.mo-river.net.

Columbia College; www.ccis.edu.

Columbia Convention and Visitors Bureau, 300 South Providence Road, Columbia, MO 65270; (573) 875–1231 or (800) 652–0987; www.visit columbiamo.com.

South Howard County Historical Society, 101 East Broadway, P.O. Box 234, New Franklin, MO 65274; (660) 848–2102; www.mo-river.net.

Stephens College; www.stephens.edu.

University of Missouri; www.missouri.edu.

WESTERN ESCAPE SIX

The Lake of the Ozarks, Missouri

Fun in the Land of the Magic Dragon / 2 Nights

Nestled in the hills of central Missouri surrounded by bluffs and forests, the Lake of the Ozarks, with its 1,150 miles of shoreline, provides everything a vacationer needs. It's hard not to find something to do at the lake; perhaps the best thing to do is . . . *nothing*. Find a place to stay, unpack, put on your swimsuit, and just lie by the lake. That's the easy thing to do.

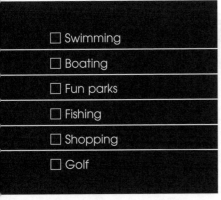

- ☐ Swimming
- ☐ Boating
- ☐ Fun parks
- ☐ Fishing
- ☐ Shopping
- ☐ Golf

In the event the urge to move hits you, you need not look far. Take a dinner cruise and watch the sun set over the mirrored waters. Shop. Poke around ancient castle ruins. Get out of the hot sun into a cool cave. Shop. Change shoes and play golf. Shop. Keep the same shoes and play miniature golf. Then there are go-carts. Did I mention shopping? Your choice of entertainment will depend on whether or not you have kids—golf course or water park, beach balls or golf balls.

The Lake of the Ozarks is also called "the Magic Dragon" because of the configuration of its shoreline. All this is just a three-hour drive away. What you want to do to make your own magic will define where you stay. This escape features a first-class bed-and-breakfast sitting on a bluff with a beautiful view and a hot tub. If you have children, however, the lake has many resorts with lake access and kitchen facilities that might better suit your needs.

Day 1 / *Morning*

Plan on leaving around 8:30 A.M. so that you can be at the Lake of the Ozarks by 11:30. Drive west on I–70 to the Kingdom City/Lake of the Ozarks exit, which is Highway 54, and follow it south to Business 54. Turn

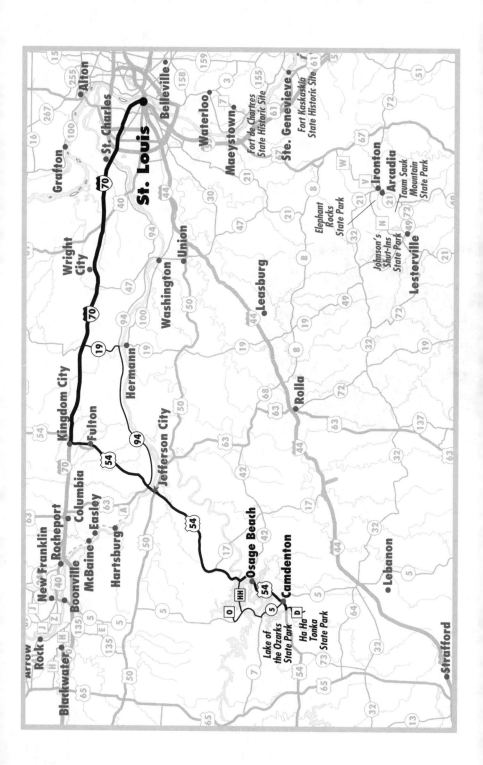

right. In less than a mile, turn into **Willmore Lodge,** the Lake Area Chamber Visitor Center. Not only can you get a lot of information on lake attractions, you can learn the history of Bagnell Dam. Built in 1930, the Adirondack-style lodge served as administrative and entertainment center for the huge Bagnell Dam project. The enormous windows give visitors a panoramic view of the lake. www.willmorelodge.com.

Turning right on Business 54 will take you across the dam to the Strip, the first commercial area on the lake after the dam opened. Boutiques, craft stores, T-shirt shops, arcades, and restaurants line this 1-mile area that has remained one of the most popular spots on the lake.

Traveling to your lunch stop will give you a good opportunity to look at a lot of what the lake has to offer.

LUNCH: Look for **Tonka Hills Restaurant,** Highway 54, (573–346–5759) on the left before you get to Camdenton. Slide into a booth and look around. You'll see mostly locals. That's a good sign. Another good sign is a ham, bean, and corn-bread plate special. The breaded tenderloin sandwich is a winner, too. Specials are $4.25 to $5.10 and sandwiches cost slightly less.

Afternoon

Big Surf Waterpark & Big Shot Raceways and Fun Park is 2 miles east on Highway 54 at the junction of Highways 54 and Y. Big Surf features an endless supply of water activities, including a wave pool, body flumes, a rapids tube ride, and a float trip. There's also sand volleyball—or you can just sunbathe on the huge deck. Little ones love the Bubble Beach Kiddie Pool. Admission: adults and children, nine to fifty-nine, $21.95; children four through eight, $16.95; seniors, $6.90; children three and under, free. Hours: end of May through first of September 10:00 A.M. to 7:00 P.M., depending on school session and weather. (573) 346–6111.

Big Shot Raceways is next door and substitutes wheels for water. NasKarts, Turbo Racers, Rookie Karats, Bumper Boats, Bumper Cars, an eighteen-hole miniature golf course, and an arcade are available for your family's entertainment. If you've spent the afternoon at Big Surf, you may want to leave this for an evening. Each ride and activity is priced separately, with no general admission. Open March through October; call ahead for hours. You can buy a Super Pass, which admits you to Big Surf with two free hours of rides at Big Shot. Adults and children nine and up, $39.95; children four through eight, $34.95. www.bigsurfwaterpark.com.

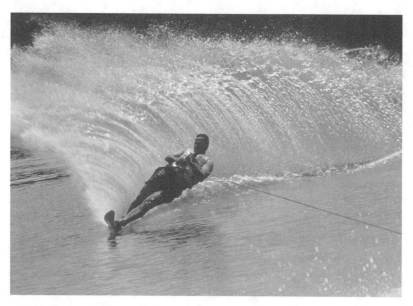

Waterskiing at Lake of the Ozarks

DINNER: **J. Bruners,** Osage Beach, Lake Road 54–40 (573–348–2966), is ¼ mile west of the Grand Glaize Bridge on Highway 54. While Bruners is known for its batter-fried lobster, chicken livers, and onion rings, this restaurant also serves up great steaks, steamed crab legs, and fresh trout and catfish. Prices start at $12.50 for chopped sirloin and go up to $35 for the lobster and crab. Open Tuesday through Saturday. The lounge opens at 5:00 P.M., with dinner starting at 5:30 P.M. Closing time is 10:00 P.M.

Evening

If you have any energy left after a day in the water and a night of good food, **The Salty Dog,** Highway 54–37 (Highway 37 is also known as Jeffries Road), Osage Beach (573–348–9797), would be a good place to end the evening.

LODGING: If a stress break is what you're looking for, **The Cliff House Inn,** Route 1, Box 885, Osage Beach, MO 65065 (573–348–9726; www.lakecliffhouse.com), perched high on a bluff overlooking the lake, provides that and more. Sit on your private deck and let your cares drift off on the breeze. There is a hot tub with gazebo for relaxing, and a full breakfast is provided in your room or on your deck. Four suites have

Jacuzzi tubs and fireplaces. No smoking. No pets. Inquire about policy for children. Rates: $105 to $140. Directions: From Highway 54 in Osage Beach, Missouri, turn onto Highway KK. Go left at "Y" (KK35). Stay left to Bay Point Village sign. Turn left (KK35P). Go ½ mile to KK35PF and turn left onto a gravel drive. Continue on gravel approximately 200 feet and you've arrived!

Day 2 / Morning

BREAKFAST: At The Cliff House Inn. What a wonderful way to start your day. Sit on your deck, enjoy a gourmet breakfast, and if you are in luck, you'll see a hawk soar over the water.

The morning would be a good time to rent a boat and explore the lake. Some boat rentals nearby are **Bridgeport Boat Rentals** (573–348–2280), **Marriott's Tan-Tar-A Marina** (573–348–3131), **Yacht Club Marina** (573–348–2296), or **Lake of the Ozarks Marina** (573–873–3705 or 800–255–5561).

If boating doesn't appeal to you, golf courses abound at the lake. The best way to choose one is to visit www.golfingmissouri.com. There also are golf packages, called "Golf Around," with discounted rates for participating resorts and golf courses on this site.

Fishing is always an option at the lake, and you can fish for free, if you have a license, at the **Lake of the Ozarks State Park,** just south of Osage Beach off Highway 54. With 85 miles of shoreline and two public beaches, you could bring a picnic and just swim, fish, and hang out all day.

After a morning of boating or golfing, drive over the **Community Bridge** that connects the east and west sides of the lake. Before the bridge was built, it would take an hour or more to get from the east side to the west. The bridge runs from the intersection of Highway 54 and HH in Lake Ozark across the lake to Shawnee Bend. Once on the west side, drive to Highway 5, turn left, and shortly after the Highway 5/Highway 7 junction at Greenview, Missouri, you'll come to the turnoff (left) to your lunch spot, Captain's Galley.

LUNCH: Captain's Galley, Highway 5, 8 miles north of Camdenton, on Lake Road 5–89 (573–873–5227). No trip to the lake is complete without at least one meal aboard a floating restaurant, and the Captain's Galley is a tried-and-true experience. Dine on wonderful fried chicken, plate lunches, and hamburgers under the Niangua Bridge. Also great piña coladas! Moderate prices.

Afternoon

After lunch, turn right (north) on Highway 5 about 10 miles to Route 0. Turn right and you will find **Old St. Patrick's Church, Cemetery and Museum,** built by Irish immigrants in 1875 using materials from the countryside, including the lumber, native stone, and limestone. It has been painstakingly restored to reflect the original era. Located on the grounds is **Mary, Mother of the Church Shrine,** a tribute to motherhood. The Mother's Wall, resembling the Vietnam Memorial in Washington, D.C., is engraved with mothers' names. A terraced amphitheater with fountains, pools, and a waterflow make this a stunning sight. For more information call (573) 374–MARY or visit www.mothershrine.org.

From the shrine turn left onto Highway 5, cross the Niangua Bridge, and drive to **Bridal Cave,** Lake Road 5–88; (573) 346–2676. More than 1,800 couples have tied the knot in the Bridal Chapel, one of the many rooms in the cave. Park rangers guide groups over lighted passageways through massive onyx formations—a beautiful natural wonder. Rates: ages thirteen and over, $12.00; ages five to twelve, $6.00. There is also a Discovery Tour, a two-hour educational program including Bridal Cave, Thunder Mountain Nature Trail, and a lantern tour of Bear Cave. Reservations needed. Flashlights also needed to complete the Bear Cave portion of the tour. Adults (ages thirteen and up), $10.00; children (ages five through twelve), $5.00; www.bridalcave.com.

From a cave to a castle. **Ha Ha Tonka State Park,** west of Camdenton off Highway 54, will stir the imagination. Once the dream of a wealthy businessman who died in a car accident, the mansion burned to the ground, leaving only the stone walls on the 250-foot bluff where it had overlooked Ha Ha Tonka springs and the lake. Visitors can explore the ruins and hike 15 miles of trails through spectacular scenery and natural wonders.

If you're ready for an afternoon pick-me-up, pick up a Turtle Sundae or Chocolate Chip Concrete at **Randy's Frozen Custard,** 1 Kings Plaza, Osage Beach, one of the best places on the lake for frozen goodies.

DINNER: You were on the water for lunch. Continue with dinner on the *Celebration,* an 80-foot yacht with open-air decks and two climate-controlled interior salons. The two-hour dinner cruise features a beef, chicken, pork, or seafood dinner with full-service bar. Dinner cruise from 7:00 to 9:00 P.M. for $32. Make your reservations by 2:00 P.M. so that you can select your entree. Other cruises are Daily Scenic, 11:00 A.M. to 12:30 P.M. and 3:00 to 4:30 P.M., $12; and Daily Moonlight, 9:30 to 11:00 P.M.,

$12. Children ten and under are half price. Cocktails are available on all cruises. Dinner cruises are Tuesday, Thursday, Friday, Saturday, and Sunday. Cruises depart from the **Confetti Pier.** Take Lake Road 52–22 to Ski Road.

LODGING: The Cliff House Inn.

Day 3 / Morning

BREAKFAST: At The Cliff House Inn.

You can't go home empty-handed, so, on your way out of town, plan a couple of hours at the **Osage Beach Factory Outlet Village** (573–348–2065), on Highway 54 heading east. With 110 outlets, it will not be hard to part with a few bucks at stores like Gap Outlet, Polo/Ralph Lauren, Tommy Hilfiger, Ann Taylor, Brooks Brothers, and Levi's Outlet. Sound good? For the home there's Dansk, Mikasa, Pfaltzgraff, and more— plus Harry & David and the Rocky Mt. Chocolate Factory. Hours: January and February, Monday through Sunday 10:00 A.M. to 6:00 P.M.; March through December, Monday through Saturday 9:00 A.M. to 9:00 P.M., Sunday 9:00 A.M. to 6:00 P.M.

After loading all your bargains in the car, turn right (east) on Highway 54 and head for Jefferson City, about 35 miles away.

LUNCH: For a good lunch and a little taste of Germany, stop in Jefferson City at **Das Steinhaus,** 1436 Southridge Drive; (573) 634–3869. For under $10 you can get a variety of sandwiches, soups, and salads. Or Wiener schnitzel, jäger schnitzel, or rouladen. Maybe just do appetizers ($4.95 to $5.95) like grilled meatballs bordelaise or veal-stuffed cabbage rolls. Going east on Highway 54, exit right at the Jefferson Street exit, turn left at the top of the ramp on Stadium Drive, and go over the highway. The next street is Jefferson; turn left, then right at the first street, Zumwalt Road. Go 1 block to Southridge Drive and you'll see the restaurant.

Afternoon

From Jefferson City take the scenic route at least part of the way back on Highway 94, which runs along the Missouri River. The road winds through the hills, then flattens out with bluffs towering on the left and lush farmlands or the river on the right. In 43 miles you'll reach the junction of 94 and Highway 19. Turn left and follow 19 to I–70, about 14 miles. Head east on I–70 for 40 miles to St. Louis.

There's More

Camdenton

Car Tours. Get off the main roads and really explore the lake and its sur-rounding countryside with a self-guided car tour. Choose one or both tours: the 50-mile River and Mountain Country tour and the 40-mile Backroads–Ozarks–style tour. Contact the Camdenton Area Chamber of Commerce (800–769–1004; www.odd.net/ozarks/cchamber) to receive the guide.

Thong Trees, Lake Road 5–87, ⁷⁄₁₀ mile from North Highway 5 on the left side. Early Native Americans marked trails with trees bent in this rather unusual way. They were also called "water trees" because they pointed to a spring or river. A large sign designates the entrance to the trail, which cir-cles around four thong trees.

Lake Ozark

Lake Cruises. Breakfast, dinner, and sightseeing cruises run daily from the Casino Pier at Bagnell Dam at 10:00 A.M., noon, 2:00 P.M., and 4:00 P.M. One-hour cruise, $8.00; two-hour cruise, $10.00. Two-hour Dinner Buffet Cruise Monday through Saturday at 7:00 P.M., $18.75. Business 54 at Bagnell Dam Boulevard; (573) 365–2020.

Sugar Creek Miniature Golf, Inc. (573–348–3810), on the Strip in Bagnell Dam. Sugar Creek Mini Golf gives you a special flavor of the Ozarks. Nestled among shaded trees and Ozark terrain, Sugar Creek offers thirty-six holes woven through scenes from the 1880s such as a church, saloon, main street, and a waterwheel.

Osage Beach

Aquatic Trail. For the adventurous boater the Missouri Department of Natural Resources has prepared a booklet showing some of the lake's prominent natural features on the Grand Glaize arm of the lake. The two-hour trip will give visitors a unique look at the lake. For a copy of the aquatic-trail booklet, write The Missouri Department of Natural Resources, Division of State Parks, P.O. Box 176, Jefferson City, MO 65102, or e-mail moparks@mail.dnr.state.mo.us.

Factory Outlet Cinema, Factory Outlet Village, Highway 54; (573) 348–1900. Movies are a hard habit to break, and besides, a good steady rain puts a "damper" on outside activities. Five screens feature current films.

Horseback Riding, Tan-Tar-A Resort, State Road KK. A thirty- to forty-minute trail ride costs $20 per person. Reservations are required. For more information call (800) 826–8272. For other horseback-riding opportunities, call the Convention & Visitors Bureau, (573) 348–1599.

House of Butterflies, Highway 54 southwest of Lake Road 54–63. Thousands of butterflies are thanking a retired Chicago couple for providing them with a haven. Vacationers appreciate it also since they are able to learn about these beautiful creatures while observing them in a garden setting. (573) 348–0088.

Lee Mace's Ozark Opry, Highway 54 and Mace Road; (573) 348–2270. For almost fifty years the Ozark Opry has been entertaining lake visitors with its home-style brand of country music, humor, and comedy. Shows offered Monday through Saturday nights, late April through late October. Hours vary with seasons. Admission: adults, $11.00; children twelve and under, $5.00.

Minor Mike's Adventure Zone, across from the Factory Outlet Village in Osage Beach; (800) 317–2126. A massive indoor play center with video games, a roller coaster, Ferris wheel, bumper cars, and a maze. Rates: $10.00 for maze, $8.00 for rides, $14.00 for both. Older children and adults can play in ***Buster's,*** which offers higher-skilled games. Age-appropriate food available from ice cream to barbecue. Hours: Monday through Thursday noon to 8:00 P.M., Friday and Saturday 10:00 A.M. to 10:00 P.M., and Sunday 10:00 A.M. to 6:00 P.M.

Ozark Caverns, Lake of the Ozarks State Park, County Road A, 8½ miles from Highway 54. Walk through the caverns and see stalagmites, soda straws, and other geological wonders, along with your basic salamanders and bats. Traditional tours, plus one for adults and one for children. Rates: adults nineteen and over, $6.00; youths thirteen to nineteen, $5.00; children six through twelve, $4.00; children five and under, free. Tour times vary with season. (573) 346–2500.

Pirate's Cove Adventure Golf, 5850 Highway 54 (573–348–4599), keeps the pirate theme going on two eighteen-hole courses. Blackbeard, the more challenging course, uses caves, waterfalls, and other obstacles and costs $6.50. Captain, the easier course, costs $6.00. Children four to twelve are $1.00 less; children three and under play free. Open daily 10:00 A.M. to 11:30 P.M. from approximately April 1 to November 1.

Shopping. Retail, specialty shops, galleries, and boutiques abound in the lake area. Many are listed in the Convention and Visitors Bureau Vacation Guide and Service Directory.

Swinging Bridge Tour. A side trip worth seeing is the Swinging Bridge, a wood-planked suspension bridge crossing the Auglaize Creek. Built in 1930 when Bagnell Dam backed up waters over country roads, the bridge is 10 miles south on Highway 42–18, a pleasant country drive.

Special Events

April. Annual Dogwood Music Festival & Art Show. Camdenton. A tradition for more than fifty years, Camdenton honors spring's arrival with a music festival that has gained wide appeal over the years. Regional entertainers, a fine-art exhibit and sale, and more than one hundred artisans. Other features include children's activities, a carnival, a parade, and lots of festival food. (800) 769–1004.

Southern Gospel Festival. Gospel music groups play gospel variations appealing to all age groups. Mainstreet Music Hall, Osage Beach. (800) 386–5253.

May. Magic Dragon Car Show. Osage Beach. Nationally known car show including street rods, customs, trucks, motorcycles, a classic auto auction, and more. Held at Lake Expo Center Grounds, Road D at the junction of Highways 54 and 42. Admission is $5.00. (800) 451–4117.

June. Cross-Over Christian Music Festival. Camdenton. National and international musicians perform Southern gospel, contemporary Christian, and Christian rock at the Stoneridge Amphitheater for four days. (800) FUN–LAKE.

August. Super Session Rock 'n' Roll Show and Dance. Osage Beach. A local group of musicians who began playing rock 'n' roll music in the lake area thirty years ago to meet college expenses return every year for an annual show. The group, now called Thirsty and The Waterboys, has evolved into a multigenerational twenty-piece band that plays music from the '50s, '60s, and '70s. (573) 392–7373 or (913) 261–7349.

September. Annual Hillbilly Fair and Annual Osage Mountain Man Rendezvous. Lake Ozark. A weekend of family fun with a parade, carnival, arts and crafts, community garage sale, festival food, and more. The Mountain Man Rendezvous honors those men who opened the West in the nineteenth century with activities including a skills contest, trader's row, and other period demonstrations. (800) 451–4117 or (573) 964–1008.

Mid-Missouri Antique Tractor Show. Near Lake Ozark. Not just tractors, but machinery and antique cars and trucks. Also arts and crafts in this old-time festival. Ten miles north of Bagnell Dam on North Eastview Drive, Eldon, ¼ mile north of Highway 54–87 Junction. (573) 480–3030.

Other Recommended Restaurants and Lodgings

Camdenton

Castleview Bed & Breakfast, 183 County Road M; (877) 346–9818. Located next to Ha Ha Tonka, this four-room home allows guests to relax in a gazebo and take walks along the lake. Full breakfast. Children over twelve welcome. No smoking or pets. Rates: $94 to $99.

The Flame Resort, State Road EE; (573) 873–5065. For a weekend or a week, this resort has sixteen housekeeping units and six luxury motel units. Indoor heated pool, recreation room, fireplaces, beach, and swimming dock. Shady grounds with walkways. Also laundry facilities. Housekeeping cabins range from $70 to $120; motel units, $50 to $120. Lower rates off-season.

Forever Resorts, Lake of the Ozarks Marina; (573) 873–3705 or (800) 255–5561. If a few days on a houseboat sounds interesting, this is the place for you. You can rent a 56-foot, 59-foot, or 65-foot houseboat, each of which sleeps ten people. The 65-foot *VIP* includes a hot tub on the upper deck. Rates range from $995 to $4,595, depending on boat and season. Located 5 miles north of Camdenton on Highway 5 at the Niangua Bridge. www.foreverresorts.com.

Greenview

Tres Hombres, Highways 5 and 7; (573) 873–5822. Well-established Mexican restaurant with a wide variety of dinners, plus steaks and burgers. Baja burritos, enchilada dinner, and fajitas reign supreme. $7.00 to $13.00.

Lake Ozark

Blue Heron, Highway HH, Horseshoe Bend; (573) 346–4646. With one of the most spectacular views on the lake, this restaurant has been a consistent favorite with vacationers for many years. Watch herons and hawks soar and circle over the lake while you dine on smoked Cornish game hen, batter-fried lobster tail, smoked trout, or any number of Blue Heron specialties. Dinners range from $18.95 to $36.00 and include salad, potato, and vegetable. Open Tuesday through Saturday. Hours: The bar opens at 5:00 P.M. and the dining room at 5:30 P.M. No reservations. Come early!

Lodge of the Four Seasons, State Road HH; (800) THE–LAKE. Entertaining guests for more than thirty-five years, the lodge offers 304 sleeping rooms, many overlooking the lake and the beautifully landscaped Japanese gardens and pool. The lodge also offers eighty-five two- and three-bedroom condominiums for nightly and weekly rental. Activities include four golf courses (one designed by Robert Trent Jones and one by Jack Nicklaus), tennis, horseback riding, excursion-boat cruises, an in-house movie theater, children's programs, a boutique, excellent restaurants, a nightclub, and much more. www.4seasonsresort.com.

Traditionally Stewart's, 1151 Bagnell Boulevard; (573) 365–2400. One of the oldest "Strip" residents, and home of the largest homemade cinnamon roll and biscuit you'll ever see. Fried chicken, catfish, and sugar-cured and country ham; also sandwiches and other plate lunches. $6.95 to $9.95.

Laurie

Chances R, Highway 5; (573) 374–8770. True lake food like frog legs and walleye. Also steaks, chicken, and chops. Breakfast buffet Saturday and Sunday. Open 6:00 A.M. to 10:00 P.M. $5.95 to $19.95.

Millstone Lodge, State Road O; (800) 290–2596. Located on the Gravois arm of the lake, the lodge has tennis, volleyball, boat rentals, a game room, and a children's playground. There is also a first-class restaurant on the premises as well as a gift shop and boutiques. Room and suite rates range from $79 to $249, depending on season.

Osage Beach

The Clown Restaurant and Topsider Lounge. Just east of the Grand Glaize Bridge off Highway 54; (573) 348–2259. One of the more active places on the lake. Features multilevel decks, food, and dancing to Top 40 music. Guests can be indoors, outdoors, or floating on the lake.

Inn at Grand Glaize, 5142 Highway 54; (800) 348–4731. With 150 rooms and suites, most with balconies and lake views, the inn offers tennis, a fitness center, game room, outdoor pool, and Cafe Glaize Restaurant. Its location in the heart of Osage Beach makes it convenient to many activities.

Potted Steer, 5985 Highway 54; (573) 348–5053. Originally a gas station, this popular restaurant is owned by Joseph Boer, who also owns the Blue Heron in Lake Ozark. Dark, very intimate bar in the basement with Dutch memorabilia. The restaurant is upstairs and is very cozy—white table-cloths, dark wood—good for an intimate dining experience. Prices range from $18.95 to $36.00, with salad, potato, and vegetable included. Specialties include many veal dishes, including osso bucco (veal shank). Beef hand-cut daily. Open Tuesday through Saturday. Hours: Restaurant open at 5:00 P.M. for cocktails, with dining room open at 5:30 P.M.; closes at 10:00 P.M. No reservations.

Tan-Tar-A Marriott Resort, Golf Club & Spa, State Road KK; (800) 826–8272. An established lake resort with double rooms and one- and two-bedroom suites from $115 to $387, depending on the season. Activities include golf, tennis, boating (including excursion-boat rides), racquetball, parasailing, swimming, two golf courses, pro shop, and much more. Package plans available. www.tan-tar-a.com.

Sunrise Beach

Lakeview Resort, HCR–69; (573) 374–5555. Located on the west side of the lake, this resort offers sand volleyball, tennis, swimming (and swimming lessons), and more. One- to six-bedroom cottages and condos from $49.95 up to $285.00, depending on season. www.lakeview-resort.com.

For More Information

Camdenton Area Chamber of Commerce, 611 North Highway 5, Camdenton, MO 65020; (800) 769–1004; www.odd.net/ozarks/cchamber.

Lake Area Chamber of Commerce, 1 Wilmore Lake, Lake Ozark, MO 65049; (800) 451–4117; www.lakeareachamber.com.

Lake of the Ozarks Convention & Visitors Bureau, 5814 Highway 54, Osage Beach, MO 65065; (573) 348–1599 or (800) 386–5253; www.fun lake.com.

Lake of the Ozarks West Chamber of Commerce, 520 North Main Street, Laurie, MO 65038; (573) 374–5500; www.odd.net/ozarks/.

Arrow Rock/Blackwater/Sedalia, Missouri

A Charming Midstate Getaway / 1 Night

Your itinerary for this easy trip can be altered to better suit your interests and the season in which you're visiting. The little town of Arrow Rock is a National Historic Landmark, and many of its buildings have retained their historic appearance. Among Arrow Rock's attractions, there's an award-winning theater presenting Broadway-caliber plays. Blackwater is a former railroad town that has lovely shops and restaurants. Sedalia hosts the International Scott Joplin Ragtime Festival in June and the Missouri State Fair for a week in August. You might want to choose to spend more time in one place than the other. Sedalia is large; Arrow Rock is small; Blackwater is smaller. Each has much to offer, and you will not want for good places to shop, eat, or relax. Right in the middle of the state, off a major east-west artery, they're easy to reach with not a lot of time spent in the car.

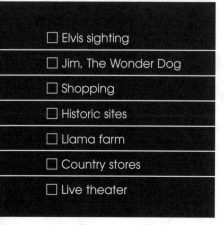

- ☐ Elvis sighting
- ☐ Jim, The Wonder Dog
- ☐ Shopping
- ☐ Historic sites
- ☐ Llama farm
- ☐ Country stores
- ☐ Live theater

Although these towns have lovely shops and restaurants, keep in mind that their hours vary. Late spring, summer, and early fall are good times to catch them open during the week; otherwise, they may open only on weekends, or they may open other times if the mood strikes. Some close for lunch. But it's all part of the area's charm.

Day 1 / Morning

Leaving St. Louis on I–70 around 9:00 A.M. will allow you enough time to stop and browse whatever interests you. Your first stop will be the **Elvis Is Alive Museum** in **Wright City,** about 30 miles west. You can't miss

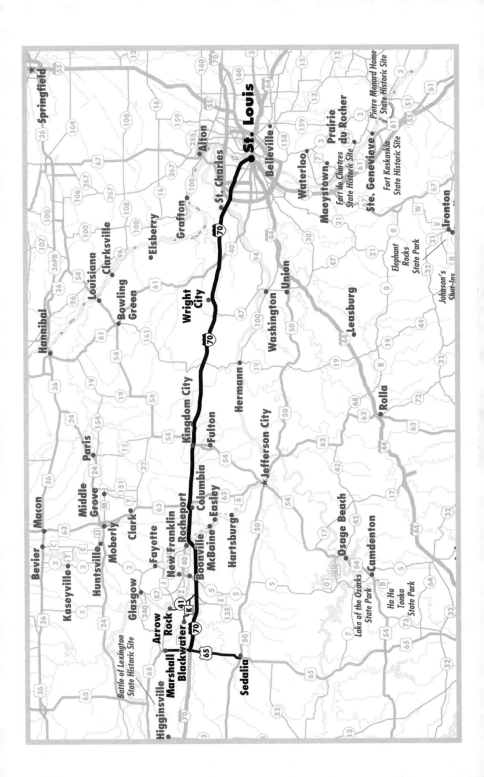

it—it has a pink Cadillac containing a cutout of Elvis in the front seat sitting out front. Admission is free, and once inside, you can look at all sorts of Elvis paraphernalia that's for sale. Another room contains a table with many additional items for purchase, plus more cardboard cutouts of celebrities. The very back room contains a coffin with a wax likeness of The King himself; a wedding altar with flowers, candles, and photographs of Elvis and Priscilla at their wedding and in happier days; plus hundreds of magazine and newspaper articles covering every facet of Elvis's life. A must-see.

Your exit (number 98) to Arrow Rock, Highway 41, is another 110 miles from the museum. Just before you reach Arrow Rock, take a quick detour to see some wonderful llamas at **River Hills Llamas;** (660) 846–2255. Go 1 mile, across the Lamine River Bridge and the railroad tracks, to Highway CC and turn right. Within ¼ mile, you will see a driveway flanked by two stone columns on the right. Follow that drive to River Hills Llamas. Llamas are beautiful, gentle, soft creatures with large expressive eyes that will melt your heart. Jim and Marcia Atkinson are enthusiastic about their multitudinous brood and will take you into the pen, where you can interact with them. The Atkinsons prefer groups, but with several days' notice, you might luck out into a tour of not only their llama farm but also their 150-year-old house, which is a showplace in itself.

Go back to Highway 41, turn right, and drive 12 miles to **Arrow Rock.** Initially named New Philadelphia in 1829, the town was a gathering place for Native Americans, then settlers traveling the Boone's Lick Trail. It later played a great part in the history of the Santa Fe Trail by serving as an outfitting post for those planning to travel west on the trail. Stop at the Arrow Rock State Park Visitor Center—on Highway 41 as you enter town—to see exhibits about Arrow Rock and the historic Boone's Lick Country.

Cozy little antiques shops and craft stores open out onto a boardwalk lining the street. Time seems to stand still in this little town. Small bungalows under large trees, gorgeous gardens, and the sound of quiet invite visitors to sit a spell.

LUNCH: Arrow Rock Tavern, 302 Main Street (660–837–3200), or the Old Huston Tavern, dates back to 1834. It was a general store, community center, and hotel before it was purchased by the State of Missouri's new park board in 1923 at the urging of the Daughters of the American Revolution. The tavern enjoys a long history of good food, and its reputation spreads far beyond the region. While waiting for your table, you can browse through the general store, stocked with goods that would have been on the shelves during the 1800s. Diners eat family-style at long tables, also as diners did in the nineteenth century. The tavern serves fried chicken, baked ham, mashed potatoes and gravy, corn, green beans, several salads, and hot bread. For dessert try their famous bread pudding and blackberry cobbler, among other offerings. The tavern also has a full liquor license. Open Wednesday through Sunday 11:00 A.M. to 8:00 P.M. Price is $12.95, not including drinks or dessert.

Afternoon

After lunch, spend some time visiting the antiques and craft shops on the boardwalk across from the tavern. Townspeople and shopkeepers are glad to share Arrow Rock's interesting history with travelers. Browse through **Aunt Yvonne's Attic,** where you'll find antiques; vintage, estate, designer, and costume jewelry; clothing and furs; and all sorts of surprises. **McAdams' Ltd.,** a former bank building, now offers a mixture of European and American antiques with antique and estate jewelry. **Santa Fe Crossing Inn & Antiques** has country furniture, historical prints, and original paintings. Look into the **Arrow Rock Country Store** for collectibles such as Bing & Grondahl, crystal, and books—a browser's heaven, as is The House of Mary B, with its many Christmas specialties.

Drive through the town to the Missouri River overlook. See Big Spring, a Santa Fe trailmark, and the Old Stone Jail built in 1873. Visit the home of nationally known Missouri artist George Caleb Bingham, who painted some of his most famous works against the Arrow Rock background. **Walking tours** are available every day from Memorial Day to Labor Day, only on weekends in April, May, September, and October, and by group reservation at other times; call (660) 837–3231. Rates: Tickets for adults cost $4.00 and are $1.00 for children.

Drive back to Main Street. One street north of Main is High Street, where you'll find the **Arrow Rock Lyceum Theater.** Housed in a former Baptist Church built in 1872, the theater is the oldest professional theater group in Missouri. The church is now a 420-seat theater that has entertained thousands of people in its more than forty-year history. Their season runs from June through October on Wednesday through Sunday evenings. Saturday and Sunday matinees start at 2:00 P.M., and evening performances at 8:15 P.M. Adult tickets are $24, seniors and students, $22, and children twelve and under, $12. Reservations advised (660–837–3311).

If you are not staying overnight here, drive back to Highway 41, turn left, and go to Route K. Follow for 3 miles to the tinier town of **Blackwater.** Founded in 1887 as a railroad town, the little town has a 1-block area of retail and craft shops, plus a couple of restaurants. Even though it is in the midst of a restoration, it remains a lovely place to visit and browse—perchance, to purchase?

The Country Collection from **Arrow Rock Antiques** has a large selection of country furniture and accessories. Don't miss **BackRoads** for elegant clutter and **Just'n Habit,** a floral, antiques, and gift shop located in a restored 1850's one-room schoolhouse. **Plum Creek,** with Amish rugs, Clay City Pottery, and Willi Raye Folk Art, is also a fun place to browse. Stop by **Chouteau Gardens,** a "pocket garden" on the main street. Sit amid the lush flowers and relax, listen to the birds, and perhaps enjoy a cold drink.

After Blackwater, follow Route K out of town and back to I–70. Go 10 miles to the I–70/US–65 junction and turn north on 65. Go 10 miles to **Marshall** and follow Business 65 into the town square. At 105 North Lafayette is a little park honoring **Jim, The Wonder Dog.** Jim, a Llewellyn setter who died in 1937, could understand foreign languages, count, and follow written directions. He also predicted the winner of the Kentucky Derby for seven years. The University of Missouri Veterinary School documented Jim's feats. A walking path with various stations telling about Jim's life circles a fountain and a statue of Jim. Tapes and books about Jim can be purchased at **Court Street Classics,** 69 South Lafayette; (660) 886–2260.

If an ice-cream cone sounds good, **One Scoop or Two Ice Cream Parlor,** located across from the park, has a good selection of ice cream and cold drinks.

Leaving Marshall, go south on US–65 for 26 miles to **Sedalia.** A frontier town founded in 1830, Sedalia was a railhead for cattle drives and a manufacturing hub. Ragtime musician Scott Joplin was born here, and the city celebrates this heritage with an annual festival.

DINNER: del-Amici (660–826–2324), in the **Hotel Bothwell,** 103 East Fourth Street, offers a varied menu with appetizers like fried mushrooms and ravioli (each $5.95). Dinner entrees include rib-eye steak ($13.95), and *Farelle di Polo con Pesto,* diced chicken sautéed with pesto, cream, and white wine in farfalle pasta ($10.95). There's also a wide selection of steaks and seafood under $17.

Jim, The Wonder Dog

Evening

A perfect way to loosen the waistline after dinner is to take a walking tour around the area. The Hotel Bothwell stands in the middle of historic downtown Sedalia and is surrounded by classic old buildings built in the late 1880s and early 1900s. A map from the **Sedalia Convention and Visitors Bureau** (800–827–5295) gives the history of each building and the best way to view them. If a nightcap is in order, however, descend the stairs of the Hotel Bothwell to **The Speakeasy** to relax and visit with other guests.

LODGING: The **Hotel Bothwell,** 103 East Fourth Street (660–826–5588), is a beautiful old hotel that opened in 1927 and has been restored to its past elegance. Windows open onto the street, and the clock in the courthouse square chimes the hour, as in days gone by. Rates: $79 to $229 (peak); $39 to $149 (off-peak). Children welcome. No pets. One floor is designated for smoking.

Day 2 / Morning

BREAKFAST: Enjoy a complimentary breakfast in the Hotel Bothwell coffee shop, with its variety of specialty coffees and fresh-baked pastries and muffins.

For a real "library" experience, visit the **Sedalia Public Library,** Third and Kentucky, the first library in Missouri to receive a grant from Andrew Carnegie. The terra-cotta and Carthage-stone building features marble and glass floors, oak woodwork, and open fireplaces.

The Gothic **Sacred Heart Catholic Church,** Third and Moniteau, built in 1893, features a breathtaking ceiling and a high, hand-carved walnut altar.

For a mixture of eclectic and antiques shopping, walk down Ohio Street. **Jambalaya's** has a mix of antique furniture and vintage clothing; for artwork, prints, and unique glassware, there's **Becca's Framing;** then go next door to **Interlude Books,** a bookstore featuring antique books. At **Smalls and Whimsies,** spend time browsing through the rows and rows of precious and maybe not-so-precious-but-really-interesting antiques and merchandise. Then have a cup of tea in their Victorian tearoom hidden in the back. **Art Impressions,** a gallery, carries artwork by area artists.

To learn about the area's important railroad heritage, visit the **Katy Depot Historic Site** at the Katy Trail trailhead. The Sedalia Depot, renovated by the Department of Natural Resources, is the home of the Chamber of Commerce and Convention and Visitors Bureau. Also a Visitors Center and The Heritage museum, the site serves as a welcome for trail riders and other area tourists.

LUNCH: For an unbelievably fine barbecue experience, stop at **Kehde's Barbecue,** Twentieth and Limit; (660) 826–2267. Fried pickles, sweet-potato French fries, and sour-cream-and-chives fries are wonderful. The Society Posh, a seasoned and buttered baked potato filled with burnt ends (smoky pieces of meat) and cheese is a new twist on barbecue. Choose from many different salads, sandwiches, or plate dinners at very reasonable prices. You can also sit in a dining car for the total railroad experience.

Afternoon

Back on Highway 65, drive north about 5 miles out of Sedalia to the **Bothwell Lodge,** a massive stone mansion standing atop the bluffs along the highway. Built between 1897 and 1928 by John Homer Bothwell, a prominent Sedalia benefactor, the lodge stands as a testament to his generosity. Now a State Historic Site, tours are held Monday through Saturday from 10:00 A.M. to 4:00 P.M. and on Sunday from noon to 5:00 P.M. Admission: adults, $2.00; children six through twelve, $1.25; under six with

paid adult, free. The park around the lodge, which is open daily from 8:00
A.M. to sunset, features hiking trails, a playground, and picnic areas.

Once back on Highway 65, drive to the I–70 junction and go east
toward St. Louis.

DINNER: If you'd like to have dinner before going home, stop in
Warrenton and go to **Brewski's,** 209 East Main Street (636–456–7678), a
charming pub in an old house in downtown Warrenton. Good pub food
including chicken wings, pastrami sandwiches, and almost every beer
known to man. Reasonable prices. (To get to Brewski's, take I–70 to exit
193. Turn right onto Highway 47, then right on to Route MM.)

Back to I–70 and east to home.

There's More

Arrow Rock

Arrow Rock Tours. Tours of the town with stops at the Sappington
Museum, Bingham House, Old Tavern, and other sites are given by the
Friends of Arrow Rock; (660) 837–3231. Adults, $4.00; students, $1.50;
children under six are free.

Camping. Camp on beautiful sites overlooking the Missouri River at
Arrow Rock State Park. For information call (660) 387–3330;
www.dnr.state.mo.us/dsp.

Prairie Park. On Route TT, 3.5 miles west of Arrow Rock. Tour the 1849
Greek Revival country home of William B. Sappington. Private residence
restored and open for tours by advance appointment through the Friends
of Arrow Rock; (660) 837–3231. $10 per person.

Blackwater

Mid-Missouri Museum of Independent Telephone Pioneers; (660)
846–4411. Located in an old bank building is a collection of old telephone
equipment, memorabilia, and other displays of local historical interest.
Open any time by stopping by City Hall on Main Street.

West End Theater, 101 Main Street; (660) 846–4411. Performances by a
local community theater group in a 1905 "plains gothic" Baptist Church.
There are three plays presented a year on the second and third Saturdays
in June, August, and October. All plays are written and directed by native
Blackwaterian Jay Turley. Ticket prices for adults, $6.00; children twelve

and under, $3.00. Complimentary refreshments at intermission. Evening performances are at 8:00 P.M.; matinees at 2:30 P.M.

Sedalia

Daum Contemporary Art Museum. Located at the State Fair Community College, 3201 West Sixteenth Street, this museum features five galleries exhibiting paintings, drawings, prints, photographs, and sculptures. Guided tours are available. (660) 530–5800; www.daummuseum.org.

Golf. Two nine-hole courses. Elm Hills Golf Course, Highway 65 and Elm Hills Road; (660) 826–6171. Rates: weekends, $6.00/nine holes, $10.00/eighteen holes; weekdays, $5.00/nine holes, $8.00/eighteen holes. Cart rental: $9.00/nine holes, $16.00/eighteen holes. Open daily 7:30 A.M. until approximately 8:00 P.M. Prairie Ridge Golf Course, Sixteenth and Prairie Road; (660) 827–5424. Rates: weekends, $8.00/nine holes, $14.00/eighteen holes; weekdays, $7.00/nine holes, $12.00/eighteen holes. Cart rental: $8.00/nine holes, $14.00/eighteen holes. Open daily 7:00 A.M. until approximately 8:00 P.M.; tee times are recommended.

Katy Trail State Park. The country's largest rails-to-trails project, with a bike trail in the old Missouri-Kansas-Texas rail bed going 223 miles east to west across Missouri. Hike or bike from trailhead east of Sedalia, then follow to Katy Depot. (800) 827–0510.

Miniature Golf. Leisure Park Miniature Golf, Arcade and Go Carts, 3208 South Ingram; (660) 826–0999. Two golf courses: $4.00 with obstacles, $3.50 without obstacles. Go carts: $4.00 for single, $5.00 for double. Swimming pool, 75 cents.

Paint Brush Prairie Natural Area; (660) 530–5500. A natural landscape 9 miles south of Sedalia on Highway 65 giving visitors a view of what the prairie looked like to homesteaders. Hiking trails throughout the area permitting viewing of native plant species and animals including prairie chickens and upland sandpipers.

Sedalia Ragtime Archives, State Fair Community College, Maple Leaf Room, 3201 West Sixteenth Street; (660) 530–5800. Ragtime and Scott Joplin memorabilia including original sheet music, piano rolls and tapes of interviews with Eubie Blake. Open Monday through Thursday 7:30 A.M. to 8:30 P.M. and Friday 7:30 A.M. to 4:00 P.M. Closed weekends and holidays.

Special Events

May. Annual Antique Show and Spring Festival. Arrow Rock. Held in the Old School House on Main Street; antiques dealers from Missouri with full range of antiques. Admission $2.00; (660) 837–3305.

Depot Days Festival. Sedalia. This festival celebrates Sedalia's railroad heritage. First-person reenactments, educational sessions, entertainment, history accounts, children's activities, and displays of model railroads and railroad artifacts. (660) 826–2222 or (800) 827–5295.

May through August (weekends). Visiting artists on the boardwalk. Arrow Rock. In coordination with Missouri Arts Council, each weekend has a different artist demonstrating period crafts. One weekend might see a candle maker, another weekend a wood-carver. Other crafts include stained glass, dried flowers, and weaving. Items also for sale. (660) 837–3335.

June. Scott Joplin International Ragtime Festival. Sedalia. Sedalia shows off its nickname as "The Cradle of Ragtime" with this nationally known five-day festival. Concerts, dances, symposiums, jam sessions, and much more crowd these days at various venues throughout the city. For complete information and tickets, call (800) 827–5295; e-mail ragtimer@scott joplin.org; www.scottjoplin.org.

July. Missouri State Pow-Wow. Sedalia. A three-day intertribal cultural gathering featuring dancing, food, and arts and crafts including silver jewelry, pottery, and paintings. Held on the Missouri State Fair Campgrounds. Camping is available. (660) 826–5608.

August. The Missouri State Fair. Sedalia. One of the state's biggest events, an eleven-day extravaganza on the 2,200-acre fairgrounds with 396 acres of exhibits. Also a mile-long midway, auto races, horse and livestock shows, nationally known entertainers, and food, food, food. (800) 422–FAIR.

September. Boonslick Folk Music Festival. Arrow Rock. A workshop and concert by musicians playing period instruments such as the fiddle, dulcimer, banjo, and guitar. Followed by Fire Department Pig Roast. (660) 837–3305.

October. Annual Heritage Craft Festival. Arrow Rock. A tradition of more than thirty years features regional craftspeople demonstrating lost period arts such as spinning, rope making, weaving, soap making, and candle making, all crafts depicting daily life as it was in the Arrow Rock of the 1880s. Historic buildings also open to the public. (660) 837–3305.

November. The Saturday after Thanksgiving, Santa comes to town, and townspeople hang natural greenery around the downtown district in Arrow Rock. Shops are open with Christmas specialty items. Carol singing and luminaries in the evening.

Other Recommended Restaurants and Lodgings

Arrow Rock

Arrow Rock Station. Fine dining in an early gas station at the corner of Main Street and Highway 41. It also features a year-round Christmas store. Dinners include steaks, pork chops, and chicken ranging from $18 to $22. Lunch served during the theater season. (660) 837–3310.

Borgman's Bed & Breakfast; (660) 837–3350. One block south of Main Street, guests can walk around historic Arrow Rock during their stay at this one-hundred-year-old home. Family-style breakfasts with home-baked breads. Four rooms with three shared baths. No smoking or pets. Rates: $55 to $60. Kborgman@mid-mo.net.

The Keeping House, 602 Van Buren; (660) 837–3335. Two suites in a charming clapboard house built in the 1840s. Each suite has its own private bath, microwave, and refrigerator. Continental breakfast provided, or guests can make their own morning feast. Rates: $95 to $125.

Schoolhouse Café. Located in the original cafeteria of the old schoolhouse on Main Street. This restaurant serves up homemade breakfast and lunch specialties at moderate prices. The schoolhouse is now the community center and rehearsal hall for the Lyceum Theater. Diners sometimes can get an audible preview of current plays while they eat! (660) 837–3331.

Ye Olde Ice Cream Shoppe. A 1950s ice-cream parlor on the Main Street Boardwalk features ice-cream specialties, deli sandwiches, soups, and salads from $4.00 to $7.50. (660) 837–3272.

Blackwater

The Iron Horse Restaurant, located in The Iron Horse Inn at the foot of Main Street. This beautifully restored, elegant dining room of this historic 1880s railroad hotel is the perfect setting for an unforgettable lunch or dinner. Lunch $4.00 to $11.00, dinner from $14.00. (660) 846–2011.

The Iron Horse Inn on Main Street. Completely renovated to the smallest detail, this charming eleven-room railroad hotel has been welcoming visitors since 1889. Incredible woodwork, period furnishings, and elegant surroundings await you. Rates: $65 to $135. (660) 846–3001.

Sedalia

Eddie's Drive-In, 115 West Broadway and 412 South Ohio; (660) 826–0155. A 1950s-style drive-in famous for steak burgers. Inexpensive.

Georgetown Inn, 22166 Highway H; (660) 826–3941. Snuggle down in an 1842 home and enjoy the peace of a country night. Five bedrooms, three full baths. Country breakfast of ham, eggs, grits, biscuits, gravy, and fruit. Children welcome. No pets, no smoking. Rates: $50 to $65.

Maple Leaf Antique Mall Tea Room, 106 West Main; (660) 826–8383. Enjoy sandwiches, salads, soups, and other home-style specials in a quaint tearoom setting surrounded by antiques. And save room for the pie! Inexpensive.

Sedalia House Bed & Breakfast, 26097 Highway HH; (660) 747–5728. A two-story colonial home amid the rolling country hills. It features five rooms with two and a half baths, and a master suite with a private bath. Rates: $65 to $80. Children welcome. Smoking permitted outside.

Walz Country Cookin' Cafe, Highway 65 North; (660) 826–4634. Find the locals and you'll find good food. A favored place, this cafe serves up home-style cooking, especially breakfasts and cinnamon rolls. Inexpensive.

Wheel Inn Drive-In, 1800 West Broadway; (660) 826–5177. A drive-in right out of the 1950s and home of the Goober Burger (a hamburger with peanut butter), a mid-Missouri landmark. Inexpensive.

For More Information

Arrow Rock State Historic Site, Arrow Rock, MO 65320 for information including camping. (660) 387–3330; www.dnr.state.mo.us/dsp.

Blackwater City Hall, 200 Main Street, Blackwater, MO 65322; (660) 846–4411.

Friends of Arrow Rock, P.O. Box 124, Arrow Rock, MO 65320; (660) 837–3231; www.arrowrock.org.

Sedalia Convention and Visitors Bureau, 600 East Third Street, Sedalia, MO 65301; (800) 827–5295; www.visitsedaliamo.com.

WESTERN ESCAPE EIGHT

Kansas City/Independence, Missouri

Missouri's Wild West / 3 Nights

Across the state, 250 miles west from St. Louis, lie Kansas City and Independence. Both enjoy a "Wild West" reputation—with cattle drives, Jesse James, and the Santa Fe Trail—and share a history as the center of Civil War guerilla activity with Quantrill's Raiders.

- ☐ Museums
- ☐ Farmers market
- ☐ Zoo
- ☐ Sunken steamboat
- ☐ Presidential history
- ☐ Historic homes
- ☐ Amusement parks

To appreciate this area would take much more than three days. Besides historical, art, and jazz museums, there's a zoo that resembles a jungle, a vibrant farmers market, a sunken steamboat and its treasures, a renovated historic train station, and a theme amusement park. And this is assuming you can keep away from the fantastic shopping areas and amazing restaurants (including that famous Kansas City barbecue) long enough to sightsee. This trip will whet your appetite enough to make you plan another trip. It's just a good thing Missouri isn't as wide as Texas.

Whether you drive or take the train, you should plan on getting into Kansas City the evening before your sight-seeing activities begin. Amtrak runs between St. Louis and Kansas City twice a day. The station is on Main Street around three minutes from your hotel, the Hyatt Regency Crown Center. If you drive, leave around 3:00 P.M. That way you can have dinner in one of the area's most well-known restaurants, Stephenson's Apple Farm. From the restaurant, go to your hotel and rest up, because you most certainly will need it.

Day 1 / Evening

DINNER: If you leave St. Louis at 3:00 P.M., you should get to **Stephenson's Apple Farm,** 16401 East US–40 (816–373–5400), by

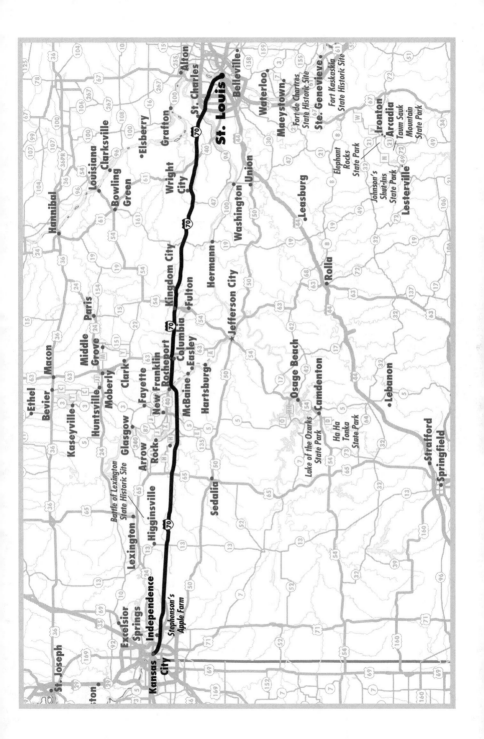

6:30 P.M., time enough for dinner. Go west on I–70 for approximately 230 miles. Take exit 14, Lee's Summit Road. Turn left at the top of the ramp and go approximately ½ mile to US–40. Stephenson's is on the corner.

Stephenson's orchards started in 1935 on old Highway 40 as a fruit stand, with apples, berries, and peaches. In 1946 the family built a restaurant, and the original stone building remains—although it has been engulfed by several renovations. The Baked Chicken 'n Butter & Cream ($13.50) alone is worth the drive. Or the Hickory Smoked Beef Brisket ($14.50). All dinners are served with apple butter and hot rolls. Entrees from $12.95 to $19.50. Hours: Monday through Saturday 11:30 A.M. to 10:00 P.M. and Sunday 10:00 A.M. to 9:00 P.M., with brunch ending at 2:00 P.M.

After dinner, drive into the city to your hotel. Take Lee's Summit Road back to I–70 and head west to I–35 South. Take the Twentieth Street exit, and drive 6 blocks on Twentieth to McGee Street. Turn right and go 3 blocks to the Hyatt.

LODGING: The Hyatt Regency Crown Center, 2345 McGee (800–233–1234), will put you in the middle of all you want to do. Large, comfortable rooms for relaxing. Restaurant, indoor and outdoor pools, and health club on-site. The hotel is also linked by way of an elevated pedestrian walkway to the Westin Crown Center, the Crown Center shops, and Union Station. No free parking. You will either have to find a place on the street, in the lot, or use valet parking for $13.50 a day. Rates start at $119. Package plans available.

Day 2 / Morning

BREAKFAST: At the Hyatt Regency. Enjoy breakfast in the Terrace, on the mezzanine level in the atrium of the hotel lobby. Standard breakfast is available along with cappuccinos, fresh pastries, and fruit.

A twenty-five-minute drive from your hotel will get you to your morning's activity, the Kansas City Zoo. (There will be maps at your hotel and you can get specific directions as well.) The **Kansas City Zoological Park** at Swope Park, 6700 Zoo Drive, I–435 and Sixty-third Street (816–513–5700), which covers more than 200 acres, has more than 1,300 animals living in such a naturalistic setting that you really have to look hard to see them. About 400 animals live in the ninety-five-acre African exhibit, which includes the Kenyan Plains with giraffes and antelopes, the Congolese Forest with leopards and lowland gorillas, and the Okavango

Delta with the elephant sanctuary. Visit Australia and see kangaroos, dingoes, emus, a sheep station, and a walk-through aviary. Other features are an IMAX Theatre, a mural of original art, an 8,000-gallon native Missouri aquarium, and a children's conservation tile wall. Admission: ages twelve and over, $7.50; seniors, $6.50; children three through eleven, $4.50; under three, free. Tuesday admission is $3.00 for all. IMAX admission: adults, $6.00; seniors, $5.00; children three through eleven, $4.00. Parking is free year-round. Summer hours (April 1 to October 14) 9:00 A.M. to 5:00 P.M.; winter hours (October 15 to March 31) 9:00 A.M. to 4:00 P.M. www. kansascityzoo.org.

LUNCH: You don't want to wait any longer for Kansas City barbecue, so head back to town and make your lunch stop **Gates Barbecue,** 3201 Main in midtown (816–753–0828), a family-owned Kansas City barbecue tradition with cafeteria-style serving. Be ready to order when they yell at you! Barbecue beef, ham or turkey sandwiches, ribs, and mutton. Also Yummy "Yammer" Pie. Open daily 10:00 A.M. to midnight. Inexpensive to moderate.

Afternoon

Explore your surroundings and walk through "The Link" to **Crown Center.** Built around the world headquarters of Hallmark Cards, this three-level center houses fifty specialty shops, twenty restaurants (from fine to casual dining), the American Heartland Theatre featuring live, Broadway-style entertainment, and the Coterie Theatre, combining live theater with educational themes for young people and a six-screen cinema. The center also hosts summer outdoor entertainment and winter ice-skating. Open Monday through Wednesday and Saturday 10:00 A.M. to 6:00 P.M., Thursday and Friday 10:00 A.M. to 9:00 P.M., and Sunday noon to 5:00 P.M. Call (800) 721–7829 or log on to www.crowncenter.com.

Learn about the humble beginnings of the Hallmark Card at the **Hallmark Visitors Center** (816–274–5672; www.hallmarkvisitor center.com) in the Crown Center complex. Exhibits show visitors the creativity and craftsmanship involved in Hallmark products. See technicians demonstrate the die-making and printing processes used in making greeting cards.

If you have children between the ages of four and thirteen, be sure you take them to **Kaleidoscope,** a hands-on art experience where they journey through the Imagination Machine to a world where they can explore under the sea, outer space, a country cottage, and a big city. Using colored paper, crayons, glue, yarn, and stickers, children can explore, create, and discover—and it's free! Sponsored by Hallmark Cards. Open Monday through Saturday. Reservations needed for the fifty-five-minute-long session. (816) 274–8300; www.hallmarkkaleidoscope.com.

Walking into the Grand Hall of the magnificent **Kansas City Union Station** is like taking a step back in time. The original marble floors, the beautiful rose and blue ceiling, the huge clock under which so many couples kissed good-bye—and "welcome home"—during World War II. Built in 1914, the station is second only to New York's Grand Central Station in size. It closed in 1985, underwent a $253-million restoration, and reopened in November 1999. But it kept its character, along with the bullet holes on the exterior from the Union Station Massacre when gunmen killed a gangster and federal agents in 1933. In place of the old ticket booth stands **Union Cafe** (816–300–2233) for casual dining. For fine dining there's **Pierpont's** (816–221–5111). Many specialty shops also line the hall.

Without a doubt, the station's biggest attraction is **Science City,** an interactive experience for all ages combining elements of museums, amusement parks, science centers, and theater. You'll find more than fifty hands-on exhibits such as designing your own newspaper front page, forecasting the weather, riding a bicycle across a rope, training for astronaut missions, exploring a space station, creeping through a cave, building a car or a robot, and traveling through the human body at Dr. Hale N. Hearty's Clinic. And this isn't all. Experience 3-D at **City Extreme Screen,** explore the galaxies at **City Dome,** and enjoy live theater at **City Stage.** Science City admission: adults, $9.00; seniors, $8.00; twelve and under, $7.00; under three, free. Science City hours: Monday through Saturday 10:00 A.M. to 5:00 P.M., Sunday noon to 5:00 P.M. Theater hours: Times vary by theater. Restaurants and shops open from morning through night. Check for exact hours. (816) 460–2020; www.sciencecity.com.

DINNER: The American Restaurant, Twenty-fifth and Grand Boulevard at Crown Center; (816) 426–1133. This restaurant is within walking distance of the Hyatt. With two French-trained, nationally recognized chefs and an adventurous menu, the American is the only Kansas City restaurant that has earned the Mobil 4-Star Award. White-clothed tables surrounded by huge windows give diners a beautiful view of the city while they enjoy such fare as Colorado lamb rack with morel mushrooms or grilled pork tenderloin with spring vegetables. For an appetizer, try the cream of crayfish soup with white asparagus and crab cake. Entrees start at $23 and the menu varies by season. A quality wine list matches the food. Very expensive, but the atmosphere and food are worth it. Hours: Lunch, Monday through Friday 11:15 A.M. to 2:00 P.M.; dinner, Monday through Thursday 6:00 to 10:00 P.M. and Friday and Saturday 6:00 to 11:00 P.M. Reservations recommended.

Evening

After this day you're probably ready to collapse, but if not, and you'd like to experience some K.C. jazz, kick back at **The Blue Room,** 1600 East Eighteenth Street (816–474–2929), located in the Historic Jazz District (Eighteenth and Vine). In the 1920s and '30s, this area was *the* place to find good jazz and blues. The club now features live jazz four nights a week, with an open-mike night on Monday night. Call for hours. www.kcmo.org/18thvine.

LODGING: Hyatt Regency.

Day 3 / Morning

BREAKFAST: You could choose the Terrace again, but since your first stop is City Market, you could munch in **Cascone's,** 20 East Fifth Street (816–842–3201), a classic American diner serving Italian sausage and pancakes. Good coffee, too.

City Market, 20 East Fifth Street, has been operating since 1857, when it started as a trading post. Now the largest open-air market in the Midwest, it features thirty-five specialty shops and restaurants. You experience a riot of color and sounds as vendors hawk their wares, from live ducks to fresh flowers and herbs to fresh fish, plus food from the Far East, pottery from South America, and clothing from the Mediterranean. Hours: March through December, 7:00 A.M. to 4:00 P.M. daily. (816) 842–1271; www.kc-citymarket.com.

Located by the City Market, the **Arabia Steamboat Museum,** 400 Grand Avenue (801–471–1856), is one of the more unusual museums in the state. After leaving Kansas City in 1856, the steamboat *Arabia* hit a snag in the Missouri River and sank, taking its cargo with it. In 1988 a group of "steamboat enthusiasts" found the ship buried in a farmer's cornfield ½ mile from the river. The group recovered more than 200 tons of cargo. The

Fresh produce in City Market, Kansas City

items were cleaned and are now on display. Looking at silverware, china, hats, and other cargo that spent almost 150 years mired in the mud and hearing the story of how they were cleaned is fascinating. Hours: Monday through Saturday 10:00 A.M. to 6:00 P.M. and Sunday noon to 5:00 P.M. Admission: adults, $9.75; seniors, $9.25; children ages four to twelve, $4.75.

Next, drive to the Eighteenth and Vine Historic Jazz District. **The American Jazz Museum** (816–474–VINE) and the **Negro League Baseball Museum** (816–221–1920) are both located at 1616 East Eighteenth Street. The Jazz Museum tells the story of jazz through interactive exhibits and displays of personal effects of jazz greats such as Ella Fitzgerald, Louis Armstrong, and Charlie Parker. Hours: Tuesday through Thursday 9:00 A.M. to 6:00 P.M., Friday and Saturday 9:00 A.M. to 9:00 P.M., and Sunday noon to 6:00 P.M. Admission: adults, $6.00; children under twelve, $2.50; $8.00 for adult admission to both museums.

The Baseball Museum uses video presentations, exhibits, and sports memorabilia to re-create the story of the Negro League. It features a seventy-five-seat theater for viewing a fifteen-minute film on the Negro League's history and has fifteen computer stations, which allow visitors to learn more about these teams. Hours: Tuesday through Saturday 9:00 A.M. to 6:00 P.M. and Sunday noon to 6:00 P.M. Admission: adults, $6.00; children under twelve, $2.50.

LUNCH: Lidia's Kansas City, 101 West Twenty-second Street; (816) 221–3722. Located in the Freighthouse District, this upscale restaurant keeps the "warehouse feeling," even with a massive fireplace, handblown chandeliers, and oversized banquettes. Food is northern Italian, and the *Pollino Nuovo* (herb-marinated grilled chicken breast with pesto, tomatoes, and fontina cheese between crusty bread slices) is very good ($9.50). Also a daily sampling of fresh and filled pastas and imported Italian dried pastas for $12.00. A complimentary luncheon Caesar salad is served tableside. www.lidiasitaly.com.

Afternoon

Let your lunch settle as you ponder the artwork at the **Nelson-Atkins Museum of Art,** 4525 Oak Street; (816) 751–1ART. As one of the top museums in the country, Nelson-Atkins has period pieces and exhibits of many cultures, but it is best known for its Asian collection with the Chinese Temple Room, furniture, porcelain, and a specially humidified gallery of delicate scrolls painting, among others. The beautifully land-scaped grounds contain a number of Henry Moore sculptures. You cannot miss the museum—it's the building with the four 5,500-pound shuttle-cocks sitting on the lawn. Hours: Tuesday through Thursday 10:00 A.M. to 4:00 P.M., Friday 10:00 A.M. to 9:00 P.M., Saturday 10:00 A.M. to 5:00 P.M., and Sunday noon to 5:00 P.M. Closed Monday and holidays. The entrance to the museum's parking garage is off Oak Street, just south of Forty-fifth Street. Parking is $3.00 with validation. www.nelson-atkins.org.

For a different perspective visit the **Kemper Museum of Contemporary Art,** 4420 Warwick Boulevard; (816) 561–3737. Opened in 1994, the museum houses a rapidly growing collection of modern and contemporary works in all types of media from artists such as Georgia O'Keeffe, Frank Stella, and Robert Mapplethorpe. Hours: Tuesday through Thursday 10:00 A.M. to 4:00 P.M., Friday 10:00 A.M. to 9:00 P.M., Saturday 10:00 A.M. to 5:00 P.M., and Sunday 11:00 A.M. to 5:00 P.M. Admission is free. www.kemperart.org.

When you say Kansas City, the first thing that comes to most people's minds is **Country Club Plaza,** that shopping haven by which all others are judged. Designed in 1922 as the country's first suburban shopping district, the Spanish architecture, fountains, and murals established this area as one of a kind. At Forty-seventh Street and J.C. Nichols Parkway, 180 shops and restaurants spread out over 14 square blocks, which can be covered by foot or horse-drawn carriage. Every Thanksgiving night, thousands of people flock to the plaza for its annual Christmas lighting ceremony, a spectacular display that has become a tradition with families for years. (816) 753–0100; www.countryclubplaza.com.

Another local tradition is going to **Winstead's,** 101 Brush Creek; (816) 753–2244. Located off the plaza, it's a local favorite that serves '50s-style hamburgers. Shopping makes you want a malt, and you could pick no better place. Open Sunday to Friday 6:30 A.M. to midnight and Saturday 6:30 A.M. to 1:00 A.M.

DINNER: Since you are on the Plaza, dine at the **Classic Cup Café,** 301 West Forty-seventh Street; (816) 753–1840. A trip to the Plaza is not complete without an outdoor dining experience at this popular restaurant. It's hard to pick from the wonderful choices. However, the Thai chicken pizza ($10.00) pleases many, as does the black-bean chili ($8.00 a bowl). Larger appetites will enjoy the porterhouse pork chop with an apple brandy cream ($19.00). And don't pass up the salad with the blackberry vinaigrette!

LODGING: Hyatt Regency.

Day 4 / Morning

BREAKFAST: Walk over to Crown Center and grab a bagel or breakfast sandwich and cappuccino at **Einstein Bros. Bagels.** Or stop in at **Golden Harvest Bakery** for hearth-baked breads, muffins, pastries, or doughnuts from Lamar's, a local icon. Both places are on Level 1. Einstein Bros. opens at 6:00 A.M. and Golden Harvest Bakery at 7:00 A.M.

You will be spending the day in **Independence,** "The Queen City of Trails," so-called because pioneers starting on the Santa Fe, Oregon, and California Trails outfitted their wagons here. And, of course, it was the home of former President Harry S Truman. To get to Independence, take I–70 East to the Noland Road exit and go north on Noland to Downtown Historic Independence. To make your day easier, stop by the Truman Home Ticket and Information Center, Truman and Main (816–254–9929) and grab a few brochures to get some background on the places you will be seeing.

The **Mormon Visitor Center,** 937 West Walnut Street (816–836–3466), tells of Mormon prophet Joseph Smith's group of pioneers who followed him to the site of Independence, which he designated as

"Zion," the center for the Mormon Church, formally known as the Church of Jesus Christ of the Latter Day Saints. Free guided tours of the center, museum, and historic sites on the square are given from 9:00 A.M. to 9:00 P.M. daily. www.lds.org.

The **Community of Christ Temple and Auditorium,** River Boulevard and Walnut Street (816–521–3030), are the headquarters of the Community of Christ. Open daily 9:00 A.M. to 5:00 P.M.

The Temple, with its spire pointing to the heavens, lures people from all over to admire the architecture and the near-perfect acoustics in the Sanctuary, which seats 1,600 people and houses a pipe organ with 5,685 pipes. Guided tours are given Monday through Saturday 9:00 to 11:30 A.M. and 1:00 to 5:00 P.M. and Sunday 1:00 to 5:00 P.M. Free organ recitals daily June through August and on Sundays September through May. www.rlds.org.

The **Church of Christ (Temple Lot and Visitors Center),** River Boulevard and Lexington Avenue (816–833–3995), occupies the original "temple lot" dedicated by Joseph Smith and his followers in 1831. Visitors can see the stone markers on display in the visitor center. Hours: Monday through Friday 9:00 A.M. to 4:30 P.M. and Saturday 9:00 A.M. to noon.

LUNCH: Drive to the **Historic Independence Square,** where you will find the **Courthouse Exchange,** 113 West Lexington; (816) 252–0344. The Dill Chicken Salad Sandwich on grilled rye is especially delicious ($5.95). Other sandwiches are available, and there's also a bountiful salad bar.

Afternoon

After lunch, walk through **Independence Square Courthouse,** where Harry Truman spent many hours as judge of Eastern Jackson County. On the first floor the **Truman Courthouse** (816–795–8200, ext. 60) is open to the public and contains displays with video presentation. Admission: adults, $2.00; seniors and youths, $1.00. Hours: 9:00 A.M. to 4:30 P.M. Friday and Saturday.

Just off the square is the **1859 Jail, Marshal's Home and Museum,** 217 North Main; (816) 252–1892. Walk into the cold, dank cells that once housed Frank James and William Quantrill. See the spot where a sheriff of one day was shot and killed and his young son injured. The museum includes a collection of artifacts and exhibits from the late 1800s. Open April through October; Monday through Saturday 10:00 A.M to 5: 00 P.M.

and Sunday 1:00 to 4:00 P.M. Closed January and February. Hours vary by season. In March, November, and December, open Tuesday through Saturday 10:00 A.M. to 4:00 P.M. and Sunday 1:00 to 4:00 P.M. Call for Christmas hours. Admission: adults, $4.00; seniors over sixty-two, $3.50; students, $1.00; children under five, free.

Next to the jail is the **Truman Home Ticket & Information Center,** Truman Road and Main Street (816–254–9929), where you can purchase tickets to see the **Truman Home.** Truman walked the 7 blocks from the impressive white Victorian home through a neighborhood of homes, shops, and churches to his office. Tour hours: Memorial Day through Labor Day, 9:00 A.M. to 4:45 P.M. daily; after Labor Day until Memorial Day, closed Monday. Admission: adults, $3.00; sixteen and younger, free. www.nps.gov/hsstr.

Even Republicans will enjoy the **Truman Presidential Library and Museum,** 500 West U.S. Highway 24; (800) 833–1225. Step into a replica of the Oval Office. See his autos, the love letters between him and Bess, the inspiring mural by Thomas Hart Benton, and the gravesites. The museum recently underwent a $22.5-million renovation. Hours: Monday through Wednesday and Friday through Saturday 9:00 A.M. to 5:00 P.M., Thursday 9:00 A.M. to 9:00 P.M., and Sunday noon to 5:00 P.M. Admission: adults, $5.00; seniors, $4.50; students six to eighteen, $3.00; children five and under, free. www.trumanlibrary.org.

A fascinating museum is the **National Frontier Trails Center,** 318 West Pacific (816–325–7575), the only museum in the nation exclusively devoted to the history of the overland trails. A film depicts the hardship the pioneers underwent on their journey west. The museum contains an authentic covered wagon along with trail diaries and artifacts. It also houses the Merrill J. Mattes Research Library, one of the largest collections in the nation documenting the overland-trail experience, as well as books on westward exploration, mountain men, Native Americans, and the railroad. Hours: Monday through Saturday 9:00 A.M. to 4:30 P.M. and Sunday 12:30 to 4:30 P.M. Admission: adults, $3.50; students six through seventeen, $2.00; five and under, free.

DINNER: If you want dinner before you start home, **V's Italiano Restaurant,** 10819 Highway 40 East (816–353–1241), serves up some mighty fine Italian food. For appetizers try the deep-fried toasted provolone cheese wedges with tomato sauce ($5.50) or garlic roasted in olive oil and served with Italian toast and cream-cheese wedges ($5.75), as well as their own Italian sausage soup ($4.50). Many other pastas and specialty entrees like Chicken Lemonata ($14.50) are also available. Prices: $8.50 for basic pasta to $20.75 for two lobster tails. www.vsrestaurant.com.

It's a three-and-a-half-hour trip home, and if you need a pick-me-up on the way, **Gasper's Truck Stop** in Kingdom City is at the halfway mark right off the interstate on Highway 54 West. Very good coffee and wonderful pies!

There's More

Independence

Bingham-Waggoner Estate, 313 Pacific; (816) 461–3491. Located on the Santa Fe Trail, this huge home rang with children's laughter and saw history unfold right at the front gate. Once owned by artist George Caleb Bingham, it has seen bloody Civil War battles. Swales from wagon wheels were recently discovered on this property, which visitors can also see. Hours: April 1 through October 31, Monday through Saturday 10:00 A.M. to 4:00 P.M. and Sunday 1:00 to 4:00 P.M. Admission: adults, $4.00; seniors over sixty-two, $3.50; children six to sixteen, $1.00; under six, free. Call for Christmas hours.

1827 Log Courthouse, 107 West Kansas Avenue, 1 block south of Historic Square (816–325–7431), was for many years the last courthouse between Independence and the Pacific Ocean. Harry Truman even held court here while the main courthouse was being renovated. Free admission.

Historic Independence Square, with its many specialty shops, craft stores, antiques shops, and restaurants.

Leila's Hair Museum, 815 West Twenty-third; (816) 252–4247. The only museum of its kind in the nation, devoted to a lost art form. Displays of articles made out of human hair, such as picture frames and jewelry. Hours: Monday through Saturday 8:00 A.M. to 4:30 P.M. Admission: adults, $3.00; seniors and children seven to ten, $1.50; under seven, free. Call for appointment.

Pioneer Spring Cabin, Southeast corner of Noland and Truman Roads; (816) 325–7111. A typical 1850s two-room log home depicting what life was like when people had regular contact with Native American tribes, settlers, migrating families, and Civil War soldiers. Free admission.

Vaile Mansion, 1500 North Liberty; (816) 325–7430. This opulent 1881 Victorian estate has all the ingredients for a wonderful novel: wealth, grandeur, loneliness, scandal, rumors of insanity, suicide, ghosts. A marvelous mansion to tour. Hours: April 1 through October 31, Monday through Saturday 10:00 A.M. to 4:00 P.M. and Sunday 1:00 to 4:00 P.M. Admission: adults, $4.00; seniors, $3.50; children six to sixteen, $1.00; under six, free. Call for Christmas hours and rates.

Kansas City

Oceans of Fun, I–435, exit 54; (800) 877–4386. Water-theme park with sixty acres of slides, wave pools, lazy rivers, and other water amusements. "Adults Only" section. Open late May through early September. Admission: adults (over 48 inches tall through age fifty-nine), $24.00; juniors four years and older and under 48 inches tall, $12.95; seniors over sixty, $16.50; after 4:00 P.M., $16.50 for any age and over 48 inches tall. Park opens at 10:00 A.M.; closing time varies. www.worldsoffun.com.

Plaza Fiesta Cruise, Ward Parkway and Wyandotte Street; (888) 741–BOAT. A new way to see Country Club Plaza—from a boat gliding along the Plaza Waterway with its waterfalls and fountains. Tours take forty minutes. Cost is $6.50. Open daily April through October from 11:00 A.M. to 10:00 P.M. and in November from 11:00 A.M. to 5:00 P.M. Holiday Christmas Lights tour, Thanksgiving through mid-January, 5:00 to 9:00 P.M.

Toy and Miniature Museum, 5235 Oak Street; (816) 333–2055. Restored 1911 mansion with miniature collection and antique dollhouses. www.umkc.edu/tmm.

Westport Shopping District. Westport Road and Broadway. Formerly a stopping place for mountain men, Indians, fur traders, and wagon trains heading west, Westport has kept its nineteenth-century charm alive with restored shops, art galleries, and restaurants on tree-lined streets with old-time street lamps. Restaurants of all types and nightclubs keep Westport hopping long after dark, making it one of the most popular areas in the city.

Worlds of Fun, I–435, exit 54; (800) 877–4386. This 175-acre theme park features the Mamba, one of the tallest, longest, and fastest steel roller coasters in the country. Also the Boomerang—a coaster going forward through loops and corkscrews, then backward, then forward again—plus other "fun" rides. Open early April through mid-October. Admission: Adults (over 48 inches tall through age fifty-nine), $35.00; juniors (four years and under 48 inches tall), $12.95; seniors sixty and older, $17.50; twilight after 4:00 P.M., $17.50 for any age and over forty-eight inches tall. Park opens at 10:00 A.M.; closing time varies. www.worldsoffun.com.

Overland Park, Kansas

Build-A-Bear Workshop, off I–35 at Eighty-fifth Street and Quivira in Oak Park Mall; (913) 307–0328. More than a store, bear makers of all ages can create their dream bear, their special companion. The Master Bear Builders will help you choose, stuff, stitch, dress, and name your very own customized bear, bunny, dog, cat, etc. www.buildabear.com.

Shawnee, Kansas

1950s All-Electric House, Johnson County Museum of History, 6305 Lackman Road; (913) 631–6709. Originally built in 1954 by Kansas City Power & Light as a showcase for modern innovations, the home has such features as an electric curtain opener and a bedside remote control for cof-feemakers. Outlets are waist-high so that high-heeled homemakers would not have to bend over to plug in the vacuum. Step into this house and step back into the fifties! www.digitalhistory.com.

Special Events

May. Harry Birthday. Independence. A celebration of Harry Truman's birthday on Independence Square. Entertainment, birthday cake in the square, children's art fair, food booths, and other activities. (816) 252–0608.

Spirit Festival. Kansas City. Local, regional, and national entertainment on multiple stages. Children's/Family Pavilion provides hands-on creative projects, displays, and exhibits. Clowns, magicians, storytellers, carnival midway. (816) 221–4444, www.spiritfest.com.

June. Annual Greek Festival. Overland Park, Kansas. One of the largest ethnic festivals held in Kansas City. St. Dionysios Greek Orthodox Community, 8100 West Ninety-fifth Street; (913) 341–7343.

Jazz Lovers' Pub Crawl. Kansas City. Jazz lovers are bussed from club to club to enjoy music and citywide partying. (913) 967–6767.

Strawberry Festival, Vaile Mansion. Independence. Antiques, crafts, flea market, entertainment, children's area, food, and lots of strawberry treats. (816) 325–7430.

July. Kansas City Blues & Jazz Festival. Kansas City. Features local, national, and international blues and jazz artists performing on four stages. Also workshops. Penn Valley Park, Twenty-seventh and Main. (800) 530–5266.

August. Annual Dawg Days Fair, Craft Show, and Flea Market. Independence. Craft booths, flea market, food, sidewalk sale, pet parade, pet adoption and pet demonstrations, plus horse-drawn wagon rides and walking tours through historic district. Main and Lexington Streets. (816) 252–0608.

September. Art Westport. Kansas City. More than 120 area artists provide paintings, sculptures, pottery, jewelry, and fabrics. Pennsylvania Avenue between Westport Road and Forty-second Street. (816) 756–2789.

Plaza Art Fair, Country Club Plaza. Kansas City. More than 190 nationally known artists display their works over a three-day event that features live entertainment and many different types of food. Call (816) 753–0100 for information.

Santa-Cali-Gon Days. Independence. Festival with more than 450 booths, three stages of entertainment, carnival, commercial vendors, and food celebrating the city's role as an outfitting post for westward-bound pioneers. Historic Independence Square. (816) 252–4745; www.independence chamber.com.

October. The American Royal Livestock, Horse Show, and Rodeo. One of Kansas City's most famous traditions since 1899. The world's largest combined show features a grand parade, rodeos, and entertainment. American Royal Complex. (816) 221–9800; www.americanroyal.com.

November. Country Club Plaza Lighting Ceremony. Kansas City. Thanksgiving night. Thousands of people each year fill the plaza to watch the flip of the switch that outlines every tower, dome, and balcony of the 14-block district in twinkling lights. The display goes until mid-January.

Mayor's Christmas Tree Lighting Ceremony. Kansas City. Kansas City Mayor turns on 7,200 white lights on the Mayor's Christmas Tree and 475,000 more white lights on Crown Center Square. Call (816) 274–8444 for date.

Spirit of Christmas Past Historic Homes Tour. Independence. A holiday tour of historic homes, including Vaile Mansion and Bingham-Waggoner Estate. Each home is decorated in period holiday fashion. Historical holiday reenactments, programs, visits with an 1800 Santa, musical performances, and home-baked holiday treats. Call (800) 810–4700 for tour information.

Other Recommended Restaurants and Lodgings

Independence

Clinton's Old Fashioned Soda Fountain, 100 West Maple; (816) 833–2625. Harry Truman's first job location. Breakfast and lunch, but their specialties are ice-cream sodas like Three Trails (chocolate, cherry, and vanilla ice cream), Green River (lime with vanilla ice cream), and Missouri Mud (chocolate with chocolate ice cream). Also shakes, malts, and sundaes and sandwiches. Inexpensive.

Pioneer Trails Country Store, 121 West Lexington; (816) 254–2466. Pick up some freshly made jams and jellies, apple butter, breads, and cookies to take back as gifts or just to nibble on in the car for the trip home.

Rheinland Restaurant, 208 North Main Street; (816) 461–5383. A German restaurant with such delicious items as the Rheinland Deli Roll, German ham wrapped around deli salad, served with potato salad and asparagus ($6.50); Hawaiian Toast, German ham on toast with pineapple and melted Swiss cheese ($6.25).

Serendipity, 116 South Pleasant; (800) 203–4299. Built in 1887, this six-room, three-story Victorian bed-and-breakfast welcomes children and has limited facilities for pets. Full breakfast. No smoking. Rates: $45 to $95. www. bedandbreakfast.com.

Kansas City

Barbecue. It's not hard to find a good barbecue place since that is one of K.C.'s trademarks. While Rosedale's, 600 Southwest Boulevard (913–262–0343), may be short on ambience, it's long on taste. Great sandwiches and ribs served with white bread. Try the corn nuggets too. Try burnt ends and sweet potato fries at Jake Edwards, 5107 Main Street (816–531–8878).

Crayola Cafe, Crown Center (located next to the Crayola Store); (816) 426–1165. The menu of this theme restaurant includes such items as PB&J Minis, Double-Decker Peanut Butter Club, and Eight-Color Salad. And there's stuff for grown-ups, too! Moderate prices.

Historic Suites of America, 612 Central; (800) 733–0612. A haven in the old Garment District of downtown Kansas City, this hotel offers suites with fully equipped kitchens and other amenities including an evening manager's reception with complimentary wine and hors d'oeuvres, complimentary breakfast buffet, grocery-shopping services, exercise facility, outdoor pool and whirlpool, and on-site parking. Rates: $105 to $245, depending on season. www.historicsuites.com.

LaFontaine Inn, 4320 Oak; (888) 832–6000 or (816) 753–4434. Beautifully restored 1910 Georgian colonial brick home in the Southmoreland Neighborhood close to Country Club Plaza, the museums, and other attractions. Wine and cheese in the evening. Coffee or tea in Butler's Pantry in the morning, followed by a freshly prepared breakfast in the dining room. Four rooms and a carriage house with three rooms, each with private bath. Some rooms have Jacuzzis. No children or pets. Smoking outside only. Rates: $125 to $159. www.lafontainebb.com.

The Quarterage Hotel, 560 Westport Road; (800) 942–4233. Located in the Westport Historic District, this classic hotel, with its oak-and-brass lobby and marble entryway, welcomes guests to the place where wagon trains passed 150 years ago. Rates ($99 to $159) include full breakfast buffet, parking, evening manager's reception, sauna, hot tub, and full-service fitness center. www. quarteragehotel.com.

Southmoreland on the Plaza, 116 East Forty-sixth Street; (816) 531–7979. Located close to Country Club Plaza and the Nelson-Atkins Museum of Art, this New England–style inn has twelve guest rooms with private baths. Some have private decks and fireplaces. Wine and hors d'oeuvres in late afternoon, hot beverages and sweets in the evening, and gourmet breakfast in the morning. No children under thirteen, no pets, and no smoking. Rates: $105 to $215, depending on season. www.southmore land.com.

For More Information

Convention and Visitors Bureau of Greater Kansas City, 1100 Main Street, Suite 2550, Kansas City, MO 64105-2195; (800) 767–7700; www.goin tokansascity.com.

Independence Tourism Department, 111 East Maple, Independence, MO 64050; (800) 810–4700; www.visitkc.com.

SOUTHERN
ESCAPES

SOUTHERN ESCAPE ONE

Ste. Genevieve, Missouri, and Prairie du Rocher, Illinois

French History in the Midwest / 1 Night

Retrace the steps of some of Missouri's and Illinois's earliest settlers just by heading south. No, not to New Orleans, but just south of St. Louis to the little towns of Ste. Genevieve, on the Missouri side of the Mississippi

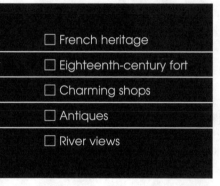

☐ French heritage

☐ Eighteenth-century fort

☐ Charming shops

☐ Antiques

☐ River views

River, and Prairie du Rocher and the surrounding areas, on the Illinois side. The French first came to the area in the early to mid-1700s as missionaries, merchants, farmers, and fur traders. But no matter what their profession, they each came with their passion for life. It showed in their food, in the way they built their homes, and in their dealings with the Native Americans. And present residents of the area take great pride in showcasing their French history. You can see it in the buildings that have been preserved as well as in some of the local cuisine. And don't be surprised if you meet a few people with decidedly French names. Some locals can trace back their roots hundreds of years. So, pack your bags, hit the road, and experience a little joie de vivre right in the Midwest!

Day 1 / Morning

Ste. Genevieve seems much farther away than it really is. It's an easy drive from St. Louis, and you'll be surprised how quickly you get there. Just hop on Highway 55 South and exit onto Highway 32, which is the second Ste. Genevieve exit (number 150). Make a left at the stop sign and you're just 6 miles from town. Highway 32 becomes Fourth Street once you're in Ste. Genevieve. The drive from St. Louis should take about one hour.

    Spend the morning getting acquainted with the history of this French colonial town through its architecture, which is considered to be some of

the best examples of the French Creole style in the United States. Because of this, and the fact that Ste. Genevieve has the largest concentration of French colonial architecture in the world (more than 150 pre-1825 structures), the entire historic district is a designated national landmark.

The first stop should be the **Boulduc House,** 125 South Main. Built in 1770, the Boulduc House is a National Historic Landmark and is considered the first most authentically restored Creole house in the nation. Its restoration is extremely accurate, according to local historians, and includes eighteenth-century furniture, a stockade fence, a frontier kitchen, eighteenth-century culinary and medicinal herb gardens, and a grape arbor. The house is open April to November, and a small admission fee is charged.

Next it's on to the **Maison Guibourd–Valle,** 1 North Fourth Street, which was built around 1784 by a pioneer French settler. Considered the most elegantly furnished home in town, you can almost imagine yourself living in Ste. Genevieve in the eighteenth century. Note the Norman trusses in the attic. Costumed tour guides will take you on a tour of this wonderful home. Make sure you see the delightful courtyard and rose garden, which contains an old stone well.

There are a number of other historical homes in town that are wonderful examples of life in Ste. Genevieve as a French settler. Space doesn't permit describing them all, so be sure to stop by the **Greater River Road Interpretive Center,** 66 South Main (573–883–7097), and pick up the brochure titled *History of French Colonial Architecture in Ste. Genevieve,* and visit as many homes as possible. They're relatively close to one another and provide a fascinating glimpse into the past. The center is open daily 9:00 A.M. to 4:00 P.M.

LUNCH: Old Towne Cafe, 104 South Main Street; (573) 883–7414. Rest your feet at this quaint European bistro and bakery just south of the Great River Road Interpretive Center. Enjoy cappuccino, quiche, sandwiches, salads, and homemade desserts in this delightfully restored building. The restaurant is open Monday through Saturday 9:00 A.M. to 4:00 P.M. (closed Sunday).

Afternoon

After lunch, stroll over to the **Church of Ste. Genevieve.** Founded in 1759, the church sits in the middle of the historic town square and is open from 6:00 A.M. to 6:00 P.M. If your eyes haven't figured out you're in a quaint community, your ears soon will when you hear the church bells ring on the hour. And for procrastinators, the bells ring fifteen minutes before Mass to make sure you're not late! Whether you make it to services or not, the Church of Ste. Genevieve is an absolutely gorgeous and historically significant building that shouldn't be missed.

Next, browse the charming shops. Ste. Genevieve has come a long way in a few short years and is now home to some eclectic stores worth seeing. You won't want to miss the **Show Me Shop,** 73 North Main Street (573–883–3096), which is dedicated to showcasing the best of Missouri with wines, cheeses, sausages, gourmet foods, gifts, and antiques. Stop in and pick up a bottle of wine for later in the evening or have a glass right in the shop.

If you like angels, you'll love **Angels of Grace, Inc.,** 109 North Main Street; (573) 883–3882. Featuring just about anything you can imagine that's angel-like, this is a great place to get a special baby or baptism gift. They also have quite a selection of personalized angel items.

If you've got a green thumb or love decorative garden accessories, stop at **Ivy and Twigs,** 199 North Main Street; (573) 883–5250. The owner bills her shop as a place for lingering. Who can argue when you're surrounded by the delicate aroma of floral potpourris and gorgeous displays of garden furniture and dried floral wreaths? **Paperwhites & Fern,** a few doors down at 173 North Main Street (573–883–5250), is an enchanting shop featuring the cottage-garden and shabby-chic styles. Items for sale include vintage linens, wicker, china, and furniture.

DINNER: Old Brick House, Third and Market Streets; (573) 883–2724. Enjoy a relaxing dinner in the oldest brick building west of the Mississippi. Take your pick from fried chicken, steaks, seafood, or sandwiches in this casual environment popular with the locals. Inexpensive.

LODGING: Main Street Inn Bed & Breakfast, 221 North Main Street; (800) 918–9199 or (573) 883–9199; www.mainstreetinnbb.com. Karen and Ken Kulberg consider their B&B the type of accommodation a husband would find comfortable. While visions of sports memorabilia and big-screen TVs come to mind, Main Street Inn B&B couldn't be farther from this stereotype. Instead, this is a delightfully refreshing B&B with spacious, airy rooms that define the statement "less is more." Built in 1882, this former hotel has been converted into eight guest rooms, all with private bath and shower. Some have a double whirlpool and fireplace, and one has a breezy, relaxing back porch. The Kulbergs have taken great care restoring the B&B, and Karen has an eye for making things just right without going overboard. From the imaginatively colored walls in the parlor to the baby grand piano in the dining room to the charmingly decorated hallway bathroom, this is the kind of place that makes you want to relax. Rates range from $85 to $125 and include a substantial, award-winning breakfast as well as complimentary wine at check-in.

Day 2 / Morning

BREAKFAST: Main Street Inn Bed & Breakfast.

After savoring an early-morning breakfast of such things as French toast, homemade breads, or breakfast casseroles, it's off to Illinois for more French sites. Take the **Ste. Genevieve-Modoc Ferry** (800–373–7007) across the Mississippi River. The ferry operates Monday through Saturday 6:00 A.M. to 6:00 P.M. and Sunday 9:00 A.M. to 6:00 P.M. The one-way fee for passenger cars is $7.00. Once on the Illinois side, take Modoc Ferry Road into Modoc. Go South on Bluff Road, which leads toward Ellis Grove at the intersection of Bluff Road and Route 3. Go right on Route 3 toward Chester and follow the signs to the Pierre Menard Home and Fort Kaskaskia.

The Illinois Historic Preservation Agency considers the **Pierre Menard Home,** 4230 Kaskaskia Street, Ellis Grove (618–859–3031), the finest example of French colonial architecture in the central Mississippi Valley. The post-on-sill frame house was built around 1800 for Menard, who eventually become Illinois's first lieutenant governor. The house is open for tours daily from 9:00 A.M. to 5:00 P.M. from April to October. It closes at 4:00 P.M. all other months and is closed most major holidays. A donation of $2.00 for adults and $1.00 for children is suggested. Don't miss the fabulous flower, herb, and vegetable gardens that surround the home. In fall the herbs are harvested and made into gorgeous wreaths and other dried arrangements. The short introductory video is also worth seeing for excellent background information.

Before leaving the area, take a quick drive up the bluffs behind the Menard Home to **Fort Kaskaskia** state historic site (signs point the way). At one time a French fort, the state has preserved the site in memory of the early settlers. Don't miss the scenic overlook of the Mississippi and Kaskaskia Rivers. It's absolutely beautiful, especially in spring and fall.

Your next stop is Fort de Chartres. Once back on Route 3, head north and drive about twenty minutes toward the town of Ruma. At Ruma,

Fort de Chartes Rendezvous, Prairie du Rocher

head east (left) onto Route 155 and go north until you reach Prairie du Rocher. Follow the sign to Fort de Chartres.

According to the Illinois Historic Preservation Agency, **Fort de Chartres** is the last of three eighteenth-century forts by that name erected next to the Mississippi River by France's colonial government. Fort de Chartres was the governmental headquarters for what was then called Illinois Country, which extended from Lakes Michigan and Superior to the Ohio and Missouri Rivers. At present, visitors can see a partially rebuilt fort, enjoy special events with reenactors dressed in French colonial military costumes, and monthly guided tours by costumed interpreters. The fort is open daily from 9:00 A.M. to 5:00 P.M.; it is closed New Year's, Thanksgiving, and Christmas Days. For additional information contact the site manager at (618) 284–7230.

Once you're ready to head home, retrace your steps back to the Ste. Genevieve-Modoc Ferry and ride back to Missouri. Head back to St. Louis on Highway 55 North.

There's More

Ste. Genevieve

La Galerie of the French Quarter Antiques Mall, 305 Merchant Street; (573) 883–2244. This mall has 10,000 square feet of antiques, French country imports, American primitives, and more.

Ste. Genevieve Museum, Merchant and DuBourge Streets, Courthouse Square; (573) 883–3461. Collections include weapons, prehistoric and historic Native American relics, old documents, and more. Admission is $1.50 for adults, 50 cents for kids.

Ste. Genevieve Winery, 245 Merchant Street; (573) 883–2800. Featuring a full line of premium and traditional wines and wine-related gifts. Open daily from 11:00 A.M. to 5:00 P.M.

Special Events

May. Kid's Day. Fort de Chartres. First weekend in May. A special weekend for children, with eighteenth-century games, contests, storytelling, and more. Free. (618) 284–7230.

June. Fort de Chartres Rendezvous, one of the largest in the country, is held the first weekend in June and includes eighteenth-century crafts, food, music, and thousands of historically dressed participants. Free. Parking is $5.00. (618) 284–7230.

August. Jour de Fête. Ste. Genevieve. Crafts, food, and music abound in this weekend-long gala. (800) 373–7007 or (573) 883–7097.

September. French Colonial Crafts and Trades. Fort de Chartres. A hands-on weekend of eighteenth-century crafts. Learn and help construct items using period tools. (618) 284–7230.

November. Autumn Celebration Arts & Crafts. Fort Kaskaskia. (618) 859–3741.

Other Recommended Restaurants and Lodgings

Ste. Genevieve

Creole House Bed & Breakfast, 339 St. Mary's Road; (800) 275–6041. A newer home made in the Creole style, this B&B features whirlpool tubs and an indoor swimming pool. Children over five welcome in the private second-story area, which is also good for large groups. Rates $95 to $155.

Inn St. Gemme Beauvais, 78 North Main Street; (800) 818–5744. This is a great place to stay if you're traveling with friends or children, as many of the eight rooms in the inn have two beds. For a more romantic getaway, request the Carriage House, with its king-size bed, double whirlpool, and kitchenette. The decor is warm and inviting with lots of exposed brick. Rates are $89 to $185.

Microtel Hotel, Highway 32; (573) 883–8884. Clean, newer budget motel that's good for families. Rates start around $40.

Somewhere Inn Time Bed & Breakfast, 383 Jefferson Street; (888) 883–9397; www.somewhereinntime.net. Delightful two-story colonial home with whirlpool tubs, in-ground pool, hot tub, and cottage that welcomes children. Rates are between $85 and $125.

Southern Hotel, 146 South Third Street; (800) 275–1412; www. southernhotelbb.com. If you don't mind your claw-foot tub and toilet right in your room (to accurately reflect the past—the tub, not the toilet!), then this is a fun place to stay and feel as though you've stepped back in time. Owners Mike and Barbara are walking historians and enjoy discussing their B&B. Great garden-related items in the Summer Kitchen gift shop. Rates are between $88 and $138.

For More Information

Great River Road Interpretive Center and Tourist Information Center, 66 South Main Street, Ste. Genevieve, MO 63670; (800) 373–7007 or (573) 883–7097.

Southwestern Illinois Tourism & Convention Bureau, 10950 Lincoln Trail, Fairview Heights, IL 62208; (618) 397–1488 or (800) 442–1488.

Arcadia Valley, Missouri

Getting Back to Nature / 2 Nights

Native Americans of the Osage tribe knew long ago what you're about to discover. They knew that the Arcadia Valley was a wonderful mix of cool breezes and clear springs, lush valleys and scenic vistas. Tucked between the St. Francois Mountains, it's a wonderfully peaceful getaway, filled with some of the best nature has to offer.

☐ Natural wonders

☐ Historical sites

☐ Outdoor activities

☐ Art and antiques

The area has gone through many ups and downs over the years. In the early 1800s the town was thick with miners who came to work in the iron and ore mines of Pilot Knob Mountain and Shepherd Mountain. By the mid-1800s the railroad had arrived and secured the Arcadia Valley as an important shipping and trading center for the region. But the Civil War was to interrupt this prosperity. In 1864 the Arcadia Valley was engulfed in the Battle of Pilot Knob, one of the ten largest battles fought in Missouri. After the war the railroad brought tourism to the valley, and many wealthy St. Louis families built summer homes in the area. And more than one church opened a summer camp, with some still in continuous operation. Many of these and other key landmarks have been preserved along with the area's abundance of natural resources. The valley is presently experiencing a rebirth. More and more people are rediscovering all it has to offer. You too can experience the magic of the area, just as Native Americans did hundreds of years ago.

Day 1 / Evening

Your best bet is to leave St. Louis after dinner for the two-hour drive to the Arcadia Valley and Wilderness Lodge, where you'll be staying. Take Highway 55 South to Highway 67 South, which is the second Farmington exit. Make a right on "W" (it's the only way you can go) and go about 8

miles to "V," where you'll make a left. Take "V" to Highway 21, where you'll go left. Drive about 20 miles until you get to Peola Road, where you'll make a left. Go about 2½ miles on Peola and you'll come to Wilderness Lodge.

LODGING: Wilderness Lodge, Peola Road, Lesterville (573–637–2295; www.wildernesslodgeresort.com), once a private residence and built in the late 1920s, is now a wonderful family getaway nestled in the foothills of the Ozark Mountains. Situated on 1,200 acres bordering the Black River, this is the perfect place to escape from the city. The lodge has more than thirty cabins that sleep from two to eight people. Rates at the lodge include dinner and breakfast each day and range from $42 per day for children to $79 per day for adults, depending on cabin selection. Canoeing, rafting, and tubing are available. Other activities include horseback riding and hayrides. On-ground activities available are the pool, hot tub, and tennis courts.

Day 2 / *Morning*

BREAKFAST: At Wilderness Lodge. Chow down on a hot breakfast of eggs, pancakes, sausage, and biscuits. Each day has a set menu (special diets can be arranged in advance of arrival) but always includes fruit, assorted cereal, juice, coffee, and milk plus a number of hot items.

Elephant Rocks State Park has been around for years—or at least the rocks have. This park, with more than 300,000 visitors annually, was created from the formation of red-granite boulders billions of years ago when molten rock was pushed to the surface from below. Erosion and weathering have caused the giant rocks, some weighing as much as 600 tons, to resemble the shapes of elephants strung end to end like circus animals—thus the park's name. Spend the morning climbing and walking around these mammoth creations and marvel in their mystery. There are a number of trails that wind through the rocks for hiking, exploration, or just sitting and enjoying the view of the valley. A wheelchair-accessible Braille trail that extends for about a mile is also located at the park. Just outside the park is the oldest recorded granite quarry in the state, which furnished stone for the Eads Bridge piers as well as the columns for the front of the Governor's Mansion in Jefferson City. The park is open daily during daylight hours. Call (573) 546–3454 for more information. To get to the park from the lodge, take Peola Road to Highway 21 South through

Lesterville to Highway N. Make a right on N and travel about fifteen minutes. Once you come to Highway 21, follow the signs to the park, just a short distance away.

LUNCH: Arcadian Cafe, 123 Main Street, Arcadia; (573) 546–2432; www.arcadiancafe.com. Plan ahead and make reservations about a week in advance for a combination lunch and guided driving tour of the Arcadia Valley. The tour is offered through **Arcadian Outfitters**—the same folks that own the cafe where you'll have lunch. The Arcadian Cafe is one of the reasons the Arcadia Valley is so charming. This little gathering spot, decorated with a hodgepodge of local memorabilia, is a welcome place to rest your tired feet and fuel up on delicious homemade soups, salads, and sandwiches. Nearly everything is good. Start off with fried dill pickles for an appetizer; then go for a bowl of chili (in season) or other great soups. Round off the meal with either the grilled chicken salad or the hot smoked-ham and cheese sandwich. Make sure you leave room for the delectable caramel apple a la mode, a concoction of batter-dipped apples served in a sundae glass with ice cream and caramel sauce. The restaurant also offers an eclectic dinner menu that includes steak and pasta and regularly has weekend evening entertainment. A small bakery with freshly made bread and pastries is connected to the restaurant. Inexpensive.

Afternoon

After you've finished lunch, the **local history tour** will begin. The Arcadia Valley is rich with interesting history as well as present-day hidden gems worth discovering. Hop on board the shuttle provided by Arcadian Outfitters for a relaxing, interesting, and fact-filled tour of the area and its residents. Stops include the **Iron County Historical Society** for a glimpse into life as an early Arcadian Valley resident. You'll tour the beautifully appointed **Green Roof Inn Bed and Breakfast,** whose delightful owner, June Haefner, enjoys showing off her many collections. You'll also visit **St. Paul's Episcopal Church,** a 125-year-old church with beautiful old-world oak interior. The multicolored painted roof is very picturesque and unusual. The tiny **Immanuel Lutheran Church** is also a treasure not to be missed. In existence for more than 150 years, the upper level of the church is still set up as an old-fashioned schoolroom, and many of the items from its early days have been preserved. The church even served as a temporary hospital during the Civil War. You'll then go to the

Green Roof Inn Bed and Breakfast, Ironton

Fort Davidson Battlefield and Museum, where you'll learn about the battle of Pilot Knob that was so important to the area.

And lest you think there aren't shopping opportunities, the tour will take you to both ends of the buying spectrum. There's **Plunder Palace,** a catchall junk/treasure shop (opinions vary!) filled to the brim with "can't live withouts" waiting to be discovered. Chances are, if you can think of it, they'll probably have it or can get it for you. This place is a real find and a delight to browse. The tour will also go to the **Urseline Academy,** a former girl's boarding school turned antiques shop and art gallery. But the highlight of the tour includes a visit to **Chanticleer Pottery** and gift shop. You may recognize these beautiful ceramic works of "kitchen and garden art" from various upscale stores in St. Louis. Here's your chance to see how the pottery is handmade and perhaps to make a purchase or two. Items range from small plates to covered casserole-type dishes to enormous garden statues, all beautifully detailed. Some of the original molds, created decades ago by the owner's mother, are still used and evoke a wonderful European country feel. Because the shop doesn't keep regular hours, visiting with the tour is the best way to see this fascinating place.

All told, the entire local-history tour takes a few hours and includes a delicious lunch from the Arcadian Cafe. Equestrian, float, and backpacking/hiking tours and accommodations are also available. Call (573) 546–2432 for more information. Advance reservations are required.

After the tour, head back to Wilderness Lodge to relax at the swimming pool or play a round of horseshoes before dinner.

DINNER: At Wilderness Lodge. Dinner menus vary by day but include such home-cooked meals as turkey with mashed potatoes and gravy, vegetables, and pie. Regardless of the selection, you won't go away hungry!

LODGING: The Wilderness Lodge.

Day 3 / Morning

BREAKFAST: At Wilderness Lodge.

On the way to your first activity of the day, stop and pick up a picnic lunch at Lenny's, Highway 21 and Peola Road, Lesterville; (573) 637–2506. This is the place to get everything you need for the journey, from lunch to snacks to drinks. Try the Black River Sub—turkey, roast beef, ham, Swiss cheese, American cheese, and your choice of toppings— the store's signature sandwich. And don't worry if you forgot a cooler. Lenny's has it all.

Head out early to **Johnson's Shut-Ins State Park.** From Lenny's take Highway 21 South through Lesterville. Make a right on Highway N and go about 8 miles to the Johnson's Shut-Ins entrance on the right. This canyonlike, water-filled playground is an extremely popular place, especially in the warm months, and only one hundred vehicles are allowed into the park at one time (all others wait until someone leaves).

It's easy to see why this place is in such demand. The brisk, clear waters of the east fork of the Black River flow through the shut-ins to create pockets of water to play in amid the smooth, slippery volcanic rock that formed millions of years ago. Located in the scenic St. Francois Mountains, the park is home to more than 1,000 recorded species of plants, which makes it Missouri's most botanically diverse state park. The first thing you'll notice as you enter the park's gate is the Shut-Ins Trail, which loops around the park. The beginning of the trail takes you to an observation deck that overlooks the upper shut-ins. This is a really great place to come with the kids, and you can easily spend the entire day splashing and playing around in nature's swimming hole. *A note of caution:* Despite the playful atmosphere and relatively calm waters, always use caution around the rocks. They're slippery, even when dry, so tennis shoes are recommended.

Also, never jump from rock to rock. It's also a good idea for children to wear approved personal-flotation devices and be supervised at all times. With a little common sense and good judgment, Johnson's Shut-Ins is a wonderfully fun place to visit. The park is open daily from 7:00 A.M. to sunset. For more information contact the park office at (573) 546–2450.

Taum Sauk Mountain State Park is your next destination. From Johnson's Shut-Ins, turn right on Highway N toward Ironton. From Highway N take Highway 21 South through Pilot Knob, Ironton, and Arcadia. Turn right on Highway CC and climb the winding road to the top, where the park and lookout tower are located. The park consists of more than 6,500 acres, including the highest point in the state at 1,772 feet above sea level. Mina Sauk Falls, the state's tallest waterfall at 132 feet, is also located here.

LUNCH: Grab your picnic lunch and head into the park for some beautiful scenery while you eat. Afterward, do a little hiking if you're up to it. For more information contact the site manager at (573) 546–7117.

Afternoon

Water is the focus of this next excursion, but not in the way you may think. The AmerenUE **Hydroelectric Power Plant** is an engineering feat and a fascinating site to explore. Carved from the top of Profitt Mountain, this fifty-five-acre reservoir is part of the unique hydroelectric pumped storage Taum Sauk Power Plant. The reservoir holds 1.5 billion gallons of water, which is enough to supply St. Louis with all its water needs for eight days. The plant is located on Highway AA, 8 miles north of Lesterville, and is well worth a drive around the lake as well as a walk around the observation area. There's also a small museum with interesting geological features and Indian collections. The plant is open March through October. From Taum Sauk Park take Highway CC down to Highway 21 South. Go about 5 miles to Highway AA and make a right. Follow Highway AA and the signs to get to either the lower lake (where the fishing is great, according to locals) or to the top lake and museum.

For your trip back to St. Louis from the power plant, take Highway AA to Highway 21 North. Take Highway W on the other side of Pilot Knob to Highway 67 North; then take Highway 55 north, toward St. Louis.

There's More

Canoeing on the Black River. You could spend an entire day or an entire weekend just floating the crystal-clear Black River. Whether you just want a canoe for a few hours or would like to have your entire canoeing weekend arranged, including food and lodging, there are a number of canoe rental companies to help make your trip fun and memorable. A sampling of companies includes Arcadian Outfitters, 123 Main Street, Arcadia (573–546–2432); Franklin Floats, Route 1, Box 9, Lesterville (573–637–2205); Twin Rivers Landing, P.O. Box 29, Lesterville (573–637–2274); and Wilderness Lodge, P.O. Box 90, Lesterville (573–637–2295).

Fort Davidson State Historic Site. The site of the Battle of Pilot Knob in 1864, this battlefield-turned-farmland has come full circle as a state historic site that honors the 1,500 men who were killed or wounded in this battle. Reenactors every third year remember this event (next scheduled for September 2004). The site has a wonderful museum and interpretive center and also offers tape-recorded driving tours. The museum is open Monday through Saturday 10:00 A.M. to 4:00 P.M. and Sunday noon to 6:00 P.M. Call (573) 546–3454 for more information.

Special Events

March. Missouri Whitewater Kayak Races. Millstream Gardens Conservation Area (Tiemann Shut-Ins) east of Arcadia Valley. (573) 546–7117.

April. Brigadoon in the Valley. Arcadia Valley. Celtic festival that includes bagpipes, dancers, food, crafts, and international entertainers. (573) 546–7690.

May. Our Town Tomorrow Spring Festival. Iron County Courthouse Square in Ironton. Music, food, auction, and carnival. (573) 546–7117.

June. 50 Bull Buck Out. Ironton. Wild rides for bulls and riders. (573) 546–2759.

September. Iron County Fair. Ironton. Features a rodeo, arts and crafts, and old trades demonstrations, food, games, and music. (573) 546–7515.

October. Old Miners Day in Viburnum. Country music, crafts, games, food, antique car show, and mine tours. (573) 244–3377.

Arcadia Valley Home and Church Tours. (573) 546–3513.

Other Recommended Restaurants and Lodgings

Ironton

Green Roof Inn Bed and Breakfast, 102 South Shepherd; (573) 546–7670. Relax on one of the many porches of this charming home. The red brick and wrought iron remind you of a New Orleans–style home. Inside are wonderfully decorated rooms filled with various antique collections. All rooms include private bath. Room rate is $75 and includes a delicious hot breakfast.

Kozy Korner Cafe, 201 South Main Street; (573) 546–7739. Excellent breakfast and home-cooked meals including wonderful homemade pies. Inexpensive.

Mimosa Drive In, North Highway 21; (573) 546–2100. An old-fashioned drive-in serving burgers, fries, and ice cream. Inexpensive.

Pilot Knob

Fort Davidson Motel, Highways 21 and V; (573) 546–7427. Clean, remodeled rooms, some with Jacuzzi tubs. Rates are $35 to $65.

Fort Davidson Restaurant, Highways 21 and V; (573) 546–2719. Everything from steak to seafood. Daily specials and a health-conscious menu are offered at this restaurant that overlooks the battlefield for which it's named. Inexpensive.

For More Information

Arcadia Valley Chamber of Commerce, 120 South Main, P.O. Box 343, Ironton, MO 63650; (573) 546–7117.

Black River Recreation Association, P.O. Box 65, Lesterville, MO 63654; (888) FLOATING.

SOUTHERN ESCAPE THREE

Southernmost Illinois: Makanda/Alto Pass

Outdoor Adventure / 2 Nights

Sometimes you just need to get out of the burbs and head to the country. A few hours away in southern Illinois lies some of the most beautiful as well as interesting scenery you could ever imagine. Here, where the juxtaposition of the highest point in southern Illinois and the low, low, lowness of swampland coexist peacefully, the air seems fresher, and the body feels more relaxed. You'll find wonderfully lush places to hike, down-to-earth folks with interesting stories, comforting food, and gorgeous scenery that makes you appreciate the great outdoors.

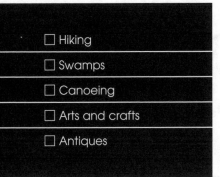

- ☐ Hiking
- ☐ Swamps
- ☐ Canoeing
- ☐ Arts and crafts
- ☐ Antiques

It's a two- to two-and-a-half hour drive to Makanda, Illinois, your weekend destination and home to Giant City State Park. Leave the night before so that you can get an early start communing with nature the next morning.

Day 1 / Evening

To get to Makanda, take Highway 40 east into Illinois. Get on Highway 64 and head east toward Nashville, Illinois. Take the Nashville exit and go south on Route 127 through the little towns of Nashville and Pinkneyville. Take Route 13 east through Carbondale. Drive through the town, staying on Route 13, and when you see the University Mall on the right, you'll know you're close. Make a right at the next road past the mall, which is Giant City Road. Go about 8 miles on this road, and it'll lead you straight into Giant City State Park. Follow the signs to Giant City Lodge and check into your cabin.

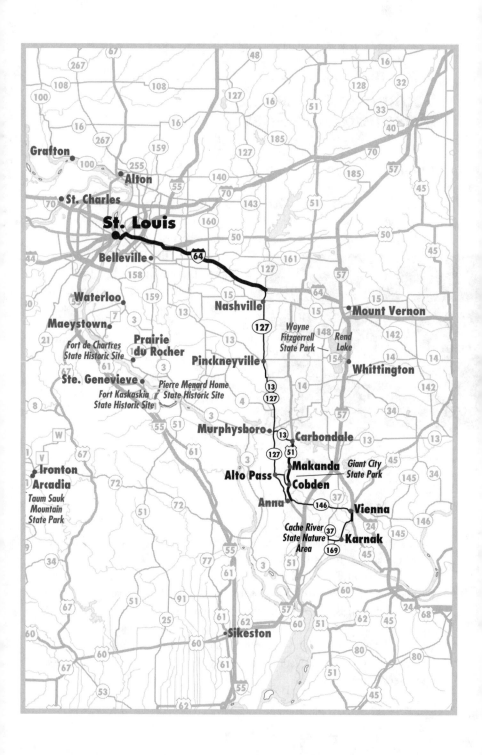

LODGING: Giant City Lodge, 460 Giant City Lodge Road, Makanda; (618) 457–4921. What could be more fun than gathering up the kids and heading to a cabin in the woods? Giant City Lodge has three types of cabins available. The Historic cabins are one-room cabins; the Prairie cabins have a separate bedroom and a second pull-down bed in the living room; and the Bluff cabins have two separate bedrooms. All cabins have a private bath, TV, phone, and minirefrigerator. Rates are between $60.00 and $105.00 for one to two people, and each additional guest costs $5.00. The cabins have been renovated and are comfortable and clean. Most have a front porch for sitting outside and relaxing. There's also an outdoor swimming pool for cabin guests to use during warm weather. (Make sure when you make your reservations that you let the lodge know you may be arriving late. The lodge closes around 8:00 P.M., but they'll see that you get in your cabin if you arrive after closing time.)

Day 2 / Morning

BREAKFAST: At Giant City Lodge. Rise and shine fairly early and head up to the lodge for a hearty breakfast in the dining room. Enjoy biscuits and gravy, eggs, pancakes with real blueberries, and other stick-to-your-ribs fare. You know you're south of St. Louis when grits appears on the menu. Fill up because you'll work it off exploring throughout the day. (Most menu items are inexpensive.)

Because you'll be on the move today and not close to many restaurants, you'll want to take a picnic lunch with you. With a little advance warning, the lodge can prepare a sack lunch. Order it as soon as you place your breakfast order, and it'll be ready to go when you are.

After breakfast it's on to **Heron Pond** and the **Cache River Wetlands** area for a fascinating glimpse at swamps and cypress. Although you'll be driving south, you're not headed to Louisiana despite how it appears. Few people realize that southern Illinois has a true swamp that's home to hundreds of rare and endangered animals as well as cypress trees well over 1,000 years old.

Leave the lodge by heading toward the little town of Makanda. You'll pass the **Makanda Boardwalk** on the left. Explore the boardwalk and its shops tomorrow, but stop in the **Makanda Country Store** for drinks and snacks before heading out. (The Country Store will also make sandwiches to go.) Continue south on Highway 51 toward Anna. At Anna make a left on Highway 146 and travel east to Vienna. Turn right on Highway 45 and

Giant City Lodge, Makanda

travel south. Watch for the brown signs leading to Heron Pond. You'll make a right turn on Belnap Road and go about 2 miles before turning right onto Heron Pond Lane (it's a gravel road). Go about a mile to the Heron Pond parking area. The trip from Makanda should take about an hour. A word of advice: If you need to use the rest rooms, now's the time; there aren't any along the trail.

Heron Pond is nestled about as off the beaten path as you can get, but it's worth the bit of extra work to find it. Part of the Cache River Wetlands area, Heron Pond is a shallow swamp covered in cypress and tupelo trees that's home to great blue herons, little blue herons, great egrets, green herons, ducks, geese, quail, and a host of seasonal migrating birds, not to mention tiny tree frogs, whose croaks sound like songbirds. The area is so important to this wildlife that in 1996 it was designated a Wetland of International Importance, only the fifteenth wetland in the United States to receive the distinction. The pièce de résistance of the trail is a "floating" boardwalk, which winds its way deep into the secluded swamp, allowing visitors to get an up-close look at this marvel of aquatic ecosystems that haven't changed in thousands of years. Pick up a self-guided-tour brochure at the beginning of the path; then take your time strolling through this easy-to-walk, well-marked trail. Listen to the quiet surrounding you.

While you'll hear birds and frogs all around, you'll be amazed that you won't hear one single sound of civilization. Step onto the boardwalk and wrap yourself in a forest of trees and breathe in the clean, fresh air while looking up through the dense canopy of treetops.

LUNCH: Picnic lunch. Eat your lunch at your car, as there aren't any picnic tables or trash cans along the path. (Please remember not to leave any trash along the hiking trail or in the woods!)

Afternoon

After finishing lunch, head back to Belknap Blacktop Road and go south toward **Karnak.** Go west on Route 169, then north on Route 37. Go west on Perks Road and follow the signs to the Lower Cache River Access Area for an afternoon of canoeing on the **Lower Cache River canoe trail.** While the upper Cache River is very difficult, if not impossible, to canoe due to tipped trees and log jams, the lower Cache is delightful. From 3 to 6 miles in length, the canoe trail takes you through another area of the cypress and tupelo swamp as well as right by the state champion bald cypress tree, which is more than 1,000 years old! The trail is marked, and canoe maps and fact sheets are available at the site headquarters in Belknap or at the refuge office on Shawnee College Road. Canoe rental is available at Cache Core Canoes and costs about $25 for the day. Cache Core is located west of the public access area and can be reached from Perks Road or Shawnee College Road. Call (618) 845–3817 for details.

DINNER: Dolly's Place Restaurant, Highway 146 just east of Route 45 in Vienna, is open 6:00 A.M. to 9:00 P.M. daily; (618) 658–9006. Relax and enjoy good country cookin' at this casual come-as-you-are cafe. Fill up on an open-faced sandwich of roast beef and mashed potatoes with gravy—and don't forget the blackberry cobbler. Inexpensive.

LODGING: After dinner, drag your weary bones back to Giant City Lodge and relax in your cabin.

Day 3 / Morning

BREAKFAST: At Giant City Lodge. Enjoy fresh fruit in season, a warm bowl of oatmeal, or maybe a hearty breakfast steak before heading out to do some more exploring.

After breakfast, head over to the park's **visitor center** (618–457–4836) for a quick movie on the history of the park. The visitor center also has an exhibit area showing examples of the wildlife in the park, a hands-on children's learning area, and an exhibit of the Civilian Conservation Corp., which built the lodge and the roads and buildings throughout the park. You can also pick up maps for each of the park's trails as well as nature-related souvenirs. The visitor center is open daily from 8:00 A.M. to 4:00 P.M.

After you've browsed the visitor center, get ready for some hiking. You can hike any trail you choose, but the Post Oak Nature Trail and the Giant City Nature Trail can easily be done in a morning. Head over to the wheel-chair- and stroller-acessible **Post Oak Nature Trail,** an easy ⅓-mile-long, asphalt-paved trail. It's very level and has a number of benches and observation platforms along the way. It's also a good place to do a little fishing if you brought your gear. The walk should take about a half hour.

Next it's on to the **Giant City Nature Trail,** for which the park was named. This trail is a little more rugged and does go up a bit of a hill, but it's worth seeing since the park's namesake is located along this trail. Giant City State Park was named for the very tall sandstone bluff walls that rise straight up from the ground. Early settlers nicknamed the area "Giant City" because to them it seemed as though the passages through the bluffs were like "streets of giants." Along this trail you'll also see Civil War–era graffiti carved into the rocks as well as Balanced Rock, a multiton boulder held in place most precariously. The Giant City Trail is 1 mile long and will take about an hour to walk.

Exit the park by heading back up toward Makanda. On your way out, stop back by the Makanda Boardwalk and browse the various artists' shops. Make sure you stop in **Angarola's Glass Design Studio,** open daily from 10:00 A.M. to 6:00 P.M.; (618) 351–0641. You'll marvel at the fabulous original works of art. If you have a few thousand dollars to spare, you may even come away with a one-of-a-kind handcrafted glass lamp. If you're a little short that day, consider a vase or candleholder, which won't set you back nearly as much. Browse the other shops as well. Most shops are open 10:00 A.M. to 6:00 P.M.; some close on Tuesday and Wednesday. For more information call **Southern Sisters,** a boardwalk shop specializing in handwoven rugs, place mats, and wall hangings, at (618) 457–8508.

Head out to Cobden, where you'll have lunch. To reach this tiny little town, continue on Highway 51 from Makanda and follow the road across new Highway 51 to old Highway 51 south into Cobden.

LUNCH: **The Appleknocker Cafe,** 111 Appleknocker Drive, Cobden; (618) 893–4846. This cafe features sandwiches and soups and is a popular spot with the locals. Prices are inexpensive.

After lunch, head back north on old Highway 51 a short distance to Skyline Drive, which leads to the little town of **Alto Pass.** Follow the signs up, up, up to the highest point in southern Illinois, **Bald Knob Mountain,** the location of Bald Knob Cross. Surrounded by the Shawnee National Forest, Bald Knob rises more than 700 feet high. The drive offers some absolutely gorgeous views of the land below and the cross off in the distance. **Bald Knob Cross** stands 111 feet tall and was built in 1963 from contributions from around the world. When illuminated at night, it is said that it can be seen over an area of 7,500 square miles. Although there's not much to do when you get up there, it's a wonderful vantage point from which to see the forest, and the sheer height of the cross is quite impressive. It is a bit windy, so dress accordingly.

After you return to the little town of Alto Pass, stop in **Austin's Antiques** at the junction of Highway 127 and Alto Pass Road (618–893–2206). This wonderful old schoolhouse holds a plethora of antiques worth browsing. The shop is open 10:00 A.M. to 5:00 P.M. on Saturday and 1:00 to 5:00 P.M. on Sunday, or by appointment.

Continue north on Highway 127 and stop into **Alto Vineyards and Winery** (618–893–4898) for a taste of some locally made wines. A little farther north up Highway 127 you'll find **Pomona Winery** at 2865 Hickory Ridge Road (618–893–2623) and **Von Jakob Vineyards,** 1309 Sadler Road (618–893–4500). These three wineries are just a few along the region's wine trail. (You can pick up a brochure of all the area's wineries at the lodge or from the Tourism Bureau.) Signs along Highway 127 point the way to each winery, and most are open April to December.

Make sure you go easy on the wine, because Highway 127 north is the first leg of your journey home. Continue north on Highway 127 to Murphysboro and Pinckneyville, where you can stop for a quick bite to eat.

DINNER: Murphysboro and Pinckneyville both have a number of fast-food restaurants from which to choose, which is your best bet in the evening.

After eating, continue on Highway 127 to Nashville, which is where you'll get on Highway 64 West. Stay on Highway 64 West until you get to Missouri. Once you cross the bridge, you can choose Highway 70, 40, 44, or 55 for the final stretch of your journey home.

There's More

Hiking and Fishing. There are so many places to hike that they're too numerous to mention. Contact the Southernmost Illinois Tourism Bureau (618–845–3777) for a detailed list of hiking and fishing areas.

Horseback Riding. Giant City Stables and Equestrian Center offers trail rides, lessons, and day camps; (618) 529–4110. Rates are $15 per hour. Hours vary, so call ahead. Kosmic Acres in Alto Pass also offers scenic trail rides through the Shawnee National Forest. The rate is $20 for a two-hour ride. Hours vary and reservations at least a few days in advance are required. Ask for address and directions when making reservations. (618) 893–2347; www.centaur.org/kosmic.

Special Events

April. Morel Mushroom Season. Contact the Southernmost Illinois Tourism Bureau (618–845–3777) for information and area lodging specials.

April through December. Spend a weekend driving the wine trail. Contact the Southernmost Illinois Tourism Bureau (618–845–3777) for a map. Many of the wineries have special activities. You can check with the Tourism Bureau for details.

July through December. Area orchards offer peach and apple picking as well as holiday activities. Flamm's Orchard in Cobden is one of the larger orchards and can be reached by calling (618) 893–4241.

August. Peach Festival, Cobden, Illinois. Held the second weekend. Food and games for all ages. Contact the Southernmost Illinois Tourism Bureau at (618) 845–3777 for information.

October. Colorfest throughout Union County; held on second weekend. Come see the glorious foliage throughout the forest.

Other Recommended Restaurants and Lodgings

There are a number of chain hotels and restaurants in the Carbondale area. Here is a sampling of places to stay.

Carbondale

Carbondale Knights Inn, 2400 West Main Street; (618) 529–2424. 128 rooms. Indoor pool and sauna. No pets. Weekend rates range from $45 to $65.

Comfort Inn, 1415 East Main Street; (800) 221–2222 or (618) 549–4244. Sixty-four rooms and indoor pool. No pets. Weekend rates start at $80.

Murphysboro

Apple Tree Inn, 100 North Second Street; (800) 626–4356. Thirty rooms and two cottages next to the inn. Picnic areas, indoor pool, hot tubs, saunas, and exercise facility. The cottages have a complete kitchen and living room. Pets allowed. Rates start at $43.50 per night for the rooms; the cottages are $85 or $125 per night depending on the number of guests.

Super 8 Motel, Route 13 East; (800) 800–8000 or (618) 687–2244. Thirty-nine rooms. Pets allowed. Rates start at $54 per night.

For More Information

Carbondale Convention and Tourism Bureau, Old Passenger Depot, 111 South Illinois Avenue, Carbondale, IL 62901; (800) 526–1500 or (618) 529–4451; www.cctb.org.

Southernmost Illinois Tourism Bureau, P.O. Box 278, Ullin, IL 62992; (800) 248–4373 or (618) 845–3777; www.southernmostillinois.com

Springfield/Route 66, Missouri

Follow "The Mother Road" / 2 Nights

Leave your books-on-tape at home for this trip, which will take you approximately 250 miles over Old US–66—where you can "get your kicks." While most of the buildings and shops that lined this famous highway are gone, it's still possible to pick out the stone foundations of what was once a restaurant or, maybe, a home. Traveling this road gives you a sense of what America must have been like fifty years ago when 66 was in its heyday.

- [ ] Caves
- [ ] Civil War battlefield
- [ ] Museums
- [ ] Zoo
- [ ] Historic districts
- [ ] Shopping

Along the way you'll visit Meramec Caverns, said to be one of the hiding places for Jesse James and his gang. If so, he picked a pretty spot to hang out.

Eventually, the road leads to Springfield, the third-largest city in the state and nestled in the heart of the Ozarks. It's also the home of Missouri's largest tourist attraction, Bass Pro Shop. If you haven't been there, don't laugh. Whether or not you fish or hunt, this place will keep you occupied for hours. Waterfalls, a wildlife museum, a first-class restaurant—even a barbershop and a McDonald's.

Good restaurants, good shopping, good cultural attractions, and good entertainment—a perfect escape.

Day 1 / Morning

By way of I–44, Springfield is 220 miles away, but Route 66, which is all double lane, may seem longer! If you're not familiar with this famous road, start at **Route 66 State Park,** 97 North Outer Road, Eureka, Missouri; (636) 938–7198. Though the park is for hiking, biking, and picnicking, the Visitors Center (formerly Steiny's Inn, a famous Route 66 restaurant) has a Route 66 exhibit, memorabilia, and books on the Mother Road. It also

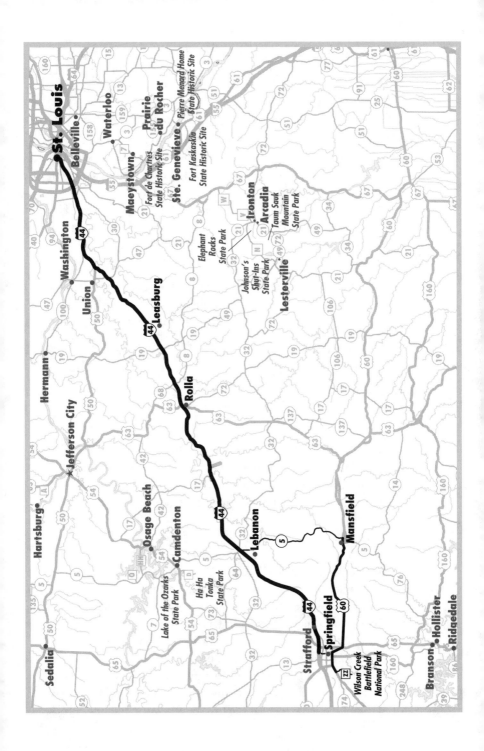

has maps, which are helpful since 66 crosses and recrosses I–44 frequently. If possible, it's a good idea to go the day before you start your trip so that you can get the information you need. The center opens at 9:00 A.M.

One of the most famous stops on Route 66 was the Old Diamonds Restaurant, near the junction of 66 and Highway 100. It is now the **Tri-County Truck Stop.** The first Diamonds was destroyed in a fire in 1948, and the owners moved it across the highway. Those in the know still stop here for greasy burgers and strong coffee. A great place for memorabilia, too.

About 30 miles farther will be **Meramec Caverns,** a five-story wonder that includes an underground waterfall and 26 miles of passages. The tour lasts approximately ninety minutes, but allow more time for the gift shop and just watching the Meramec River. Admission: adults, $12.50; children five through eleven, $6.25; children under five, free.

LUNCH: After the Caverns, you'll probably want lunch. Another 10 miles down Route 66 will find you in Sullivan, Missouri. Get off 66 and onto the north outer road heading west, and **The Du Kum Inn** (101 Grand Center; 573–468–6114) will be on your right. It's always nice to find a place frequented by the locals, and The Du Kum Inn is one of those places. Great onion rings and hot-plate lunches at low prices—an outstandingly fine tuna salad sandwich, too! Inexpensive.

Afternoon

Driving along, you can see gas stations that once thrived, now covered over with vines, weathered barns leaning to one side, and small towns ignored by the thousands of cars passing a few miles away on the interstate. The road is in pretty good shape, although a road crew doing patch jobs might slow you down.

Keep a close eye on the signs HISTORIC ROUTE 66. They don't pop up as often as they should, which means you could take a little unplanned side trip. The road goes right through Rolla, Missouri, borders I–44 on the south for a few miles, and then goes over to the north again.

At **Lebanon, Missouri,** on City Route 66 East, sits a landmark, the **Munger Moss Motel,** enjoying a resurgence of business because of the road's popularity. Across the street, stop at **Wrink's Food Market,** where you can get Valomars candy bars and a cream soda or root beer. Shelves are packed with "66" antiques and collectibles from old glass soda bottles to signs and books. There's even a deli if you want a sandwich. Wrink has good stories to tell, like how popular the market was with "St. Louis folks"

The Meramec River at Meramec Caverns

going to the Lake of the Ozarks. But that was before I–44 and the turnoff many miles east, making the trip shorter.

Back on 66 and in 35 miles, you'll come to **Exotic Animal Paradise,** Strafford, Missouri (888–570–9898), a 400-acre drive-through animal park with camels, ostriches, emus, llamas, and many other species roaming free. The park also has a petting zoo. Get your camera ready! Open all year from 8:00 A.M. to dusk. Admission: adults, $10.99; children three through eleven, $6.99; seniors, $8.99. Allow about sixty to ninety minutes for this tour.

You are now about 12 miles from Springfield, Missouri, and are to be congratulated for mastering this segment of Route 66—America's Main Street.

DINNER: Reading the menu at **The Gallery Bistro,** 221 East Walnut (417–866–0555), might take some time with such choices as Tiger Tenderloin (grilled beef tenderloin medallions and tiger shrimp with chipotle sauce served with a Parmesan potato cake), or Citrus Curry Salmon with jasmine rice. Or mushroom-sage cream soup. Or a giant cilantro snow-crab cake with basil greens and Southwest aioli. The tenderloin is $21.95 and the salmon $15.95, but the taste is priceless. A good wine list, too.

LODGING: The Walnut Street Inn, 900 East Walnut (800–593–6346), is an 1849 Queen Anne Victorian house in the middle of the **Walnut Street Historic District.** The inn has fourteen rooms, some of which feature Jacuzzis, fireplaces, and balconies, but all have TVs, full baths, and ultra-comfy beds and surroundings. Rates: $89 to $169. www.walnut streetinn.com.

Day 2 / Morning

BREAKFAST: At the Walnut Street Inn. Served in two dining rooms with large windows, breakfast is cheery, delicious, and plentiful. Quiches, casseroles, fruits, juices, and muffins (especially the cappuccino ones) are served by hosts Gary and Paula Blankenship, who like to visit with guests, if they have time. Try to hit the 8:00 A.M. seating because you have a full day ahead.

This morning you will go to a Civil War battlefield and museum 10 miles southwest of Springfield. Take Sunshine Street to Highway 60; go left on Route MM, then left on Route ZZ for 2 miles. Your first stop is **General Sweeny's Museum of Civil History** (417–732–1224), the only private museum in the United States that tells the story of the Civil War in the West. If you weren't interested in the Civil War before seeing this collection, you will be. If you already are a Civil War buff, you might not leave this museum for hours. These exhibits take you through the Civil War, beginning in the 1850s with skirmishes in Kansas. Read accounts of battles such as Shiloh, Corinth, and Vicksburg as well as Wilson Creek and see artifacts from these and other battles. See original weapons, clothing, flags, and medical supplies. Admission: adults, $3.50; children five to eleven, $2.50; seniors, $3.00. Summer hours: Wednesday through Sunday 10:00 A.M. to 5:00 P.M. Closed Monday and Tuesday. Closed November through February. www.civilwarmuseum.com.

Leaving the museum, turn left to **Wilson Creek Battlefield–Museum;** (417) 732–2662. Fought on August 10, 1861, to gain control of Missouri, this battle left more than 2,300 Union and Confederate soldiers dead or wounded. At the Visitors' Center a short film and other displays describe events leading up to the battle. The self-guided auto tour will take you on a 4.9-mile loop with stops along the way at historic points on the battlefield. Admission: $3.00 per person, $5.00 per car. Open all year, seven days a week, 8:00 A.M. to 5:00 P.M.; www.wilsonscreek.com.

Return to Highway 60 and go back to Springfield. Your next stop is **Bass Pro Shop,** 1935 South Campbell Avenue; (417) 887–7334. At 300,000 square feet, this is truly the "grandaddy of all outdoor stores." Besides clothes, equipment, boats, campers, and gifts, there's a trout pool, a four-story waterfall, a Missouri River exhibit, an Ozark stream with a ninety-six-pound snapping turtle, a freshwater aquarium, and a 30,000-gallon saltwater aquarium. You can continue browsing the showroom indefinitely. Just when you think you've seen it all, you turn a corner and something new pops up. But, when you decide it's time to move on, head to the **American National Fish and Wildlife Museum** right next door to Bass Pro. This 92,000-square-foot museum features live animals, educational and interactive exhibits, and much more. It's a must-see for people of all ages. Admission: adults, $11.25; children four to eleven, $7.75; children under four, free. www.outdoor-world.com.

LUNCH: Time for lunch? You don't have to go far. **Hemingway's Blue Water Café** on the fourth level of the Bass Pro Shop satisfies any craving—be it fish or fowl, salads or sirloin—at prices from $5.95 for most sandwiches to $10.95 for London broil and crab legs. Or you could try the luncheon buffet, which includes roast beef, fried catfish, and an array of salads, vegetables, breads, and desserts. Adults, $7.95; children five to ten, $2.95; children under five, free. Hemingway's also has a dinner buffet for $16.95 (adults) and $5.95 (children). Sunday brunch offers soup and salad bar, roast beef, Belgian waffles, various egg dishes, and a dessert bar; served from 9:00 A.M. to 3:00 P.M. Adults, $11.95; children, $3.95; four and under, free.

Afternoon

After lunch, your next stop is the **Missouri Sports Hall of Fame,** 5051 Highland Springs Boulevard (¼ mile east of Highway 65 on Highway 60); (417) 889–3100. You'll find Missouri heroes like Ozzie Smith, Bob Gibson, Stan Musial, Payne Stewart, and many others in interactive displays. Broadcast a game with Jack Buck, Joe Garagiola, and Harry Caray. Experience having a baseball thrown at you at 90 miles per hour. Memorabilia from baseball, football, basketball to golf, auto racing, and fishing. Odds are you won't make it out of this gift shop empty-handed, either. Admission: adults, $5.00; students, $3.00; seniors, $4.00. Open Monday through Saturday 10:00 A.M. to 4:00 P.M. and Sunday noon to 4:00 P.M.

If the day should be a little hot, a drive through **Fantastic Caverns,** 4872 North Farm Road 125 (417–833–2010), will not only provide relief but a beautiful drive. As America's only ride-through cave, the caverns give a spectacular view of what happens when an underground river meanders for millions of years. Riding on jeep-drawn trams in a cool 60 degrees, visitors go from room to room while the guide explains the formations, including the Auditorium room, a vast natural theater. Admission: adults, $15.95; children six to twelve, $8.95; children five and under, free. Open daily all year except Thanksgiving Day, Christmas Eve, and Christmas Day, 8:00 A.M. to dusk. www.fantastic-caverns.com.

DINNER: Kick back in **The James River Grill,** 1155 East Battlefield Road, (417–890–0024), a laid-back, fun restaurant serving locally grown or produced products from a wood-fired open kitchen. Start with their specialty, fried green tomatoes served with a banana rum BBQ sauce. Choose from many barbecue selections from smoked pork shoulder to baby back ribs, or get the sampler for $17.49. Save room for their deep-dish apple pie with homemade cinnamon ice cream, voted Springfield's best dessert. Open Sunday through Thursday 11:00 A.M. to 10:00 P.M. and Friday and Saturday 11:00 A.M. to 10:30 P.M.

LODGING: The Walnut Street Inn.

Day 3 / Morning

BREAKFAST: At the Walnut Street Inn.

Before heading back to St. Louis, visit the **Dickerson Park Zoo,** 3043 North Fort; (417) 864–1800. Besides seeing hundreds of wild animals up close, visitors see animals native to the Ozarks, such as black bears, bobcats, and otters, in their native environment. While emphasizing many animal-conservation programs, the zoo is internationally known for its Asian Elephant Breeding Program. Other programs involve cheetahs, wolves, and lemurs. Open daily April through September, 9:00 A.M. to 5:00 P.M. and October through March, 10:00 A.M. to 4:00 P.M. Admission: adults, $5.00; children three to twelve, $3.00, under three, free; seniors, $4.00. www.dickersonparkzoo.org.

Head back on Highway 60 to Mansfield, Missouri, and the **Laura Ingalls Wilder Museum and Home,** 3068 Highway A; (417) 924–3626. A 50-mile drive from Springfield, this attraction is a must-see for those fans of the Wilder books and TV series *Little House on the Prairie*. The museum contains Laura's handwritten manuscripts, photographs, Pa's fiddle, and other artifacts. Open March through October, Monday through Saturday 9:00 A.M. to 5:00 P.M. and Sunday 12:30 to 5:30 P.M. Admission: adults, $6.00; children six to eighteen, $3.00; children under six, free; seniors, $5.00.

Drive back through Mansfield to Highway 5 North and follow it to Lebanon, 46 scenic, but hilly and curvy, miles. At Lebanon go east on I–44 to Rolla, 55 miles.

LUNCH: Eat in Rolla at the Maid Rite, 1028 Kingshighway; (573) 364–1434. (This street is also part of Historic Route 66. You probably recognize it.) This is the perfect, Route 66 way to have lunch—the original "loose meat" sandwich. In business since 1955, the restaurant also serves roast beef, barbecue, fried chicken, shakes, and, of course, the Maid Rite, which costs only $1.09. Cheap eats!

Afternoon

If you ate enough sandwiches, that should hold you for the two-hour trip back to St. Louis. Or if you're in the mood for another cave, take exit 214 at Leasburg (30 miles from Rolla) and visit **Onondaga Cave State Park;** (573) 245–6600. A naturalist who explains the geologic and natural features of the cave leads the seventy-five-minute tour. Admission: adults, $7.00; students, thirteen to nineteen, $5.00; children six to twelve, $3.00; under six, free. Hours: 9:00 A.M. to 5:00 P.M.

There's More

Battlefield Mall, 2825 South Glenstone Avenue; (417) 883–7777. One of Missouri's largest shopping centers with more than 170 specialty stores and restaurants, including Dillard, Famous Barr, and JCPenney.

Commercial Street Historic District. Home of the Frisco Railroad Museum (573–866–7573), with more than 2,500 items of Frisco Railway–related items displayed in re-created dioramas, two cabooses, a boxcar and a Frisco dining car. This 6-block Federal Historic District contains antiques shops, restaurants, flea markets, and the Ozark Model Railroad Association. In the middle you can "train watch" from a footbridge, built in 1902, which spans thirteen sets of railroad tracks.

Discovery Center, 438 St. Louis Street (417–862–9910), an interactive, hands-on museum for kids and adults. Dig for dinosaur bones in the Paleo-Lab; learn about energy in EnergyWorks; learn about the body in BodyWorks. In Discovery Town write your own newspaper, control traffic, and learn about banking and other town activities. Hours: Wednesday through Friday 9:00 A.M. to to 5:00 P.M., Saturday 10:00 A.M. to 5:00 P.M., and Sunday 1:00 P.M. to 5:00 P.M. Admission: adults, $5.00; children three to twelve, $3.00; seniors, $4.00.

Galloway Village, south of Battlefield Road on Lone Pine Avenue. Once an 1800s mining town, the renovated village includes shops containing handcrafted gifts and clothing and antiques. Stroll along the Greenway, stop for tea, and browse the shops.

Golf. Springfield has seven public courses. Call (800) 678–8767 for locations, rates, and packages.

The History Museum for Springfield-Greene County, City Hall Building, 830 Boonville; (417) 864–1976. A collection of more than 8,000 items connecting past to present with permanent and rotating exhibits. Hands-on areas in Native American, Civil War, and Victorian galleries. Open Tuesday through Saturday 10:30 A.M. to 4:30 P.M. Admission: adults, $3.00; seniors and students, $2.50; children, $1.00. www.historymuseumsgc.org.

Juanita K. Hammons Hall for the Performing Arts, 901 South National Avenue; (417) 836–6776. The place for touring Broadway shows, children's productions, jazz, classical, pop, and rock productions.

Landers Theatre, 311 East Walnut Street; (417) 869–1334 or (417) 869–3869. Missouri's oldest and largest civic theater, constructed in 1909, and an example of baroque Renaissance/Napoleon style of architecture and decoration, the Springfield Little Theater presents six plays each season at the Landers. Call for times and ticket prices.

Ozark Greenways. Walking, biking, hiking trails developed by Ozark Greenways dedicated to preserving Ozarks' natural heritage. Call for trail guides. (417) 864-2015; www.springfield.missouri.org/gov/ozarkgreenways.

Remington's New Country Entertainment, 1655 West Republic; (417) 889–4500. Kick up your heels on a 4,000-square-foot dance floor, take country dance lessons, or watch any of the four big-screen TVs. Open

Wednesday through Saturday 5:00 P.M. to 1:30 A.M. and Sunday 5:00 P.M. to midnight. Must be over twenty-one.

Walnut Street Historic District Walking Tour. Prepared by the Historical Site Board, this walking tour along Walnut Street showcases a century of changing building styles and tastes. Interspersed between the historic homes are a few galleries and specialty shops such as Collections Gift Shoppe, offering gift items by Crabtree & Evelyn, Mary Engelbreit, and area artists, and Bailey & Beck, with framed art, gifts, and books by Thomas Kinkade plus other gourmet gift items. The Springfield Convention and Visitors Bureau, 3315 Battlefield Road (800–678–8767), has the District Walking Tour Guide.

Special Events

February. Sertoma Chili Cookoff. Downtown Springfield. Dozens of individuals and organizations enter their chili in this competitive and wacky fund-raiser benefiting the Boys and Girls Clubs.

March. Spring Fishing Classic, Bass Pro Shop's Outdoor World. Expert guest celebrities, seminars, special programs for children. Free admission. (417) 887–7334.

April. Frisco Days. A 6-block-long festival celebrating the coming of the Iron Horse. Trains, horse-and-buggy rides, antique bicycles and automobiles, reenactments. Free admission.

International Beer Festival, University Plaza Convention Center. Sample more than one hundred brands of domestic and imported beer. Hors d'oeuvres provided by Springfield's leading restaurants are served. (417) 881–1215 or (417) 869–3869.

Rock n' Ribs BBQ Festival. This BBQ extravaganza features rock 'n' roll, blues, and jazz music; barbecue competitions; Best Bloody Mary and Margarita contests; drawings; children's entertainment; and more! (417) 866–6600.

May. ArtsFest on Walnut Street. A celebration of visual and performing arts with more than one hundred regional and local artists. (417) 869–8380 or (417) 831–6200.

National Street Rod Association Show. Ozark Empire Fairgrounds. More than 1,600 pre-1949 street rods. Sixty commercial exhibits. Swap meets, crafts shows, and displays. (800) 678–8767.

June. Route 66 Music Festival. Three-day music and camping festival featuring big-name entertainment. Held on Route 66/Chestnut Expressway west of Springfield. (888) 875–9772.

July through August. Ozark Empire Fair. Fairgrounds. Missouri's second-largest fair. Live music, livestock competition, exhibits and food, midway. (417) 833–2660.

August. Moonlight Tour at Wilson's Creek. A living-history night program. Park guides lead visitors by lantern around the Wilson's Creek battlefield, showing the field conditions after the Battle of Wilson's Creek. Visitors will see the field hospital, headquarters with prisoners, and other vignettes. (417) 732–2662.

September. Greater Ozarks Bluesfest, downtown Springfield. Two days of blues featuring local, regional, and national talent. Includes outdoor concert and Blues Crawl. (417) 869–3869 or (417) 869–8558.

October. Cider Days, Walnut Street. A fall celebration with crafts from regional and local artists. (417) 831–6200.

December. First Night Springfield, downtown Springfield. Entertainment for the whole family including music, masquerade, gospel, cloggers, mimes, and more, plus food. (417) 831–6200.

Other Recommended Restaurants and Lodgings

Springfield

Aunt Martha's Pancake House, 1700 East Cherokee Street; (417) 881–3505. Locally owned with thirty-five years' experience of serving the area's best pancakes. Inexpensive.

Bijan's, 209 East Walnut; (417) 831–1480. An eclectic menu with eclectic decor. Moderate prices.

Churchill Coffee Company and Cafe, Coffee Estate, South Glenstone Avenue; (417) 823–8203. Daily roasted coffee and incredible cinnamon rolls, gourmet soups, wraps, and sandwiches. Inexpensive.

Courtyard by Marriott, 3527 West Kearney; (800) MARRIOTT. Indoor pool with health club. Children eighteen and under free. Rates: $79.95 to $89.95.

Gailey's Drugstore, 220 East Walnut; (417) 862–1755. A Springfield original. Hamburgers, old-fashioned fountain drinks, ice-cream sodas, and the best malts you've ever had. Inexpensive.

Lamplighter Inn, 1772 South Glenstone; (800) 749–7275. Restaurant on premises, outdoor pool. Children twelve and under free. $49.94 to $54.95.

The Mansion at Elfindale, 1701 South Fort; (800) 443–0237. Victorian mansion with thirteen suites in a European–style bed-and-breakfast. Rooms have private baths. No smoking or alcohol. Rates: $45 to $135.

Mille's Turn of the Century Cafe, 313 South Jefferson; (417) 831–1996. Casual and classy with steaks, seafood, chicken, and a good selection of vegetarian dishes. Specialty salads with homemade dressings. Moderate prices.

The Repair Shop Restaurant and Saloon, 2251 East Kearney Street; (417) 866–5254. An original with a horseshoe bar and log room with unique furnishings. Organic steaks and true local flavor. Moderate prices.

Springfield Brewing Company, 305 South Market Avenue, in historic downtown; (417) 832-TAPS. Delicious food with good beer brewed on-site. Try the Shanghai Pasta ($8.50) or Santa Fe Cheddar Ale Soup ($3.95); great pizzas like smoked cheddar, bacon, and tomato or the Southwest, with chorizo sausage and black beans ($7.95). Billiard tables, cigar room, and live music on weekends. Rooftop beer garden is exceptional in good weather. Inexpensive to moderate.

Virginia Rose Bed & Breakfast, 317 East Glenwood; (800) 345–1412. Country Victorian B&B with four rooms decorated with period furnishings. Private baths. Parlor with books, games, and puzzles—and a piano for those who play. Breakfasts such as egg strata or quiche, fruit, and fresh-baked muffins or biscuits. Rates: $65 to $100.

For More Information

Springfield Convention and Visitors Bureau, 3315 East Battlefield, Springfield, MO 65804; (800) 678–8767; www.springfieldmo.org.

SOUTHERN ESCAPE FIVE

Branson, Missouri

Luxury in the Ozark Mountains / 3 Nights

Not including Branson in a guidebook written about weekend getaways from St. Louis would be an oversight, yet there are literally dozens of travel books that focus on Branson as a vacation destination. So why mention it

- ☐ Big Cedar Lodge
- ☐ Beautiful scenery
- ☐ Relaxing retreat
- ☐ Family fun

here? Well, if you're like me, you'd really enjoy getting away to the majestic hills and lush foliage of the Ozarks. But also like me, you'd rather have dental surgery than watch country-music performers singing their hearts out up and down Highway 76. After all, that's what Branson's all about, right? Well, yes and no. Yes, there are numerous shows that could easily consume all your waking hours if you choose. But no, the Branson area is not only about glittery costumes and country music. It's also about wooded hills, prairie grasses, cool lake breezes, and gorgeous sunsets. It's about getting away from reality, pampering yourself, eating some great food, and spending time alone or with your family. You *can* go to the Branson/Table Rock Lake area and never step foot in a country-music show if you prefer. So if you always thought Branson was only about "pickin' and grinnin'," take a new look and come away with a wonderful getaway.

Day 1 / Morning

Because of the long drive, you'll want to get an early start. I'd recommend leaving by 9:00 A.M. Depending on where you're located, the trip will take about four hours, not counting stopping for lunch. You'll take I–44 West for the majority of your trip. The scenery is lovely to look at, especially in spring, when the redbud and dogwood trees are in bloom. Once you reach Springfield, take Highway 65 south toward Branson, about 35 miles away.

Your first stopping point, Big Cedar Lodge, is about 10 miles south of Branson off Highway 65. Follow the signs and make a right on Highway

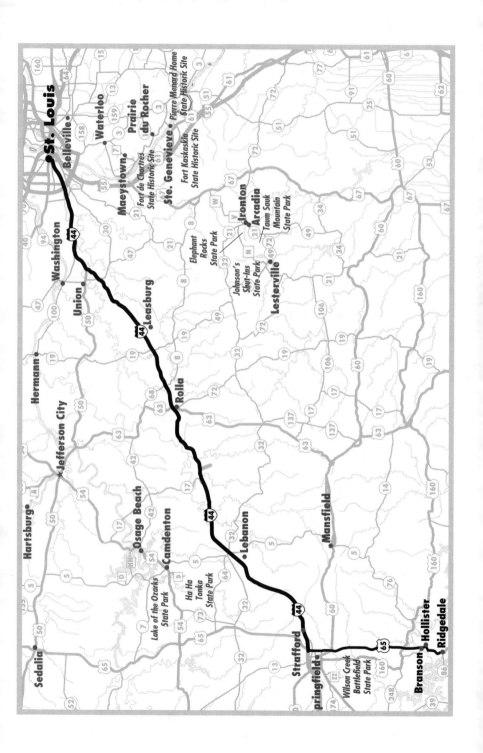

86. Continue on a mile or two and you'll see the sign for Big Cedar Lodge. Make a right at the entrance sign and follow the signs for registration in the main lodge.

LUNCH: Depending on how hungry you are, you can either stop in Lebanon, about two and a half hours from St. Louis, or continue on to Springfield for lunch. Either town has plenty of chain restaurants that'll get you in and out quickly. If you decide to drive straight through, the Devil's Pool Restaurant at the Lodge has a varied and inexpensive menu.

Afternoon

LODGING: Big Cedar Lodge, 612 Devil's Pool Road, Ridgedale; (417) 335–2777; www.big-cedar.com. What started as a modest fishing lodge in the 1930s has developed into a wilderness retreat with amenities. Accommodations range from hotel-type rooms to luxury multibedroom, free-standing cabins, with rates across the board from $69 to $619, depending on the room and season. (A cabin, with full kitchen and two bathrooms is great for families.) The outstanding feature of Big Cedar Lodge is the attention to detail that is paid to virtually everything on the property. Local craftspeople were hired to design and create the hundreds of stained-glass windows that can be found throughout the lodge; each slightly different, they pay tribute to the animals, trees, and water that surround the area. Also, because the lodge is environmentally friendly, you won't see much plastic here. Instead, trash cans are woven wooden baskets complete with a collection bag for recycling. Materials used throughout the property are rustic yet comfortable, and many were handmade. Most rooms and all cabins have a view of Table Rock Lake, and many have outdoor balconies or decks. The level of detail, the quality of the workmanship, and the friendly, helpful staff most definitely make Big Cedar a first-class operation.

After you've checked in and gotten settled, you'll want to stretch your legs before dinner. Not to worry. There are plenty of walking paths and even more hills around Big Cedar Lodge, so spend some time exploring the grounds. A 1-mile walking trail offers an easy and enjoyable walk, or you may want to browse through the surrounding gardens. Make sure you pick up a brochure on Big Cedar's gardens if you're interested in knowing more about the plants. The booklet was prepared in response to the most commonly asked questions about the flowers and plants that grow nearly everywhere around the lodge. If your timing's right, you may be able to tag along on a garden tour conducted by the staff (check with guest services for times). Or consider a quick game of tennis or a dip in the pool; the outdoor heated pool is open March through December and overlooks Table Rock Lake. There's also an outdoor hot tub.

DINNER: Top of the Rock Restaurant, 150 Top of the Rock Road, Hollister; (417) 339–5321. If a relaxing dinner with a fabulous view is your idea of starting off your getaway right, then you've come to the right place. Top of the Rock Restaurant, which is owned by Big Cedar Lodge, is a comfortably elegant, yet relaxed, restaurant with one of the best views of Table Rock Lake. Request a seat by the window, or better yet, sit outside on the terrace with its cool breezes and cozy stone fireplace. The restaurant has a varied menu that includes pastas, wood-fired pizzas, beef, and chicken. Kids' meals are also available. House specials include a rotisserie half chicken that just falls off the bone and a twin fillet of beef tenderloin that's so tender you can cut it with a fork. Specials vary nightly. The restaurant is open daily 11:00 A.M. to 9:30 P.M. Dinner entrees are in the moderate to expensive range. Reservations accepted. You can take the Lodge's courtesy shuttle to the restaurant (check with guest services) or exit the Lodge onto Highway 86 and head back toward Highway 65. Take a left on the road just before Highway 65, Top of the Rock Road. The restaurant is about a mile from the Lodge.

Day 2 / Morning

BREAKFAST: Devil's Pool Restaurant, Big Cedar Lodge. Take a stroll across the swinging bridge to this former summer-cabin-turned-lodge-restaurant for breakfast before starting your day. Enjoy hearty fare such as eggs, biscuits, or pancakes or, if you prefer, a light fruit salad. Prices are inexpensive.

While you could easily spend your entire day relaxing at Big Cedar Lodge, consider heading over to **Silver Dollar City** if you're in the mood for a little excitement (or if the thought of relaxing around the lodge has your kids pacing the floor and complaining "there's nothing to do!"). Silver Dollar City is by definition a theme park. But unlike most theme parks, Silver Dollar City is like an old-fashioned village complete with more than fifty shops featuring top-notch craftspersons who make everything from candy and musical instruments to furniture and blown glass. Set in the late 1800s era, costumed artists and craftspeople work their magic on treasures they hope you'll buy.

Silver Dollar City amusement park

Of course, the kids will want to explore the rides. Here's their chance to hop aboard roller coasters, log flumes, white-water rafts, and more. There's even an area with tamer rides, just for younger kids, as well as a playground and sandbox area. **Marvel Cave** is also part of the park. Discovered in the 1500s, Marvel Cave is a registered National Landmark that you can explore during a guided walking tour. Silver Dollar City also offers a number of musical shows at various locations throughout the park.

This is a great place to go if you want to cover a lot of territory—shopping, fun for the kids, entertainment, food—in a short amount of time. And don't worry too much about the heat. Unlike most theme parks, Silver Dollar City is covered in shade trees that really help keep the temperature manageable. Plus the park offers water-misting stations, free cups of water for the asking, and lots of water rides to keep you cool. One-day passes are $35 plus tax for adults and $24 plus tax for kids ages four to eleven. Children ages three and under are free. Silver Dollar City is located at 399 Indian Point Road, Branson; (417) 334–7263 or (800) 952–6626; www.silverdollarcity.com. Hours of operation vary but are generally 9:30 A.M. to 7:00 P.M.

Since you'll be at the park only part of one day, you may want to use the following plan to hit what I consider to be the park's highlights: Enter the park between 9:30 and 10:00 A.M. and head toward the left to the American Plunge for a fun "log flume" ride the whole family can enjoy. On the way, glance in the Mountain Outfitter's Gun & Knife Shop to see and hear the blacksmith reciting poetry while plying his trade. Continue to the northwest corner of the park for BuzzSaw Falls, the world's first liquid coaster—a combo rapid-water ride with dry-coaster thrills. Plan on getting wet! Smaller kids will enjoy Tom Sawyer's Landing in the center of the park. Nearby, stop for lunch.

LUNCH: Enjoy some excellent BBQ at **Riverside Ribhouse,** just next to Tom Sawyer's Landing. The BBQ pork-and-beef sandwich is served on a delicious bun baked at the park's bakery. This excellent sandwich includes sides like coleslaw or applesauce. Prices are in the inexpensive range. Kids' meals are available.

Afternoon

Next head over to the northeast corner of the park to the Geyser Gulch Tree House. Here you and your kids can shoot oversized water guns into a lake, play in water activities, and shoot giant foam-ball launching rockets. Plan on getting wet again! Just south of Geyser Gulch is the Hillcreek Pottery and Painted Garden shop. Both adults and kids will enjoy watching potters create bowls, cups, and more right before your eyes. The craftspeople are friendly and genuinely welcome questions. And the shops are air-conditioned, which is an added bonus if you need a break! Wind your way back toward the entrance of the park and stop at Hazel's Blown Glass Factory for a firsthand look at glass being fired; then continue toward the park's entrance to Brown's Candy Factory to see fudge or peanut brittle being made. Finally, if time permits, consider exploring Marvel Cave, but note that the tour takes about an hour and includes climbing up and down a lot of steps.

After your day at Silver Dollar City, head back to the cabin and clean up before dinner.

DINNER: Dixie Stampede Dinner and Show, 1 mile west of Highway 65 on Highway 76, Branson; (800) 520–5101 or (417) 336–3000; www.dixiestampede. com. Reservations recommended. At first the concept of eating my dinner in a horse arena didn't appeal to me. The idea of a herd of stomping stallions galloping by me eyeing my meal and sending up clouds of dust into my dinner seemed way too unsanitary and far too hokey for me. But I must admit, the Dixie Stampede Dinner and Show turned out to be quite entertaining without the slightest bit of dust or aroma of horses to compete with the meal. My hat is off to the young people who flew by me while balancing on one knee atop charging steeds or hanging upside down under the belly of a bronco. The premise of the show is a North vs. South Civil War thing. Without getting heavy-handed, the show mixes talented horse riders with dancing belles and beaus of the ball, all amid a Southern plantation backdrop. Riders compete in trick riding, buckboard racing, ostrich races, and corny comedy while you dine, minus silverware, on rotisserie chicken with all the down-home fixin's. (Vegetarian meals available upon request.) This is wholesome entertainment with some very impressive riding. Admission, which includes a musical preshow, dinner, and show is $35.99 plus tax for adults and $19.99 plus tax for kids. Make reservations for the 8:00 P.M. show. Other show times are 5:30 P.M. and matinees on select dates.

LODGING: Big Cedar Lodge.

Day 3 / Morning

BREAKFAST: Get up early and grab a quick bite to go at **Nowell's Grocery Store** on Highway 65 in **Hollister,** between Big Cedar and Branson (you can't miss it on the east side of the street), or at one of the many fast-food restaurants in Branson before heading out for a morning of exploring Lake Taneycomo on a **guided kayaking tour.**

According to **Trek the Ozarks,** almost anybody can comfortably paddle a kayak, which is probably why kayaking is the fourth-fastest-growing sport in the United States. Much better than noisy motorboats, kayaking is a great way to explore the calm, cool waters of Lake Taneycomo and an excellent way to see wildlife in their habitats without disturbing them. Plus it's fun exercise!

The four-hour tour begins with a brief kayaking lesson followed by a guided tour of the lake. Kids ages eight to twelve do best sharing a two-person kayak with the guide, who is experienced in working with youngsters this age. The tour is not recommended for kids under age eight. Rates are $68 per person for a half day ($40 for kids riding along in a two-person kayak) and include all equipment such as personal flotation devices, plus a snack and transportation to and from the lake. Call (417) 335–4455 for reservations. Most questions about the tour can be answered by reviewing the Web site at www.trektheozarks.com. Trek the Ozarks is located at 1200 State Highway 248, Branson. From Big Cedar head north on Highway 65 and exit at Business 65 going west, which becomes State Highway 248. Trek the Ozarks is located within the Downhill Bikes and Accessories shop on the right.

LUNCH: Farmhouse Restaurant, 119 West Main, downtown Branson; (417) 334–9701. No doubt you've worked up an appetite, so chow down on country cooking the locals enjoy. Catfish, hearty breakfast fare, grilled sandwiches, chicken-fried steak, a salad bar, and blackberry cobbler have been keeping the front door swinging for years. Entrees are inexpensive.

Afternoon

Before you leave this quaint little business district of Branson's, stop in **Dick's Oldtime 5 & 10,** or as most people call it, The Dime Store, 103 West Main Street; (417) 334–2410. One of only a handful of dime stores I can think of, Dick's has more than 50,000 items from toys to crafts to housewares to souvenirs. It's tons of fun to explore. Don't miss the large display of paper dolls in the back corner.

Spend the rest of the afternoon relaxing back at Big Cedar. Consider some time at the spa if you would like a massage or manicure. A twenty-minute chair massage is $25; manicures begin at $25. The spa also offers wraps and other spa treatments. Because the spa is small, it's best to make reservations at least one week in advance or when making your lodge reservation; call (417) 335–2777 for reservations.

DINNER: *Showboat Branson Belle,* White River Landing, 4800 State Highway 165, Branson; (800) 775–BOAT or (417) 336–7171. You can accomplish two things at once—dining and entertainment—when you board the *Showboat Branson Belle.* Once aboard this beautiful, and huge, paddle-wheel boat, you'll have a delicious meal prepared right in the ship's on-board galley while enjoying a variety of family-friendly entertainment. Between dinner and the evening entertainment, kids love the chance to go to the top of the boat and meet the captain in the pilothouse. Many people are surprised to learn that the *Showboat Branson Belle* is a true stern-wheeler, propelled through the water only by by its two huge paddle wheels and steered by a 10-foot-wide captain's wheel. You'll also have a chance to gaze out over Table Rock Lake from the shaded top deck before heading back to your seat for the evening's entertainment. For a more luxurious dining experience, spend a little more and dine in the private

Paddle Wheel Club Room, with an upgraded menu and outstanding views of Table Rock Lake and the paddle wheels. Dinner and entertainment begins at $44.50 for adults, $21.20 for kids. Lunch is $38.15 for adults, $19.10 for kids. Special dietary needs can be accommodated, and a children's menu is available.

Evening

If time allows, and you really feel you can't leave Branson without seeing at least one show, consider **Spirit of the Dance** at 8:00 P.M. This is a high-energy show in the spirit of *Riverdance,* featuring a dynamic blend of Irish dance with dashes of flamenco, red-hot salsa, and jazz. Spirit of the Dance is at the Bobby Vinton Blue Velvet Theatre, 2701 West Highway 76, Branson; (888) GO–BRANSON or www.gotobranson.com for tickets.

LODGING: Big Cedar Lodge.

Day 4 / Morning

BREAKFAST: Devil's Pool Restaurant, Big Cedar Lodge.

After breakfast, head on over to Cedar Mountain Stables, just up the hill from the registration area. There's nothing like **horseback riding** to really see the Ozark Mountains up close and personal. Guides will take you on a one-hour tour through the woods that includes a beautiful view overlooking Table Rock Lake. This is especially great to do during fall, when the leaves are changing color. Horseback rides are $22 per person. If you'd prefer to put a little more distance between you and Mr. Ed, a carriage ride around the Big Cedar grounds is a comfortable alternative. A twenty-minute ride runs $12.50 per person. If you're at the lodge during summer, don't miss the evening-campfire wagon tours. You begin with a ride in an antique hitch wagon and head down a wooded trail to a rustic campsite along the lake. Cowboys will entertain you with songs while you roast marshmallows and drink cool sarsaparilla. Evening-campfire wagon tours are $15 per person. Kids three and under are free.

After a pit stop in the gift shop, it's time to head back home. The drive should take about four hours, not including a stop for lunch.

LUNCH: St. Louis Bread Company, 1651 North Bishop (Highway 63 North); (573) 368–4499. This newer "BreadCo" is a place for a quick and great-tasting sandwich or cup of soup. Prices are inexpensive. The Bread Company is about two hours out of Branson in Rolla. Take the third Rolla exit (number 186) and go right about 4 blocks; the restaurant will be on the right.

There's More

Branson

Branson Scenic Railway, 206 East Main Street; (417) 334–6110 or (800) 2TRAIN2. Experience the beauty of the Ozarks aboard a restored 1940s and 1950s train. Saturday-evening dinner excursions available as well. Tickets are $20.25 plus tax for adults, $10.25 plus tax for kids to age twelve.

Ride the Ducks, 2320 West Highway 76, next to McDonald's and Wal-Mart; (417) 334–DUCK. If you want a quick "lay-of-the-land" tour the kids will love, entertainment, and a cruise on the lake, you can get it all when you ride the ducks—converted DUKW army amphibian vehicles used in World War II that roll on land and float on water. Cost is $14.95 for adults, $7.45 for kids.

Ridgedale

Dogwood Canyon Nature Park, 612 Devil's Pool Road; (417) 335–2777 (same address and phone number as Big Cedar Lodge and just a short 16-mile drive away); www.dogwoodcanyon.com. Hop on Highway 86 West; the park will be on the left. The entrance is just over the crest of a hill, so keep your eye out for signs. The park is a private wilderness refuge that encompasses more than 9,000 acres of Ozark wilderness. Take a tram tour of the park and discover American bison and Texas longhorn as well as white-tailed deer and wild turkey. You'll even cross over a beautiful covered bridge built by the Amish. Tour prices are $23.95 for adults and $9.95 for kids.

Special Events

May through June. Silver Dollar City Great American Music Festival. See and hear performers from around the country. (417) 334–7263 or (800) 952–6626; www.silverdollarcity.com.

June through August. Silver Dollar City National Children's Festival. All kinds of crazy kids stuff including Scooby Doo, Veggie Tales, and an Extreme Stunts bike and roller blade exhibition. (417) 334–7263 or (800) 952–6626; www.silverdollarcity.com.

November through December. An Old Time Christmas. Silver Dollar City. Carolers and special Christmas activities. (417) 334–7263 or (800) 952–6626; www.silverdollarcity.com.

Radio City Rockettes Christmas Spectacular at the Grand Palace. Branson. (800) 5–PALACE or (417) 33–GRAND.

Other Recommended Restaurants and Lodgings

Branson

Bradford on the Lake, 2601 Indian Point Road, Branson; (800) 864–6811. Family-run motel 1½ miles from Silver Dollar City. Updated decor, two outdoor pools, hot tub, and complimentary continental breakfast. Good for families who don't mind sharing a room and are just looking for a clean, comfortable place to stay. Rates are $49 and $59 year-round.

Château Grille, Château on the Lake, 415 North State Highway 265, Branson; (417) 334–1161, ext. 2050, or (888) 333–LAKE. Treat yourself to a culinary delight with menu items that include grilled lobster tail, rack of lamb, salmon, or the special Grand Menu, all expertly prepared. Children's menu available. Expensive, although the children's menu is very reasonable.

Château on the Lake, 415 North State Highway 265; (417) 334–1161 or (888) 333–LAKE; www.chateauonthelakebranson.com. Elegant French-looking château on a mountaintop overlooking Table Rock Lake. Luxuriously appointed rooms start at $109 to $169 per night depending on the season.

For More Information

Branson/Lakes Area Chamber of Commerce and Convention & Visitor's Bureau, P.O. Box 1897, 269 State Highway 248, Branson, MO 65615; (417) 334–4136 or (800) 214–3661; www.explorebranson.com.

SOUTHERN ESCAPE SIX

Memphis, Tennessee

Blues, Barbecue, and Graceland / 2 Nights

The "Home of the Blues" and "The Birthplace of Rock 'n' Roll" is how Memphis bills itself, and, once you visit, you won't disagree. Many attractions are music-oriented, but there is so much more for those persons who don't live and die by the guitar. Downtown Memphis is especially visitor-friendly. You can park your car the entire weekend and not want for something to do. Mud Island, Beale Street, Peabody Place, the Pinch Historic District—these attractions and more, plus restaurants and coffeehouses, are all within walking distance.

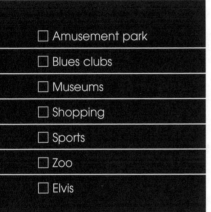

□ Amusement park

□ Blues clubs

□ Museums

□ Shopping

□ Sports

□ Zoo

□ Elvis

Besides blues, rock 'n' roll, and Elvis Presley, Memphis has its roots deep in the Civil War and Civil Rights movement. You can see its ties to history at Mud Island River Park and the National Civil Rights Museum at the Lorraine Motel, site of Dr. Martin Luther King's assassination.

The Memphis Pink Palace Museum, once the dream mansion of a Memphis entrepreneur, now houses an IMAX theater, planetarium, and natural and cultural exhibits.

There are many "musts" on your Memphis visit. One is, of course, Graceland, home of "The King," and the other—the Peabody ducks at the famous Peabody Hotel.

Day 1 / Morning

Plan to leave St. Louis by 8:30 A.M. Memphis is approximately a five-hour drive south on I–55, and you will arrive in Sikeston, Missouri, at 11:30, in time for lunch.

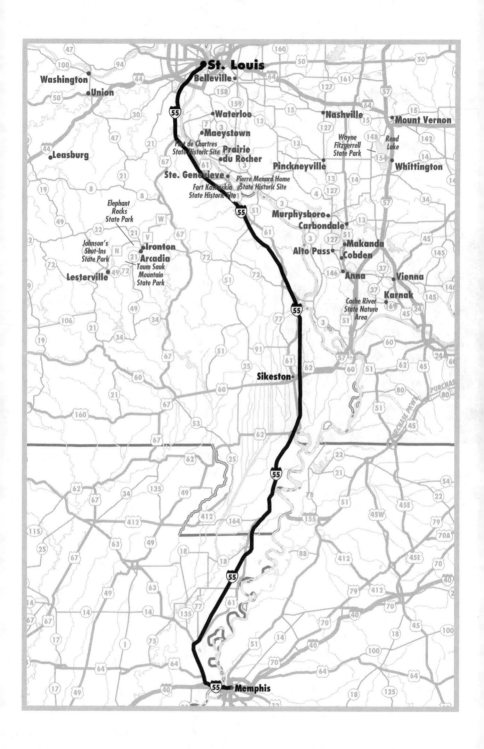

LUNCH: This won't be just any lunch. You will eat at **Lambert's Cafe,** 2515 East Malone (573–471–4261), home of the "Throwed Rolls." And they do throw them—hot rolls fresh from the oven come sailing over patrons' heads to your waiting hands. These rolls go wonderfully with the crispy fried chicken, pork chops, or meat loaf. Besides coming with mashed potatoes and gravy, turnip greens, corn, or any of the other seventeen vegetables offered, you get "Pass-Arounds" like fried potatoes and onions, black-eyed peas, fried okra, and sorghum for your rolls. If you still have room after that lunch, get one of their larger-than-life cinnamon rolls (called hubcaps) to take with you! Prices are moderate and include lots of fun! While you're waiting for your feast, take in some of the wall decorations that include hundreds of license plates, some of which are quite old, from every state. (To get to Lambert's, take exit 67 toward Sikeston. Turn left onto US–62. The restaurant is about 3 blocks away.)

Afternoon

Return to I–55 for the rest of your drive to Memphis. Plan on checking into your hotel first.

LODGING: The **Talbot Heirs Guesthouse** (901–527–9772) is located in downtown Memphis at 99 South Second, across from the Peabody Hotel. Coming into Memphis on I–55 South, cross the bridge and take the Riverside Drive exit to downtown. Once you're on Riverside, head south to Union Avenue and turn left. (If you turn right, you'll be in the river.) Take Union to Second Street and turn right (it's one-way). The hotel is on the right.

This small hotel with nine suites, each one uniquely decorated, will put you within walking distance of most of what Memphis has to offer including Beale Street, the National Civil Rights Museum, Mud Island, and the Gibson Guitar Factory. Rates for the guest house range from $150 to $250 per night. The hotel does not have a parking lot, but you can put on your flashers and double-park in the front to unload your luggage. Then drive 1 block to Peabody Place, turn right, then right again into the All Right Garage. Parking rates are about $5.00 per day.

Since you've been in the car a few hours, your first visit should be to **Mud Island,** a fifty-two-acre park in the Mississippi River. You can take the Monorail to Mud Island. To get to the **monorail station,** turn left out of Talbot Heirs and walk 1 block to Union Avenue. Go west on Union to Front Street, take a right, go about 6 blocks, and cross the street. This

Mud Island

monorail, incidentally, was the same one seen in the movie *The Firm,* which was filmed in Memphis.

Once at Mud Island you can experience 1,000 miles of the Mississippi Delta by walking along the 5-block replica of the lower Mississippi River, complete with water and beach as it spills into the Gulf of Mexico. The Mississippi River Museum features eighteen galleries depicting life along the Mississippi beginning 10,000 years ago. Board a reconstructed 1870s steamboat. Experience gunfire from the deck of a Civil War gunboat. Listen to the music of Memphis—jazz, soul, blues, and rock 'n' roll. Take a guided tour of *The Memphis Belle,* World War II's most famous B-17, which was the first B-17 to complete twenty-five successful bombing missions. Open April through October. Spring/fall hours: Tuesday through Sunday 10:00 A.M. to 5:00 P.M. Summer hours: open daily 10:00 A.M. to 8:00 P.M. Admission for adults (thirteen through fifty-nine), $8.00; for children (five through twelve), seniors (sixty-plus), and those with disabilities, $6.00; children four and under, free. (800) 507–6507; www.mudisland.com.

After Mud Island take the monorail and start the walk back to Talbot Heirs. Before you reach your room, explore the **Peabody Place Retail** and **Entertainment Center.** Stretching from the Mississippi riverfront to the Peabody Hotel and Beale Street, it is connected by skyways, corridors, and a trolley station. Attractions include a twenty-two-screen movie theater, an IMAX 3-D theater, numerous retail stores, and restaurants.

Return to your room and relax before dinner. Each room has a full kitchen with a refrigerator stocked with cereal, milk, yogurt, soda water, and juice. There's even ice cream in the freezer, and the coffeemaker is ready to fill. If you give the innkeeper a grocery list before 11:30 A.M., he will have groceries delivered to you for a $20 charge if you want to eat in.

If it's 5:00 P.M., cross over to the **Peabody Hotel** and watch the ducks climb out of their fountain, waddle down the red carpet to the elevator, and go to the roof. They'll return at 11:00 A.M. the next morning! As the story goes, in the 1930s, the former hotel manager and a good friend returned from a hunting trip and decided to put live duck decoys in the fountain. At present, the ducks come from a farm and are switched every three months.

DINNER: For an elegant dinner in an elegant house, **Cielo's,** 679 Adams (901–524–1886), is the place. Located in historic Victorian Village, Cielo's used to be a private home. Now visitors dine by candlelight in quiet, intimate rooms. The food is spectacular—with appetizers such as zucchini stuffed with crab relish and marinated shrimp; entrees like tangerine glazed duck, roasted sweet potatoes, and flash-fried spinach or pork tenderloin with horseradish mashed potatoes; and the desserts! Cappuccino cheesecake, Key lime cheesecake, Godiva chocolate, and peanut-butter cake are a few selections. Closed Monday.

Day 2 / Morning

BREAKFAST: Take advantage of the food in the room for breakfast or hop across the street to the **Cafe Expresso** at the Peabody Hotel, where you can get breakfast muffins, breads, lattes, and cappuccinos. Reasonable prices.

You have a full day, so prepare to get to **Graceland,** 3734 Elvis Presley Boulevard, for the 9:00 A.M. tour. It's about a twenty-minute drive from the Talbot Heirs Guesthouse. For the full effect you should buy the Graceland Platinum Tour, which includes the mansion tour, a tour of Elvis's custom jets, the *Hound Dog II* and *Lisa Marie,* and the auto museum with Elvis's cars, including the famous pink cadillac. Cost for the package is $25.25 for adults, $22.75 for students and seniors (sixty-two-plus), $12.75 for children seven through eleven, and free for children six and under. Whether you are an Elvis fan or not, you will come away with a definite feel for the power of The King. There is also a restaurant and several gift shops. Open Monday through Saturday 9:00 A.M. to 5:00 P.M. and Sunday 10:00 A.M. to 4:00 P.M.; closed Thanksgiving and Christmas Day. The mansion is closed Tuesday from November through February, although other attractions are open. Call (800) 238–2000 for reservations or visit www.elvis-presley.com.

Your next stop will be **Sun Studios,** 706 Union Avenue, thought by many persons to be the actual birthplace of rock 'n' roll since this was where Elvis was discovered. You'll hear informal outtakes of Jerry Lee Lewis, Johnny Cash, Roy Orbison, and others in addition to Elvis. Hold the microphone Elvis held. Walk on the floor where he walked—the studio and office are virtually unchanged since Elvis walked through the doors in 1953. The studio is open every day from 10:00 A.M. to 6:00 P.M. Admission $7.85. (800) 441–6429; www.sunstudio.com.

LUNCH: Return to your parking garage and walk to **Elvis Presley's Memphis,** 126 Beale Street, for lunch. In addition to burgers, chicken, steaks, and appetizers, you can get The King's favorite—a fried peanut butter and banana sandwich. Mighty tasty! Also try the fried dill pickle chips. Prices range from $10 to $20. They also serve a Gospel Brunch on Sunday from 11:00 A.M. to 2:00 P.M. (901) 527–6900; www.epmemphis.dom.

Afternoon

You'll be on **Beale Street,** so walk down a couple of blocks to **A. Schwab's Dry Goods Store,** founded in 1876. Their motto is "If you can't find it at Schwab's, you're better off without it." You'll find such varied treasures as Fels Naphtha soap, cotton stockings, dresses, hats, hot sauce, relish, and hair clippies (49 cents each or twelve for $1.00).

Walk back up Beale Street to the **Main Street Trolley Station** and take the next trolley (50 cents regular fare, 25 cents for seniors and those with disabilities) to the **National Civil Rights Museum.** Located at the **Lorraine Motel,** site of the assassination of Dr. Martin Luther King, this museum offers a powerful history of the Civil Rights movement through audiovisual aids, exhibits, photographs, art, and documents. Dr. King's room and the one adjoining have been kept exactly as they were April 4, 1968. A wreath hangs on the railing where King fell. Allow at least ninety minutes for this tour. Hours from September through May are Monday, Wednesday, Thursday, and Friday 9:00 A.M. to 5:00 P.M.; Sunday 1:00 to

5:00 P.M. June through August hours are Monday, Tuesday, Wednesday, Thursday, Friday, and Saturday 9:00 A.M. to 6:00 P.M.; Sunday 1:00 to 6:00 P.M. Adults, $8.50; seniors and students with ID, $7.50; children six through twelve, $6.50; children three and under and museum members, free. Museum is free on Monday 3:00 to 5:00 P.M. from September through May, and 3:00 to 6:00 P.M. from June through August. Call (901) 521–9699 or visit www.civilrightsmuseum.org.

You have a couple of choices now. If you have children, you can hop back on the trolley and go to **The Fire Museum of Memphis,** 118 Adams Street; (901) 320–5650; www.firemuseum.com. Children really enjoy this museum built in an old Memphis firehouse. Or you could take the trolley to the **Gibson Guitar Building,** 1 block south of Beale Street.

At the Fire Museum you can go in the Fire Room and see what it's like to experience a variety of severe fires, or you can visit the Safety House and see how to fireproof your house. You can slide down a pole and take a virtual ride on a fire truck. Hours are Tuesday through Saturday 9:00 A.M. to 5:00 P.M. and Sunday 1:00 to 5:00 P.M. They are closed on Monday. Rates are $5.00 for adults, $4.00 for seniors and ages three through twelve; children two and under are free.

At the **Gibson Guitar Factory,** you can tour the factory through sixteen different stations of the guitar-making process, from fitting and sanding through tuning and packing. Tour is by appointment only. Thursday through Saturday 11:00 A.M., noon, 1:00 P.M., and 2:00 P.M.; Sunday through Wednesday 1:00 P.M. Admission is $10 per person (twelve and over).

While you're there, don't miss the **Memphis Rock 'n' Soul Museum.** In partnership with the Smithsonian Institute, the museum lets visitors track the history of rock 'n' roll from its blues roots in the 1930s to its birth in the 1950s and through its growth to the present. Located inside the Gibson Guitar Factory Building. Open Monday to Sunday from 10:00 A.M. to 6:00 P.M. Admission: adults, $8.50; seniors, $7.50; youths (five to seventeen), $5.00.

Back to the Talbot Heirs Guesthouse for a little rest and relaxation before dinner.

DINNER: A visit to Memphis is not complete without dinner at **The Rendezvous,** a local institution for barbecue. Open since 1948, this restaurant specializes in "dry" ribs, as opposed to the wet sauce of most types. And they are delicious. Start dinner with a platter of barbecue smoked sausage and cheese and crackers. They don't take reservations, and if you want to avoid waiting for well over an hour, get there by 7:00 P.M.; (888) 464–7359. Moderate prices.

Evening

Again, if you have children, your evening's entertainment will differ. Kids would enjoy **Putt-Putt Family Park,** 5484 Summer Avenue; (901) 386–2992; www.puttputtmemphis. com. Three miniature golf courses, a PGA-recognized 120-tee golf range, laser tag, video games, go-carts, all the things kids—and adults—can enjoy. You will have to get your car out for this attraction. Open all year 8:00 A.M. to midnight.

For couples a night on Beale Street visiting different clubs and hearing Memphis blues as it should be heard will be memorable. Start with **B.B. King's Blues Club,** 143 Beale Street (901–524–5464); then move to the **Rum Boogie Cafe,** 182 Beale Street (901–528–0150) for music to get you on your feet, or **This Is It,** 167 Beale Street (901–527–8200).

LODGING: Talbot Heirs Guesthouse.

Day 3 / Morning

BREAKFAST: You have a couple of places to see this morning that could take some time, so you might want to do breakfast in your room or at the Peabody again. Since you're retrieving your car from the garage, you might want to try **The Arcade,** 540 South Main (901–526–5757), Memphis's oldest cafe, open for breakfast seven days a week; or the **Yellow Rose Cafe,** 58 North Mid-America Mall, Main Street on the trolley line near Court Square (901–527–5692), open Monday through Friday.

Your first stop is the **Memphis Pink Palace Museum and Planetarium.** This huge mansion was designed by Piggly-Wiggly founder Clarence Saunders to be his dream house. He fell into bankruptcy, however, and never completed his dream. The house was given to the city to become a museum. A magnificent hand-carved miniature circus with moving parts is amazing. Other exhibits include audiovisuals and dioramas depicting Memphis's development over the last several hundred years. If time permits, see the Planetarium and try to catch a show at the IMAX theater. Current admission for the museum is $8.00 for adults, $7.50 for seniors age sixty-plus, and $5.50 for children ages three to twelve. Hours vary by season, so call (901) 320–6320 or (901) 763–IMAX, or visit www. memphismuseums.org.

Next is the **Memphis Zoo** in Overton Park, 2000 Galloway. More than 2,800 animals representing 400 countries call the seventy-acre zoo home. The zoo features many unique attractions such as Animals of the Night, where visitors see such nocturnal animals as bats, blind cave fish, and naked mole rats; Primate Canyon, with an Oriental pagoda and replica for an African fishing village for its inhabitants; the Dragon's Lair, where you can observe Komodo dragons; and the beautiful Butterfly Garden. Open March through October 9:00 A.M. to 6:00 P.M.; November through February 9:00 A.M. to 5:00 P.M.; during summer on Saturday and Sunday, open until 9:00 P.M. Ages twelve and up, $10.00; sixty and up, $9.00; ages two to eleven, $6.00; under two, free. (901) 276–9453; www.memphis zoo.org.

Before heading out on your 300-mile trip back home, stop for lunch at **Huey's,** 77 South Second Street, just down from the Talbot Heirs. Great burgers, grilled chicken sandwiches, salads, and other pub grub. Kids will have a great time putting toothpicks in straws and shooting them at the ceiling, where they will stick—along with thousands of other toothpicks. Inexpensive.

For a stretch and a snack, Cape Girardeau, about three hours from Memphis, would be the place.

There's More

Baseball. St. Louis Cardinal fans can enjoy seeing their Triple A farm club, the Memphis Redbirds, play in Autozone Park at Third and Madison. Single game ticket prices range from $5.00 on "the Bluff" to $15.00 for the Infield Club. There are five price levels in between. Call (901) 721–6000, or visit www.memphisredbirds.com.

Basketball. The NBA has landed in Memphis with the Memphis Grizzlies playing fast-paced ball at the Pyramid Arena. Single tickets are $9.00. Call (800) 4NBA–TIX or visit www.grizzlies.com.

The Children's Museum of Memphis, 2525 Central Avenue. An interactive discovery museum for children and their parents featuring a grocery store where kids can choose their items and go to the checkout, a fire truck to climb on, a dental office, and a tool bench. Hours: Tuesday through Saturday 9:00 A.M. to 5:00 P.M., Sunday noon to 5:00 P.M. (901) 458–2678; www.cmom.com.

C.H. Nash-Chucalissa Archaeological Museum. 1987 Indian Village Drive. A reconstructed fifteenth-century Indian village that shows you life in that era. Also includes an archeological park and museum. (901) 785–3160. Hours vary seasonally. Adults, $5.00; seniors and ages four through eleven, $3.00; under four, free.

Memphis Brooks Museum of Art. Overton Park, 1934 Poplar Avenue. Located in a historic register building, this museum has a permanent collection spanning twenty centuries and is one of the top twenty-five collections in the United States. Major changing exhibitions. (901) 544–6200; www.brooksmuseum.org.

Memphis Queen Riverboats. Take a paddle-wheel cruise on the Mighty Mississippi. Open year-round, you can choose from dinner, sight-seeing, day-trip, and moonlight cruises. Downtown at Monroe and Union Avenues at the trolley stop. Adults, $12.50; seniors, $11.50; children ages four through seventeen, $9.50. (800) 221–6197; www.memphis queen.com.

National Ornamental Metal Museum. 374 Metal Museum Drive. The only museum of this type in the United States devoted entirely to display and preservation of fine metalwork. See the art, see artists work, and learn how metalwork is done. (901) 774–6380; www.metal@wspice.com.

Oak Court Mall, 4451 Poplar Avenue (901–682–8928), offers a full complement of high-end specialty stores including Banana Republic, Ann Taylor Loft, Starbucks, and more. Anchored by Dillard's and the region's largest Goldsmith's. South Main Street has many new art galleries and shops such as The Village Boutique, which offers the most elegant unique and up-to-date African fashions, as well as Elvis's old hangout, the Arcade Restaurant.

The Pinch Historic District. North Main Street from the Memphis Cook Convention Center to North Parkway. An entertainment area featuring restaurants and bars with live entertainment every weekend.

Shopping. For shoppers, Memphis is a mecca for money dropping. Wolfchase Galleria, 2760 North Germantown Parkway (901–388–5542), Memphis's newest mall, features 120 specialty shops with thirty-five exclusives. Visit www.wolfchasegalleria.com. Also the Village of Chickasaw Oaks (3092 Poplar Avenue; 901–794–6022), is a replica of a 1776 village, offering boutiques, gourmet coffee shops, restaurants, and a French bakery.

Slavehaven/Burkle Estate Museum. A tiny house built in 1849 said to be a way station for slaves running to the North. See secret cellars where slaves hid and trapdoors to the escape route. Call (901) 527–3427 for appointment.

W.C. Handy Home, 352 Beale Street, the home of "The Father of the Blues." Handy raised six children in this small "shotgun" house before moving to New York. (901) 522–1556 or (901) 527–8784. Summer hours, 10:00 A.M. to 5:00 P.M. Tuesday through Saturday; winter hours, 11:00 A.M. to 4:00 P.M. Tuesday through Saturday.

Special Events

April. Africa in April Cultural Awareness Festival. Church Park on Beale Street, 1 block south of the entertainment district. A five-day festival honoring a different African country each year with exhibits, art, music, dance, and seminars. (901) 947–2133.

May. Memphis in May, an annual monthlong salute to a different country each year with each weekend featuring its own event: The Beale Street Music Festival, International Weekend, World Championship Barbecue Cooking Contest, and Sunset Symphony. Call (901) 525–4611 for times and locations.

August. Elvis Tribute Week at Graceland, a weeklong celebration of the "King," his life, and music. Special events culminate in the Candlelight Vigil. (800) 238–2000.

September. The Mid-South Fair, Mid-South Fairgrounds, featuring more than sixty rides, 150 vendors, and 200 exhibitors. Mainstage concerts with name entertainment, livestock shows, and rodeo. (901) 274–8800.

October. Arts in the Park, a three-day festival in the Memphis Botanical Garden featuring more than 800 visual and performing artists and an artist market with more than 150 national artists. (901) 761–1278.

Other Recommended Restaurants and Lodgings

Automatic Slim's Tonga Club, 83 South Second Street; (901) 525–7948. Located next to the Talbot Heirs. If lively and spicy Southwestern cuisine is your cup of tea, this is the place for you. Also features Caribbean food. Moderate.

Blues City Cafe, 138 Beale Street; (901) 526–3637. Delicious barbecue ribs, tamales, chili, and an especially wonderful crawfish au gratin. Great for late-night dining after cruising Beale Street.

Buckley's Downtown Grill, 117 Union Avenue, (901) 578–9001. Award-winning menu features steaks and pasta. Voted "Best Meal for the Money" for two years. Moderate.

Elvis Presley's Heartbreak Hotel, 3677 Elvis Presley Boulevard; (877) 777–0606; www.heartbreakhotel.com. Located across the street from Graceland and next to the other Elvis attractions, this 128-room hotel features free Elvis movies, a heart-shaped outdoor pool, and a continental breakfast. Packages including the Graceland Tour are available with shuttle stops to other attractions. Rates: $105 per night.

Hampton Inn & Suites, 175 Peabody Place; (901) 260–4000. The Hampton Inn offers 144 finely appointed rooms and suites, complimentary breakfast, and a location off historic Beale Street within walking distance of the city's business district. Amenities include continental breakfast, indoor pool and spa, and fitness center. www.hamptoninn.com.

Interstate Barbecue, 2265 South Third Street; (901) 775–2304; www.interstatebarbecue.com. Serves wonderful barbecued pork, beef brisket, and pork ribs, plus turkey, chicken, and barbecued bologna. Open 11:00 A.M. to 11:00 P.M. Monday through Saturday.

Isaac Hayes—Music*Food*Passion, located in Peabody Place Entertainment Center, 150 Peabody Place; (901) 529–9222. Get into the soul of Memphis with live music every night or Sunday Jazz Brunch. Feast on lip-smackin' smoky barbecue, beef brisket, and Isaac Hayes's own personal specialties.

Memphis Marriott Downtown, 250 North Main Street; (800) 228–9290; www.mariotthotels.com/memdt. Recently renovated and attached to the convention center, this hotel has a full-service restaurant, lobby lounge with music, health club, and indoor pool, among other niceties. Rates start at $64.

The Peabody, 149 Union Avenue; (800) 732–2639. Home of the famous Peabody Ducks and known as "The South's Grand Hotel," this hotel has four restaurants, a shop, and an athletic club with indoor pool. Rates: $150 to $270.

Sleep Inn at Court Square, 40 North Front Street; (800) SLEEP–INN. Downtown's newest hotel, with a free continental breakfast. Also on the trolley line. Rates start at $89.

For More Information

The Memphis Convention and Visitors Bureau, 47 Union Avenue, Memphis, TN 38103; www.memphistravel.com.

Memphis Convention and Visitors Bureau Travel Center, 119 North Riverside Drive; (901) 543–5333 or (800) 8–MEMPHIS.

EASTERN
ESCAPES

EASTERN ESCAPE ONE

Belleville/Maeystown/Waterloo, Illinois

A Drive through Little Germany / 1 Night

Some of the most picturesque and historically significant communities in the area lie just over the river in Illinois. Monroe County, which includes Belleville, Maeystown, and Waterloo, is an area rich in German history. The Germans settled in southwestern Illinois in the early to mid-1800s and brought with them many traditions that still exist, from food to music to housing design.

☐ German heritage

☐ Wineries

☐ Shopping

☐ Tours

The German settlers were attracted to the area by reports from relatives of the area's excellent growing conditions for crops. Most of them went to work for descendants of the original pioneers, who paid wages with land instead of money. Ultimately, German farmers held most of the land in Monroe County. Because of this, present-day Monroe County is the least populated of all the counties contiguous to St. Louis.

Over the past twenty years, residents of the area have made a concerted effort to preserve this strong German heritage. From the local historic districts in Belleville to the entire town of Maeystown, the desire to keep something from the past and share it with visitors is evident.

Day 1 / Morning

The most direct way to get to Belleville is to get on Highway 270 going east toward Illinois. Highway 270 becomes Highway 255 as you get closer to the Jefferson Barracks (JB) Bridge. Take the bridge over the Mississippi into Illinois, continuing on I–255 south. Take Route 15 East toward Belleville; then exit onto Route 159 North, which takes you into the heart of Belleville. When you come to the "square," which is actually a traffic circle, merge into traffic, go a quarter of the way around, and turn right onto

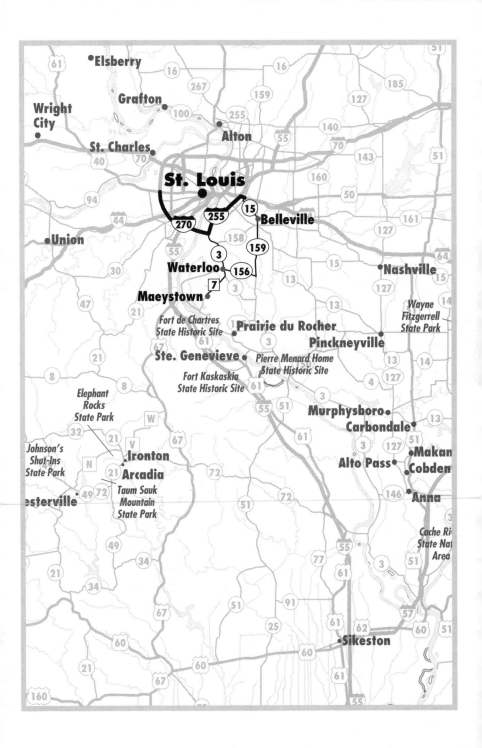

East Main. Park on the street or in any of the free visitor parking lots located on the side streets and you're there. The drive from St. Louis should take about twenty-five minutes.

Begin your trip by taking a walking tour of the longest continuous main street in the United States, according to the Belleville Tourism Office. Up and down the street you'll find charming shops for browsing and antiquing. Don't miss **Keil's,** 26 East Main Street. It's a wonderful example of a general store from a bygone era. From saws to sewing needles, you can find it at Keil's. In the **Belleville Antique Mall,** 208 East Main Street, take a ride in the still-operating birdcage elevator, one of only two in the country. Don't miss **Ben's Floral and Crafts,** 12 East Main Street, an enormous arts-and-crafts store, along with **The Thomas Kinkade Art Gallery.**

LUNCH: The Pie Pantry Eatery, 310 East Main Street; (618) 277–4140. Relax and enjoy a casual lunch at this downtown landmark. Choices include soups, sandwiches, salads, and, of course, pie. Try the chicken salad served on toasted raisin bread along with a cup of soup. Favorite pies include pecan, chocolate chip, and lemon meringue. Inexpensive.

Afternoon

Take a **walking or driving tour of Belleville's German–American Folk Houses.** Belleville is home to a large number of these unique homes, built in the mid-1800s, and has taken great care over the years to preserve them. A detailed brochure on this self-guided tour is available from the Belleville Tourism office, 216 East A Street, Belleville, IL 62220 (800–677–9255), or if you prefer, one can be mailed to you in advance of your trip.

The tour begins at the corner of Survey and Fulton Streets at 602 Fulton (618–234–0600), which is the **Emma Kunz House Museum.** Built in 1830, it's Illinois's oldest dated brick Greek Revival home and is a classic example of an ethnic German "Street House." From there you'll head south on Survey Street, west on Adams, south on Charles, north on Freeburg, and east on Adams; then it's a quick turn north on Charles. Complete your route by going east on Garfield, southeast on Mascoutah, then southwest on Fulton, ending back at the Emma Kunz House Museum. The tour should take about an hour.

After the tour it's on to **Maeystown.** From Belleville take Route 159 south to Hecker. Turn right onto Route 156 West, which takes you through Waterloo to Wartburg Road. Turn left on Wartburg/Maeystown Road. The drive should take thirty to forty-five minutes. You've reached Maeystown when you cross over the little stone bridge. Yes, this hidden little treasure of a town is real—and, yes, it's been here all this time without you knowing about it. But fewer people will be able to plead ignorance about this authentic 1800s German hamlet if David and Marcia Braswell have their way. Owners of The Corner George Inn Bed and Breakfast, David and Marcia are helping to spread the word about this charming little village getaway as well as educate their guests on the German history of the area.

Listed on the National Register of Historic Places, the village of Maeystown has more than sixty significant buildings dating back to the 1800s, including the Corner George Inn, a sweet shop, a restaurant/tavern, a church, a museum, visitor center, general store, and a craft shop. Take some time to browse around town or walk across the stone bridge to the nature trail for a short hike.

DINNER: Dreamland Palace, 3043 State Route 156, Foster Pond; (618) 939– 9922. If the true German experience is what you want, then Dreamland Palace is the place to be for dinner. Located just 4 miles west of Waterloo and about a fifteen-minute drive from Maeystown, Dreamland Palace is the essence of traditional German food in a relaxed, homey atmosphere. Start your meal off with a German wine or one of several German beer selections. If you enjoy beef, the sauerbraten, a house specialty, is superb, and the potato pancakes over which it's served are outstanding. The portions are large, and the food is rich, but if you've saved room, make sure you try the apple strudel with caramel sauce; it's the essence of comfort food. Entrees are in the $12-to-$15 range for dinner. The restaurant is open Wednesday through Saturday 11:00 A.M. to 9:00 P.M. and Sunday 11:00 A.M. to 8:30 P.M.

LODGING: The Corner George Inn, corner of Main and Mill; (618) 458-6660; www.cornergeorgeinn.com. Lovingly restored by David and Marcia Braswell in 1989, The Corner George Inn was originally built in 1884 as a hotel and saloon. After the turn of the century, the hotel became a residence and the saloon became the village general store. The original hotel now boasts three guest rooms with private baths. Four additional suites are located in nearby cottages and buildings. Each room or suite has

General store in Maeystown

its own personality, so get a description of each before you choose. The summer kitchen is a little house separate from the main inn and is charmingly rustic with a bath and toilet right in the room, surrounded by privacy screens. For a little more luxury, consider one of the suites with a whirlpool tub. Children are welcome in the Pfeifer House suite, thanks to its two bedrooms, a sitting room, and a bathroom. This is also a great option for two couples traveling together. Rates are $79 to $159.

Day 2 / Morning

BREAKFAST: The Corner George Inn. Breakfast is served in the 600-square-foot ballroom-turned-dining-room and is likely to include French toast, fresh fruit, sausage, and peach coffee cake.

After breakfast, head back up to Waterloo for a stroll around the square, which is home to the historic **Monroe County Courthouse.** Tour the historic district, which includes the **Peterstown House,** 275 North Main Street; (618) 939–4222. Peterstown House is the location for the only stagecoach stop still intact in the area. Then stop in the **Bellefontaine Home and the Monroe County Historical Society,**

709 South Church (618–939–5230), for a complete history of the area as well as that of Waterloo's sister city, Porta Westfalica, Germany.

Afternoon

It's on to **Schorr Lake Vineyard & Winery,** 1032 South Library Street; (618) 939–3174. Take Illinois Route 3 to South Library Road, go west on South Library Road for ³⁄₁₀ mile, and you're there. All the wines at Schorr Lake Vineyard are "estate grown and produced." By producing all their own fruits, the owners work to create the highest quality and most consistent wines possible. Enjoy a glass of blackberry port or chardonelle while overlooking the lovely Schorr Lake. The winery is open April through December on Friday, Saturday, and Sunday from noon to 6:00 P.M. or by appointment.

Next, it's on to the **Waterloo Winery,** 725 North Market Street; (618) 939–5743; www.waterloowinery.com. Enjoy a tour of the winery followed by a sampling of the newest releases before choosing a bottle or two to take home. The winery is open year-round, Wednesday through Sunday from noon to 5:00 P.M.

LUNCH: JV's, 117 North Main Street; (618) 939–7127. Stop into this neighborhood favorite for great sandwiches and salads. Try the house specialty, a Mackie burger topped with melted Swiss cheese, bacon, grilled onions, and mushrooms. Inexpensive.

Before heading home, do a little browsing in the local stores. **Mill Street Treasures,** 125 West Mill (618–939–3125), offers antiques, gifts, and handmade keepsakes. **Echoes of the Past Antiques,** 116 East Third (618–939–6160), is located in a German-style home dating from the 1850s just across from the Monroe County Courthouse. Echoes specializes in Victorian furniture and glassware as well as country furniture and decorative items. For a real country store experience, there's none other than **Horn's Country Store,** 205 South Moore (618–939–7219). Whether you're looking for primitive furniture, bakery items, seeds, bird feed, or pet food, you'll find it at Horn's.

To get back to St. Louis, just hop on Illinois Route 3 heading north and follow the signs to Highway 255 into St. Louis. You'll cross over the JB Bridge, and you're back in Missouri. The trip home should take about forty-five minutes.

There's More

Belleville

Belle-Clair Fairgrounds, 200 South Belt East; (618) 233–0052. The location of the St. Clair County Fair and so much more. The indoor exposition hall hosts year-round events including a flea market every third full weekend of the month.

Eckert's Country Store & Farms, 3101 Greenmount Road (on Route 15 East); (618) 233–0513; www.eckerts.com. Pick your own apples, peaches, and berries. The kids will love the petting farm and play area complete with kid-size tractors to drive. There's also a family-friendly restaurant, a country market, a custard shop, and a new garden center.

National Shrine of Our Lady of the Snows, 442 South DeMazenod Drive (located at Illinois Route 15 at Route 157); (618) 397–6700. One of the largest outdoor shrines in the country, Our Lady of the Snows has more than 200 landscaped and wooded acres with several devotional areas for people of all ages and faith traditions. A beautiful place for a leisurely walk or drive.

Old Town Market, East Main at Mascoutah Avenue; (618) 233–6769. Stop by for locally grown, seasonal produce as well as for art by local artists at this old-fashioned open-air market. Open every Saturday 8:00 A.M. to noon, May through October.

Victorian House Museum, 701 East Washington Street; (618) 234–0600. Built by German immigrants, this Victorian-era home now houses locally made nineteenth-century furnishings as well as a changing display for a glimpse into the history of St. Clair County.

Waterloo

Illinois Caverns State Natural Area, 4369 G Road; (618) 458–6699. Some of the most interesting parts of Illinois lie underground. With more than one hundred recorded caves, Monroe County has more caves than any other county in Illinois. According to the state's department of natural resources, Illinois Caverns contains an extensive array of spectacular cave formations, and many are actively growing. Special site rules require visitors to use adequate safety equipment, and visitors should plan on getting their feet wet. Illinois Caverns is open year-round. Visitors are required to read and sign a cave exploration permit before entering the cave. Permits are available at the cave or by calling the site interpreter. Call about required safety equipment before arriving or request a brochure that lists the details.

Special Events

April. Eckert's Strawberry Festival and Craft Show. Eckert's Country Store & Farms, Belleville. (618) 233–0513.

May. Fruehlingsfest. Maeystown. Watch as crafters demonstrate their talent at this spring festival. (618) 458–6660.

Old Belleville Days. Belleville downtown area. Games, crafts, music, and food. (618) 234–0600.

June. Monroe County Fair. Held at the fairgrounds just west of Waterloo. (618) 939–5300.

Porta Westfalica fest in recognition of the town's sister city in Germany. Waterloo. (618) 939–5300.

September. Apple Fest. Eckert's Country Store & Farms, Belleville. (618) 233–0513.

October. Oktoberfest. Maeystown. Experience the sights, sounds, and smells of autumn while browsing through arts-and-crafts displays and demonstrations. (618) 458–6660.

December. German Christmas. Maeystown. Participate in a traditional German Christmas with carolers and a Christmas market. (618) 458–6660.

Other Recommended Restaurants and Lodgings

Belleville

Amarillo Tex, 104 West Main; (618) 233–2550. Mosey on up to the bar for some Tex-Mex and a margarita at this fun cafe.

Bellecourt Place, 120 North Jackson; (618) 233–8490. Enjoy dining in a beautiful historic church in the heart of Belleville.

Quebec City Bistro, 108 East A Street; (618) 257–2915. French cafe serving quiche, crepes, sandwiches, and soups. Oui, Oui!

Victory Inn Bed & Breakfast, 712 South Jackson Street, Belleville. (618) 277–1538. Restored 1877 home has three guest rooms, all with private bath. Rates from $60 to $115. www.victoryinn.com.

For More Information

Belleville Tourism, 216 East A Street, Belleville, IL 62220; (800) 677–9255; www.belleville.net.

Southwestern Illinois Tourism & Convention Bureau, 10950 Lincoln Trail, Fairview Heights, IL 62208; (800) 442–1488.

EASTERN ESCAPE TWO

Mt. Vernon, Illinois

A Stroll through History / 1 Night

Mt. Vernon is a charming little city at the crossroads of two major highways in southern Illinois. Because of its location, you could easily mistake this as a drive-by town or nothing more than a place to stop for the night before traveling on. But then you'd miss the little and not-so-little gems that make this town a great getaway. Mt. Vernon has a rich and plentiful American Indian and pioneer history as well as a multitude of antiques shops in and around town. Art also plays a big role in this southern Illinois town, including the hundreds of works by national and international artists on display at the Mitchell Museum at Cedarhurst. And because of its fertile soil, southern Illinois seems to be the perfect spot for growing grapes, which has resulted in a number of award-winning wineries within a few minutes' drive of Mt. Vernon.

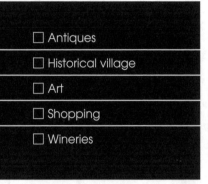

☐ Antiques

☐ Historical village

☐ Art

☐ Shopping

☐ Wineries

Day 1 / Morning

Leave St. Louis around 8:00 A.M. in order to arrive in Mt. Vernon between 9:30 and 10:00 A.M. It's an easy drive of a little more than 100 miles, depending on where you're coming from in St. Louis. Head east on any of the major highways and cross over the Poplar Street Bridge into Illinois from downtown St. Louis. Get on Highway 64 East. Highway 64 and Highway 57 merge just outside Mt. Vernon. You'll want to go south on Highway 57 and shortly thereafter exit at the Mt. Vernon exit and go left on Highway 15, which is also called Broadway. Continue east on Broadway to Twelfth Street and make a left (north); then make a left at Richview Road heading west. Once you pass the Mitchell Museum and Cedarhurst, make a quick right on Twenty-seventh Street and follow the

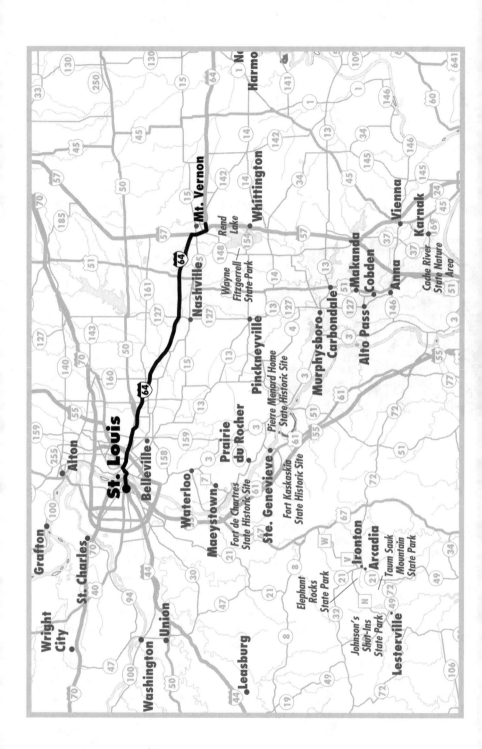

signs for your first stop at the **Jefferson County Historical Village,** 1411 North Twenty-seventh street; (618) 246–0033.

The Historical Village is the clever idea of the Jefferson County Historical Society. The village is designed to showcase artifacts such as old log cabins, rope beds, and primitive medical equipment from the region in a setting that is similar to its original period. Visitors can stroll through the village alone or with a volunteer guide and see firsthand how the pioneers and early settlers lived in this part of the state. You'll see log-cabin homes, the first log jail in the county, a one-room school, a medical building, a general store, and other period buildings as well as a museum and interpretive center. Kids will love buying candy in the old general store, or a special postcard printed on an old-fashioned printing press. The guides have a wealth of knowledge and really make the place come to life. If you're lucky, you just might be visiting when the blacksmiths demonstrate their craft. Admission is free, but donations are accepted, which directly benefit the Jefferson County Historical Society. The village is open May through October, weekends only. Saturday hours are 10:00 A.M. to 4:00 P.M. and Sunday hours are 1:00 to 4:00 P.M. Tours are also given year-round on weekdays by appointment.

Cedarhurst Sculpture Park and the **Mitchell Museum** are your next stop. Exit the Historical Village and go right on Twenty-seventh Street back to Richview Road. Turn left and make an immediate left into the museum complex. This private art collection belongs to the estate of the late John and Eleanor Mitchell, longtime residents of southern Illinois. The Mitchells were world travelers and quite the adventurers, having climbed mountains in Switzerland and Germany and hunted big game in Africa. The Mitchells had no heirs and upon their death left a vast collection of late-nineteenth-century and early-twentieth-century paintings, sculpture, and decorative arts to their namesake museum for the benefit of residents and visitors in southern Illinois.

Begin in the museum, where you can browse through the permanent collection that includes works by Mary Cassatt, George Bellows, and John Singer Sargent. The museum frequently hosts touring exhibits, which in the past have included art from Trinidad and Tobago as well as other international destinations. The Children's Gallery is a popular place, with such diverse exhibits as pop-up books, a contemporary exhibit of kites, and art from Special Olympics athletes.

Next, step outside to the ninety-acre estate to stroll through the sculpture park. In addition to the permanent collection, the park has an ongoing exchange program with artists from around the world, so the outdoor collection is always changing. This is a wonderful place for strolling around and admiring the seamless blend of art and nature. Cedarhurst also sponsors a chamber-music-concert series with performers from all over the world.

Cedarhurst and the Mitchell Museum are located on Richview Road; (618) 242–1236. Hours are 10:00 A.M. to 5:00 P.M. Tuesday through Saturday and 1:00 to 5:00 P.M. Sunday; closed on national holidays. Admission to the museum and sculpture park is free.

LUNCH: Hunan Chinese Restaurant, 2405 Broadway; (618) 244–0977. All that international art just begs for an international lunch. Hunan is a local favorite and serves a wide variety of traditional Chinese dishes. Exit Cedarhurst and make a left on Richview Road. Make a right on Centralia Road/Twelfth Street and a right on Broadway. The restaurant will be on the left about 12 blocks down and is open daily. Inexpensive.

Afternoon

Don't leave downtown Mt. Vernon without stopping into **Flota's Antiques,** 901 South Tenth Street/Route 37. Open Monday through Thursday and Saturday 9:00 A.M. to 5:00 P.M., this is the place locals go to hunt for antiques. With more than 400 pieces of furniture in stock plus primitives, glass, china, dolls, and more, it's not to be missed. Flota's is located 8 blocks south of Route 15/Broadway on Route 37/Tenth Street. From Hunan Chinese Restaurant head east on Highway 15/Broadway and make a right on Highway 37/Tenth Street heading south. Flota's is 5 blocks down on the right at the corner of Tenth and Lamar Avenue. Call (618) 244–4877 for more information.

Close by is **Wheels Through Time Museum of Vintage Motorcycling,** 1121 Veterans Memorial Drive; (618) 244–4118; www.dales-hd.com. Much more than a warehouse filled with rows of motorcycles, the Wheels Through Time Museum is one of only a handful of places in the country where visitors can learn about the motorcycle and its place in the early days of transportation. Each display not only focuses on a motorcycle, but on the memorabilia, history, and artwork of its era. This creative displaying allows both motorcycle enthusiasts and nonenthusiasts alike to appreciate the role these two-wheeled vehicles played in the early days of the twentieth century. The museum is open 9:00 A.M. to 5:00 P.M.

Horse at Cedarhurst Sculpture Park

Monday, Tuesday, Thursday, and Friday and from 9:00 A.M. to 4:00 P.M. Saturday; closed Sunday and holidays. Call ahead on Wednesday if you'd prefer to visit that day. From Flota's make a right on Veteran's Memorial Drive heading west. The museum is located directly behind Dale's Harley-Davidson, which is the third building on the left. Admission is free.

Outlet shopping is the next order of business. Mt. Vernon is home to the **Rend Lake College Marketplace,** I–57 and I–62 (exit 95); (618) 244–9525. Open Monday through Saturday from 9:00 A.M. to 9:00 P.M. and Sunday from 11:00 A.M. to 7:00 P.M. You can take your pick of more than ten stores, where you'll find bargains at every turn. The outlet is home to a number of women's clothing stores such as BonWorth (618–242–9020) and Dress Barn (618–242–9041). BrassWerks (618–242–8215) is where you'll save 50 percent off all merchandise. College Golf Outlet (618–242–3001) will save you a bundle on your next set of clubs or other golf accessories. And Kountry Depot Krafts (618–244–4113) carries primitive, country, and Victorian crafts.

To get here from Wheels Through Time, make a left heading west on Veteran's Memorial Drive; make a right on Forty-second Street heading north, and then make a left on Highway 15/Broadway and head west. Cross over Highway 57 and take the first right on the service road (Potomac Boulevard) once over the highway. This will lead you directly to the mall, which will be on the left.

DINNER: Lone Star Steakhouse & Saloon, Rend Lake College Marketplace, I–57 and I–62; (618) 244–7827. Conveniently located at the Rend Lake College Marketplace is this fun-loving chain restaurant serving Texas-size portions of grilled steaks, chicken, pork, and seafood. For starters try the Tumbleweed Onion. Sweet and batter-fried, these strips of onion are addictive, especially when dipped in the special sauce that accompanies them. If you like prime rib, you'll fine some awesome options here; but come early because once they're out, they're out. For a side item go for the baked sweet potato filled with butter and cinnamon sugar—a real treat. The staff is friendly and occasionally bursts into song when inspired by familiar tunes that play throughout the restaurant and bar. Inexpensive to moderate.

Evening

Just next door to the restaurant is **Cherry Creek Golf Center.** This is a great place to wind down the evening playing miniature golf. Grab a club and start swinging. Admission is $4.00 for adults, $3.00 for kids under seventeen, and free for kids under five. The center is open daily from 8:00 A.M. to 10:00 P.M. Call (618) 246–9502 or (618) 244–9525 for more information.

LODGING: Hampton Inn, 221 Potomac Boulevard; (618) 244–2323. For reservations call (800) HAMPTON or the hotel directly. Conveniently located to just about everything in Mt. Vernon, the Hampton Inn offers a host of amenities including free continental breakfast, free local calls, and free HBO, ESPN, and CNN. There's an indoor pool and spa, and some rooms are equipped with whirlpool tubs. Rates range from $64 to $75.

Day 2 / Morning

BREAKFAST: Hampton Inn. Enjoy a quick and easy continental breakfast in the lobby before heading out for a day of antiquing, arts and crafts, and wine tasting.

The first stop is the **Polished Plank Antique Mall,** located just 1 mile west on Highway 15 from the intersection of Highway 57 and Highway 64. From the hotel turn right onto Potomac Boulevard and then right on Highway 15 heading west. Polished Plank is less than a mile on the right. With more than eighty-five dealers and 10,000 square feet of space, you can get lost for hours browsing through all sorts of antiques from Depression glass to advertising memorabilia to salt-and-pepper shakers. Polished Plank is open from 10:00 A.M. to 6:00 P.M. Monday through Friday and 10:00 A.M. to 5:00 P.M. Saturday and Sunday and can be reached by calling (888) 524–3077.

LUNCH: Grab an early lunch at **El Rancherito,** a local favorite for authentic Mexican food. El Rancherito is located at 4303 Broadway; (618) 244–6121. From Polished Plank, make a left on Highway 15 and head east. Cross over Highway 57. Once over the highway, the restaurant will be on the right just a few blocks down. Inexpensive. (If Mexican isn't your thing, take heart. Mt. Vernon has just about every kind of fast food restaurant up and down Broadway, so everyone should be able to find something that suits them.)

For more shopping, cross back over Highway 57, and continue east until you reach Route 37. Go left, heading north, to **Tom & Jerry's Antiques** on Route 37 in Whittington (618–629–2824). More than fifty dealers offer a wide selection of antiques, furniture, glassware, collectibles, pottery, and primitives. Tom & Jerry's is open in summer from 10:00 A.M. to 5:00 P.M. Monday through Saturday and 1:00 to 5:00 P.M. Sunday. Winter hours are 10:00 A.M. to 4:00 P.M. Monday through Saturday; closed Sunday.

Just north of Tom & Jerry's on Route 37 is a great place to take a break. Stop into **Pheasant Hollow Winery** (618–629–2302) for a sampling of southern Illinois wines. Nestled among the trees, this quaint little winery is a delightful venue for relaxing with friends. There's usually something going on besides wine tasting, which could include anything from a Cajun festival to bonsai tree trimming. Wine selections range from a dry Vidal to a sweet peach wine and many variations in between. The winery is open from 10:00 A.M. to 8:00 P.M. Monday through Saturday and noon to 8:00 P.M. on Sunday.

To check out another winery, head south on Route 37 to Highway 154 West, where you'll find the entrance ramp for Highway 57 heading south. Hop on and head toward Benton, about five minutes away. Exit at number 71 and go left, heading east toward Benton on Route 34. Continue down until you see Stuyvesant Street on the right. Turn in and follow the signs to **Spring Pond Vineyards,** 13772 Spring Pond Road, Benton; (618) 439–9176. Stop in for a sample of their wines before heading back to Mt. Vernon.

Reverse your steps and head north on Highway 57 for the twenty-minute trip back. Take the Route 15/Broadway exit and go right. Take the first left by Steak 'n' Shake onto North Forty-fourth Street and follow the signs to **GenKota Winery,** 301 North Forty-fourth Street, Mt. Vernon; (618) 246–WINE. Although GenKota looks out over the highway, it's a quaint, relaxing tasting room with a wide front porch and oversize swings, perfect for relaxing and sipping a glass of award-winning Chambourcin, Sunset Rose, or Drake Port. They also offer a nice selection of wine-related merchandise.

DINNER: Applebee's Neighborhood Grill & Bar, 105 Potomac Boulevard, Mt. Vernon; (618) 244–7510. This is a relaxed, fun place that offers lots of choices to please most anyone's taste. Steaks, grilled chicken, soups, and salads are the usual fare. From GenKota Winery make a right onto Route 15. Cross over Highway 57 and take the first right once over the highway onto Potomac. Applebee's will be on the left. Inexpensive to moderate.

To return to St. Louis, exit Applebee's by making a right onto Potomac and a left onto Route 15. The entrance for Highway 57 North will be on the left. Reverse your steps from St. Louis, and the trip home should take about one and a half to two hours.

There's More

Appellate Courthouse, Main and Fourteenth Streets; (618) 242–3120. Constructed in 1857 as the southern division of the Illinois Supreme Court. Abraham Lincoln successfully argued a famous tax case here. Also used as an emergency hospital in 1888 by Clara Barton. Tours available by advance reservation.

Brehm Memorial Library, 101 South Seventh Street. Research local history and genealogy. Call (618) 242–6322 for more information.

Special Events

May. Cedarhurst Family Festival. Mt. Vernon. Performances by area high school and college jazz bands, storytelling festival, children's art area, and more. (618) 242–1236.

July. Southern Illinois Fair & Expo. Mt. Vernon. Tractor pulls, rodeo, demolition derby, and more. (618) 242–0870.

September. Cedarhurst Art and Craft Fair. Mt. Vernon. Juried event with more than 150 crafters from across the United States. Kids' corner, music, food. (618) 242–1236.

October. Pioneer Days at the Jefferson County Historical Village. Mt. Vernon. Civil War reenactment, period traders, music, and crafts. (800) 252–5464.

Other Recommended Restaurants and Lodgings

Comfort Inn, 201 Potomac Boulevard; (618) 242–7200. Rates are $53 to $98. Ninety-five rooms, indoor pool and hot tub, free continental breakfast. Smoke-free rooms and family suites available.

Holiday Inn, 222 Potomac Boulevard; (618) 244–7100 or (800) HOLI-DAY. Rates are from $63 to $99. Two hundred thirty-six rooms, indoor pool, hot tub, restaurant, smoke-free rooms available.

Mom's Cafe, 1920 South Tenth Street; (618) 244–9777. Down-home cooking including great breakfasts. Locals love it. Inexpensive.

Triple E. Barbeque, 37 Sam Mateer Road; (618) 244–7500. Another popular spot; casual. Inexpensive.

For More Information

Mt. Vernon Convention & Visitors Bureau, P.O. Box 1708, Mt. Vernon, IL 62864; (800) 252–5464; www.mtvernon.com.

EASTERN ESCAPE THREE

Rend Lake/Whittington, Illinois

A Wet and Wild(life) Weekend / 1 Night

Sometimes I just want to get away to the water. I can't do the beach in a weekend. And The Lake of the Ozarks is farther away than I can manage on short notice. Once I discovered Rend Lake, I knew I had found the

- ☐ Boating
- ☐ Wildlife viewing
- ☐ Golf
- ☐ Arts and antiques

perfect compromise. Not too far from St. Louis, Rend Lake is a great place to go with the family, as a couple, or with friends. This 19,000-acre man-made lake has virtually no development on it, which makes it seem very remote. Plus, it's surrounded almost completely by a state park filled with great things to see and do. To top it all off, the lake is located next to a number of quaint small towns that are home to eclectic antiques shops, wineries, a beautiful public golf course, and the Southern Illinois Arts and Crafts Marketplace and Gallery.

Day 1 / Morning

Head out around 8:00 A.M. for the two- to two-and-a-half-hour drive to Rend Lake in southern Illinois. Drive east on any of the major highways and cross over the Poplar Street Bridge into Illinois from downtown St. Louis. Get on Highway 64 East. Highway 64 and Highway 57 merge just outside Mt. Vernon. You'll want to go south on Highway 57 for about fifteen minutes past Mt. Vernon; then you'll get off the highway at the Whittington exit (number 77) and make a right on Route 154. Make a left onto Gun Creek Trail and then a quick right into the parking lot for the **Southern Illinois Arts and Crafts Marketplace and Gallery.** This is such an interesting place to visit because you don't expect to find an art gallery and store in the middle of a field. Nonetheless, 900 artists and craftspeople from all over Illinois show and sell their wares in this beautiful building designed just for them. This is a great place to buy one-of-a-kind jewelry, pottery, china, paintings, decorated tile, and carved wood.

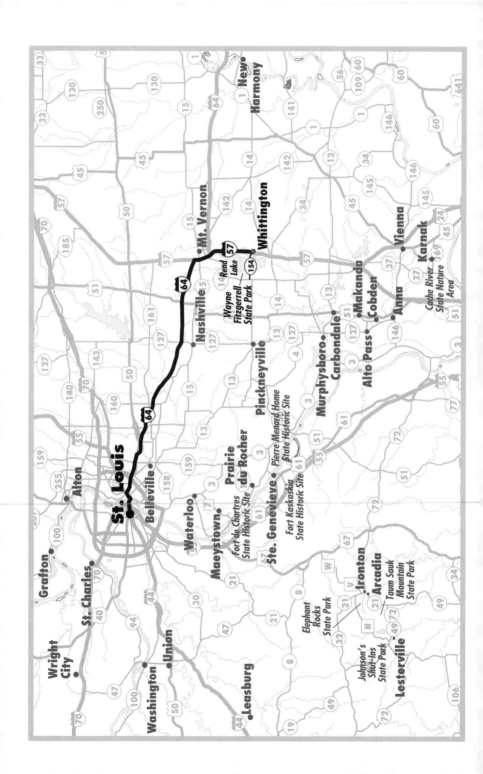

Adjacent to the marketplace is an art gallery displaying additional works by Illinois artists. The building also houses a gift shop with great kids' items as well as other souvenirs and lots of visitor information. You can easily spend an hour or so just browsing. The marketplace and gallery are open daily 9:00 A.M. to 5:00 P.M. For more information call (618) 629–2220.

To get to your lunch destination from the Marketplace, exit the parking lot and head east on Route 154. Cross over Highway 57 toward Route 37. Go left (north) on Route 37 about 1 mile, and Burton's Cafe will be on the right.

LUNCH: Burton's Cafe, 13427 Ewing Road (at the intersection of Route 37 and Ewing Road), Whittington; (618) 629–2515. There's lots to do today, so grab an early lunch at this diner, a local favorite. Although Burton's is nothing fancy to look at, it serves some of the best catfish I've ever had. The fillets have a delicate, crispy, cornmeal breading and are served piping hot along with sides of delicious homemade fried potatoes, hush puppies, and coleslaw. Burton's is also known for pies, especially its white pie—a creamy custard variety with a hint of almond and vanilla. Closed Sunday and Monday. Inexpensive.

Afternoon

Grab your suit and head over toward Rend Lake for an afternoon of **pontoon boating.** To rent your boat, head to Rend Lake Resort. Drive south on Route 37 to Route 154. Make a right on Route 154 heading west. Cross over Highway 57 and continue on Route 154 right to the entrance of Wayne Fitzgerrell State Park. The resort is about 4 miles into the park. The gift shop at the resort rents pontoon boats for $100 for up to four hours. (You will be staying at the resort this evening, but check-in time is not till 3:00 P.M.) Even novice boaters do pretty well driving these barge-like watercraft, which allow enough elbow room to fit a family and all its gear. This is a great way to see the lake firsthand, soak up some sun, and feel your cares melt away. The lake is also a great place to fish, and there are even some beaches with roped-off swimming areas where you can take a dip in the lake if you like. Make sure you pick up a map of the lake and surrounding areas at the gift shop. The map details where things are along the lake and lists standard lake markers, which are universal boating symbols worth noting. Brochures are also available by calling the Rend Lake Visitor Center at (618) 439–7430.

If smaller watercraft are your style, the gift shop also rents paddle boats for $6.00 per hour, aqua cycles for $10.00 per hour, and water mice, which are pint-size speed boats perfect for two, for $25.00 per hour. Serious anglers may prefer renting a 16-foot fishing boat for $45.00 for a half day. The gift shop can be reached by calling (800) 633–3341.

DINNER: Seasons on the Green, 12476 Golf Course Road; (618) 629–2454. Enjoy a variety of dinner items at this comfortable restaurant located next to the Rend Lake Golf Course. Steaks, grilled chicken, seafood, and a variety of soups, salads, and sandwiches along with a full bar make for a relaxing meal. Request a seat that overlooks the golf course, or if the weather permits, dine on the patio to get a better view of this beautifully landscaped public course. Inexpensive to moderate.

Evening

After dinner, head back to Rend Lake Resort for a **horse-drawn carriage ride** around the property. Weekend evenings in the summer offer guests the opportunity to take a relaxing ride around the grounds for just $5.00 per person. Inquire at the gift shop about carriage-ride hours.

LODGING: Rend Lake Resort, 11712 East Windy Lane (in Wayne Fitzgerrell State Park); (800) 633–3341. To be about as close to the water's edge as you can be is the best reason to stay at Rend Lake Resort. The resort offers standard motel rooms, cabins, and "boatels." The boatels are the best of the three choices because they offer a private balcony that sits right on the water's edge. Some boatels offer lofts with a master suite upstairs and a sofa bed on the main level. Some have fireplaces and wet bars. The cabins offer a less intimate view of the lake but have the added benefit of a little more privacy, as there are only two adjoining rooms per structure. The motel rooms are much farther away from the lake, and there is little if any view of the water. The resort offers two restaurants, a gift shop, swimming pool, children's pool, boat rentals, and courtesy dock. Rates for the boatels are between $93 and $97. Cabins run $93, and the standard motel rooms range from $78 up to $103 for the spa suite, which includes a Jacuzzi tub. The boatel rooms book up early, so plan ahead. But don't fret if you're a last-minute traveler. Cancellations do happen, so you may get lucky.

Day 2 / Morning

BREAKFAST: **Windows Restaurant** at Rend Lake Resort. Take a leisurely stroll from your room to the main restaurant at the resort for a hearty breakfast. You can choose from standard breakfast fare including omelets, pancakes, eggs, and biscuits. If the weather permits, choose a seat out on the deck for an up-close look at the water and early-morning anglers.

Morning's a great time to go fishing. Even if you haven't assembled a collection of top-notch fishing equipment, you can still have a good time angling with a basic rod and reel. But don't forget to buy a fishing license. (Illinois fishing licenses cost just a few dollars and are available at a variety of locations around the lake.)

Next you can spend the morning appreciating all that nature has to offer. Rend Lake and its surrounding area is a mecca for **wildlife viewing.** More than 40,000 acres of water and land provide a diverse habitat for all sorts of wildlife: Canada geese, white-tailed deer, ring-necked pheasant, numerous shorebirds as they make their spring and fall migrations, and many, many birds, ducks, bald eagles, and even an occasional pomarine jaeger (a wildcatlike creature). Rend Lake area is also home to one of the largest nesting colonies of great blue herons—one of the few rookeries in southern Illinois. If you're in no particular hurry, you can drive around Rend Lake with no specific destination in mind. Look for the binocular logo signs that will help you locate wildlife viewing areas. Or you can pick up the brochure titled *Watchable Wildlife,* which details fourteen observation sites, either at Rend Lake Resort or **Rend Lake Visitor's Center** (618–439–7430).

One particularly interesting wildlife-watching area is at the **Spillway Overlook** by the Visitor's Center. Here you can view the main dam spillway. You may just see ring-billed gulls, canvasbacks, and golden-eyes, as well as purple martins. The pomarine jaeger has also been spotted in this area. To get to the Spillway, hop on Highway 57 South and drive about five minutes to the Benton exit (number 71). Make a right and head west on Route 14 about 2.5 miles and turn right on Rend City Road. Drive north 3 miles to Main Dam Road and turn right. Follow the signs to Rend Lake Visitor's Center.

Head back out to Route 14 and go east toward the little town of Benton, where you'll find some interesting antiques shops. Route 14 runs directly into the public square, a traffic circle around the Franklin County Court House. To the right as you enter the circle, you'll find **The Goodie**

Shop, 806 Public Square; (618) 438–3071. This little shop is crammed with antiques, collectibles, and furniture. The shop, which is open from 10:00 A.M. to 5:00 P.M. Monday through Saturday and 1:00 to 5:00 P.M. on Sunday, is well worth a little side trip.

Swing back to Rend Lake Resort for a quick bite of lunch at the casual Reilly's. To get there, reverse your steps from the Visitor's Center and head back to the resort.

LUNCH: Reilly's Lounge at Rend Lake Resort, 11712 East Windy Lane, Whittington; (800) 633–3341. Just next door to Windows, Reilly's serves basic sandwiches and salads for a fast meal while you're on the run. Inexpensive.

Afternoon

Not far from the resort is **Rancho Bandera Stables,** 11094 Ranger Road; (618) 629–2260. Horseback riding is a great way to see the park up close and personal. Guides will lead you on a trail ride through the park along paths reserved just for the horses. One-hour rides are $18 per person, and half-hour rides are $12. From the resort make a right on Ranger Road. You'll see a white sign marked stable about 2 miles down on the left. Turn into the parking lot, and you're there.

Head back to St. Louis by continuing out of the park. Make a left on Route 154 and a left onto Highway 57 North. The trip home should take about two hours.

There's More

Benton

Jacqueline's General Store, 702 North McLeansboro Street; (618) 435–4444. Fine gifts, antiques, gourmet foods, dolls, linens, glassware, and more. Open Monday through Saturday 9:00 A.M. to 5:00 P.M.

Rend Lake Marina, 8955 West Dam Lane; (618) 724–7651. Pontoon, personal watercraft, and fishing-boat rentals.

Ina

Ina Antique & Collectibles, 106 West Third Street; (618) 437–5018. This little store is filled with pottery, quilts, furniture, glassware, lamps, crocks, and more. Open 9:00 A.M. to 5:00 P.M. Thursday through Tuesday.

Whittington

Rend Lake Golf Course, 12476 Golf Course Road (618–629–2353) is a beautiful twenty-seven-hole public course that is considered one of the finest in the Midwest. The course is considered challenging for the accomplished player yet enjoyable for the beginning golfer. The course has been rated as the number-one public golf facility in the Gateway PGA. Greens fees start at $36 and include a cart. Club rental is available, and a driving range is open until 11:00 P.M. nightly.

Wineries. Three wineries are located in the general Rend Lake area. Pheasant Hollow Winery in Whittington (618–629–2302) is on Route 37 just north of Route 154 at Exit 77 east of Highway 57. GenKota Winery is located in Mt. Vernon, 301 North Forty-fourth Street (618–246–WINE), and Spring Pond Vineyards, 13772 Spring Pond Road (618–439–9176) is in Benton.

Special Events

January through April and September through November. Some of the best retrievers, beagles, and bird dogs compete for national honors at the bird dog field trials. Whittington. (618) 629–2320.

May. Largest flea market in southern Illinois with more than 150 dealers. Sesser. (618) 625–5813.

May through September. Summer Sunset Series. Benton. Local entertainers are spotlighted in a summer-long series of Saturday-evening programs set on the shores of Rend Lake at the Visitor's Center Amphitheater. (618) 439–7430.

June. Rend Lake Days Homecoming. Sesser. Features country music, carnival, dancing, parade, and horse show. (618) 625–6213.

October. Children's Festival of Arts and Crafts. Whittington. Artists work with children in hands-on experience. Basket weaving, kite making, food, gift shop. Held at Southern Illinois Artisan Shop. (618) 625–5813.

Other Recommended Restaurants and Lodgings

Benton

The Buzz Espresso Bar & Deli, 601 Public Square; (618) 438–2899. This urbanesque coffee bar and sandwich shop is a great choice if you're visiting during the week. Open Monday through Friday 7:30 A.M. to 5:00 P.M. Closed Saturday and Sunday. Live music on selected Friday and Saturday nights. Inexpensive.

Whittington

Seasons Lodge and Condominiums at Rend Lake Golf Course. Nicely furnished casual rooms with outdoor pool and patio area. Optional spa and fireplace suites. Rates are $69 to $129. Call (800) 999–0977 or (618) 629–2368. Seasons also has condominiums for rent. Two-bedroom, two-bathroom condos are $240 per day; three-bedroom, two-bath are $260 per day, and three-bedroom, three-bath are $280 per day.

For More Information

Mt. Vernon Convention & Visitor's Bureau, P.O. Box 1708, Mt. Vernon, IL 62864; (800) 252–5464; www.southernillinois.com.

EASTERN ESCAPE FOUR

Springfield, Illinois

An All-American Getaway / 1 Night

If you're looking for a quintessential American experience, few Midwestern towns can rival Springfield. More than any other town, it can lay claim to Abraham Lincoln, having been the town where he lived much of his adult life and where he practiced law. And it's thanks to him that Springfield is the state capital. Lincoln and eight of his friends were successful in passing a bill that ultimately moved the state capital from Vandalia in 1837. Springfield is a wonderful town for spending a few days going back in history, but it is also very much living in the present. It's a town where you can enjoy creative cuisine and wonderful accommodations provided by a new generation of Springfield residents.

- ☐ The Old State Capitol
- ☐ Abraham Lincoln historic sites
- ☐ Frank Lloyd Wright architecture
- ☐ Lively downtown

Day 1 / Morning

The drive to Springfield should take between an hour and a half and two hours, depending on where you live in St. Louis. The distance from downtown St. Louis to Springfield is about 100 miles. Leave home around 9:00 A.M. in order to get into Springfield and see a sight or two before lunch. Just head north into Illinois on Highway 55 and stay on Highway 55 the whole way. As you get close to Springfield, you'll see signs for Sixth Street/Business 55. You'll want to get into the left-hand lane. Sixth Street is the main entrance into town, and the exit becomes the left lane of Highway 55. Follow Sixth Street toward downtown. Between Adams and Washington Streets there is an underground parking garage. Pull into the garage and park. You're perfectly situated to see many of the downtown sites.

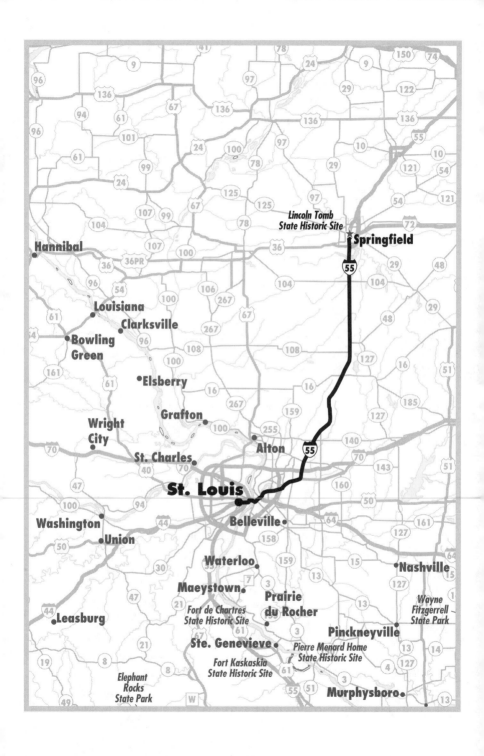

First stop is **The Old State Capitol** (217–785–7961), which sits between Adams and Washington Streets (just above the underground parking garage). Completed in 1854 for the modest sum of $260,000, the Old State Capitol is where Abraham Lincoln gave his famous "House Divided" speech and was the center of Illinois government from 1839 to 1876. At that time the building was the grandest in Illinois, and because of Lincoln's involvement, it is considered among the most important nineteenth-century public buildings in the United States. The well-informed interpreters take a genuine interest in educating visitors about the building and the time period. A donation of $2.00 for adults and $1.00 for children is requested. The Old State Capitol is open daily March through October from 9:00 A.M. to 5:00 P.M. and November through February from 9:00 A.M. to 4:00 P.M. Closed most major holidays and government holidays. Call to be certain.

LUNCH: Exit The Old State Capitol from the south and walk across Adams Street, which is a pedestrian plaza between Fifth and Sixth Streets. Stop in for lunch at **The Feed Store,** 516 East Adams; (217) 528–3355. Here you'll find a cozy, relaxed sandwich, salad, and soup shop. Place your order with the hostess and then have a seat. Undecided? The chicken salad sandwich on French bread is outstanding, as is the seafood chowder. If you can, leave room for the extra-moist and flavorful apple cake topped with caramel icing; it's superb. Lunch with drink and dessert is around $8.00 to $10.00.

Afternoon

Just a few doors down from The Feed Store, at the corner of Sixth and Adams, are the **Lincoln–Herndon Law Offices;** (217) 785–7289. Abraham Lincoln practiced law here for nearly ten years, beginning around 1843. This historic site is the only surviving structure in which Lincoln maintained working law offices, and he tried cases in the building's federal court located below his office. The Law Offices' hours are the same as The Old State Capitol—daily March through October 9:00 A.M. to 5:00 P.M. and November through February 9:00 A.M. to 4:00 P.M. Closed most major holidays and government holidays. Call to be certain.

Around the corner on Sixth Street are a few specialty stores worth exploring. **Tinsley's Dry Goods** offers a variety of Lincoln souvenirs. **Del's Popcorn** is the place for homemade popcorn and candy, as well as a good place to stop in for a quick soda. **Caffe Panini,** 231 South Sixth

Street (217–522–0488), is a great option for a cup of coffee or sandwiches and salads to go.

If the weather is good, you can walk the few blocks to the Lincoln Home National Historic Site. From the corner of Sixth and Monroe, walk 1 block south on Sixth Street to Capitol Avenue; go east 1 block on Capitol. On the left you'll pass the First Presbyterian Church (217–528–4311) at Seventh and Capitol Avenue. Inside you can view the **Lincoln Family Pew,** as well as fine examples of Tiffany stained-glass windows. The **Lincoln Home Visitor Center** sits across the street at 426 South Seventh Street; (217) 492–4241, ext. 221. The Visitor Center is open daily from 8:30 A.M. to 6:00 P.M. with extended hours in summer. The center is closed New Year's Day, Thanksgiving, and Christmas. Orientation programs and exhibits offer insight into Lincoln's life in Springfield as well as a look at his home as it appeared in 1860. Obtain your free tickets here for entrance into the Lincoln Home

Tour the **Lincoln Home National Historic Site** next. The home and its 4-block cobblestone neighborhood is where Abraham and Mary Todd Lincoln lived for seventeen years. In 1988 the home underwent an extensive restoration process to preserve its beauty and national significance. The tour provides a wonderful insight into the life of this famous president as well as what life was like in the mid-nineteenth century. The Lincoln Home is open daily from 8:30 A.M. to 5:00 P.M., with extended hours spring, summer, and fall; closed New Year's Day, Thanksgiving, and Christmas.

Depending on your ticket time for the Lincoln Home tour, stroll around the historic neighborhood and explore the **Dean House** and the **Arnold House,** which are home to exhibits on Lincoln as well as America during the mid-nineteenth century. If time permits, walk over to the **Lincoln Depot** (Great Western) on Monroe Street between Ninth and Tenth Streets. This is where Lincoln gave his famed farewell address in 1861 as he bid his Springfield friends and neighbors good-bye. Who knew he would never return to Springfield again in his lifetime? The depot is open daily April through August from 10:00 A.M. to 4:00 P.M. Admission is free.

DINNER: Cafe Brio, Sixth and Monroe; (217) 544–0574; www.cafe brio.com. After a long day of touring, this energetic hot spot in the heart of downtown Springfield will perk you up. Serving Latin, Mediterranean, and Caribbean cuisine, Cafe Brio's menu is imaginative, and the decor is spirited and fun. Most everyone will find something they'll enjoy eating, whether it be seafood, tacos, or filet mignon. Appetizers include tamale cakes and blackened salmon tostada. Entrees include rotolo, which is a puff pastry layered with mozzarella, asiago, and ricotta cheeses and baked. Desserts are equally inventive and include hot chocolate-silk pie and brown-sugar tortilla. Dinner entrees average $13. Cafe Brio is open for lunch and dinner Monday through Saturday and for brunch on Saturday and Sunday.

LODGING: The Inn at 835 Bed & Breakfast, 835 South Second Street; (888) 217–4835 or (217) 523–4466; www.innat835.com. Built during the Arts and Crafts movement as Springfield's first luxury apartment building, the inn is now home to ten rooms/suites individually named after different flowers and decorated accordingly. Rooms include private bath, color TV, and phone; some have whirlpool baths, fireplaces, and private verandas. This is a delightful place to stay when you want the pampering and one-of-a-kind feeling of a B&B but feel more comfortable in a hotel-type environment with a TV, phone, and front-desk staff. The inn is located 3 blocks from the state capitol complex, which makes for easy walking to area attractions. Rates from $114.99 to $194.99 include wine and cheese in the evening, cookies at night, and a full breakfast in the morning. (The batter-dipped French toast is warm and crunchy, reminiscent of a funnel cake, and the smoked bacon is heavenly.) The inn welcomes children ages twelve and older. Special pampering packages are also available.

Day 2 / Morning

BREAKFAST: The Inn at 835 B&B. Sleep in and enjoy a late breakfast around 9:00 A.M.

After breakfast head over to the **Dana-Thomas House,** 301 East Lawrence (217–782–6776), for a fascinating tour of what many people consider to be the best preserved and most complete of Frank Lloyd Wright's early "Prairie" houses. Although not a Lincoln site, the Dana-Thomas House is uniquely American and has ties to one of Springfield's most well-known families. Built between 1902 and 1904 by wealthy Springfield socialite Susan Lawrence Dana, the house is an unbelievable example of what happens when you mix extraordinary talent with an open checkbook. Ask about the hammered copper vase that sits above the entryway; the story is fascinating. Parking is provided on Cook Street at

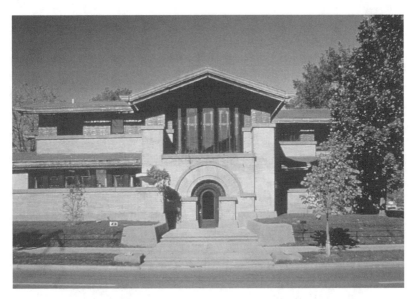

Dana-Thomas House, Springfield

Second, or you can walk the few blocks from the Inn at 835 by heading north on Second Street and then east 1 block on Lawrence. The House is open Wednesday through Sunday 9:00 A.M. to 4:00 P.M. A donation of $3.00 is requested. When you leave, don't miss the **Sumac Shop** (217–744–3598) in the carriage house for wonderful examples of art glass, books, and Frank Lloyd Wright–related gifts and reproductions.

Next stop is **New Salem,** a home to Lincoln for about six years and currently a reconstructed village where he spent his early adulthood. Take Cook Street back to Second and go north to Jefferson; turn left onto Jefferson Street and take Jefferson all the way to the west end of town. After you cross over Veteran's Parkway, you'll see signs for Route 97, which is about a mile away. Turn right onto Route 97 and take it all the way to **Lincoln's New Salem State Historic Site** in Petersburg. The entrance to New Salem is on the left. The drive is about 20 miles and takes about thirty minutes.

LUNCH: Enter the village parking lot and stop in the conveniently located McDonald's for a quick lunch before exploring New Salem.

Afternoon

After lunch, head into New Salem's **visitor center,** R.R. 1; (217) 632–4000. Make sure you watch the twenty-minute video of Lincoln's life and times in New Salem before exploring the village. The informative video gives a good overview of why Lincoln came to New Salem, what he did in this commercial village, and why he left. After the video either browse the displays or head into the village.

Each of the reconstructed homes stands on what is believed to be its original site, so it's fascinating to survey the village and see just how it probably would have looked in Lincoln's time. Inside many of the buildings you'll see interpreters in period costumes taking on the role of cooper, blacksmith, or other commonly held jobs in the early nineteenth century. Wander around the village and peek into each building for a fascinating glimpse back in time. New Salem is open seven days a week. From March through October, hours are 9:00 A.M. to 5:00 P.M.; from November through February, 8:00 A.M. to 4:00 P.M. The site is free to visitors, but donations are accepted.

As you leave New Salem, you can turn left at Route 97 for the 2-mile drive into **Petersburg's** town square. Spend a little time browsing this quaint village. There are a variety of antiques shops in the square and a few restaurants where you can get a drink or snack before heading back to town.

Your last stop before leaving Springfield is **Lincoln Tomb** in Oak Ridge Cemetery. Head back toward Springfield on Route 97. As you get closer into Springfield, Route 97 becomes Jefferson. Turn left onto Bruns Lane and then turn right onto North Grand Avenue; turn left onto Monument Avenue, which will lead you straight into Oak Ridge Cemetery. Signs will lead you to the tomb. The tomb is open daily 9:00 A.M. to 5:00 P.M. March through October and closes at 4:00 P.M. November through February; closed most major holidays; (217) 782–2717. This is the final resting spot for Lincoln, his wife, and three of his four sons.

When you leave the tomb, exit the parking lot to the right and follow the road to the Walnut Street exit. Turn right onto Walnut Street and follow it to Veteran's Parkway. Turn left onto Veteran's Parkway and continue down Veteran's Parkway toward the mall and various chain restaurants if you'd prefer to eat before leaving town. When you're ready to leave, just continue south on Veteran's Parkway to I–72/36. Take 72/36 East/Decatur exit and then take 72/36 East to I–55, and you're on your way home.

There's More

With so much to see and do in Springfield, it's easy to turn this getaway into a two-night trip. Here are a few more options:

Executive Mansion, 410 East Jackson; (217) 782–6450. See where Illinois's governor lives. Tour sixteen rooms open to the public, including the State Dining Room and the Lincoln Bedroom. Open Tuesday and Thursday 9:30 to 11:00 A.M. and 2:00 to 3:30 P.M., Saturday 9:30 to 11:00 A.M.; closed most major holidays. Free.

Illinois State Museum, Spring and Edwards Streets; (217) 782–7386. Includes the special exhibit "At Home in the Heartland." Open Monday through Saturday 8:30 A.M. to 5:00 P.M. and Sunday noon to 5:00 P.M.; closed most major holidays.

Trolley Car. If you'd prefer a motorized drive to each of the sites, take a ride on an open-air trolley. Tickets are sold at several downtown locations. Call (217) 789–2360 for a list of stops and ticketing locations.

Special Events

Monthly. Saturday Evening Theater at The Old State Capitol. Usually the second Saturday of the month. Historical music and drama performances followed by a reception and candlelight tour through this beautiful historic site. (217) 785–7960.

June through August. Theater in the Park. Lincoln's New Salem State Historic Site, Petersburg. Weekends, June through August. Enjoy an evening of outdoor entertainment in this lovely setting next to the pioneer village. Call (217) 632–4000 for more information.

August. Illinois State Fair, Illinois State Fairgrounds. Springfield. (217) 782–6661.

September. International Route 66 Mother Road Festival. Springfield. www.route66fest.com.

October. Candlelight tour of New Salem, Lincoln's New Salem Historic Site. Petersburg. (217) 632–4000.

Other Recommended Restaurants and Lodgings

Petersburg

The Oaks Bed and Breakfast, 510 West Sheridan; (217) 632–5444 or (888) 724–6257. As you drive into Petersburg, you can't miss this regal house high atop the hill. Five rooms, including a suite, all with private bath and gourmet breakfast. Children welcome. Rates: $70 to $125.

Springfield

Holiday Inn Express Hotel and Suites, 3050 South Dirksen Parkway; (217) 529–7771 or (800) HOLIDAY. Free continental breakfast. Children under eighteen stay free with parents. Pool, game room. Rates: $59 to $75.

Mansion View Inn & Suites, 529 South Fourth Street; (217) 544–7411 or (800) 252–1083; www.mansionview.com. Includes thirty-two two-room suites, some with Jacuzzis. Free continental breakfast. Located in downtown Springfield across from the Governor's Mansion. Rates: $59 to $129.

Renaissance Springfield Hotel, 701 East Adams Street; (217) 544–8800 or (800) HOTELS-1. Downtown hotel adjacent to the convention center, within walking distance of historic sites. Indoor pool. Rates: $69 to $137.

For More Information

Springfield Illinois Convention & Visitors Bureau, 109 North Seventh Street, Springfield, IL 62701; (800) 545–7300 or (217) 789–2360; www.visit-springfieldillinois.com.

EASTERN ESCAPE FIVE

New Harmony/Evansville, Indiana, and Henderson, Kentucky

A Tale of Three River Towns / 2 Nights

Tucked away along the Wabash River in Southern Indiana is New Harmony, founded in 1814 by George Rapp, leader of a German Lutheran group called the Harmonie Society, to prepare for the Second Coming of Christ. The group built their community on neatly planned streets; planted formal gardens, orchards, and fields; and constructed mills. They supplied all their own needs and sold the surplus to other settlers.

- ☐ Historical community
- ☐ Museums
- ☐ Camping
- ☐ Parks
- ☐ Shopping
- ☐ Biking
- ☐ Antiques
- ☐ Prehistoric site

While Harmonie thrived, some of the group became disenchanted after ten years when Christ did not arrive. Robert Owen, who also wanted to create a new order where education and social equality would prosper, purchased the town. New Harmony remains a charming village, devoid of fast-food and retail chain stores.

Historic properties, festivals, theater, art exhibitions and galleries, and shopping give visitors a taste of the town's history. Walk through the Roofless Church, visit the ultramodern Atheneum, walk the Labyrinth. You don't even need a car—you can walk to all these attractions and more.

Also on a river—the Ohio—35 miles east is Evansville. Here you can see one of the best-preserved prehistoric Native American settlements in the United States at Angel Mounds State Prehistoric Site. Explore various types of architecture at the Riverside Historic District. Learn about steamboats, railroad, and river-town life at the Evansville Museum of Arts & Science. Take a short drive across the river to Henderson, Kentucky, and observe hundreds of birds in their natural environment at John James

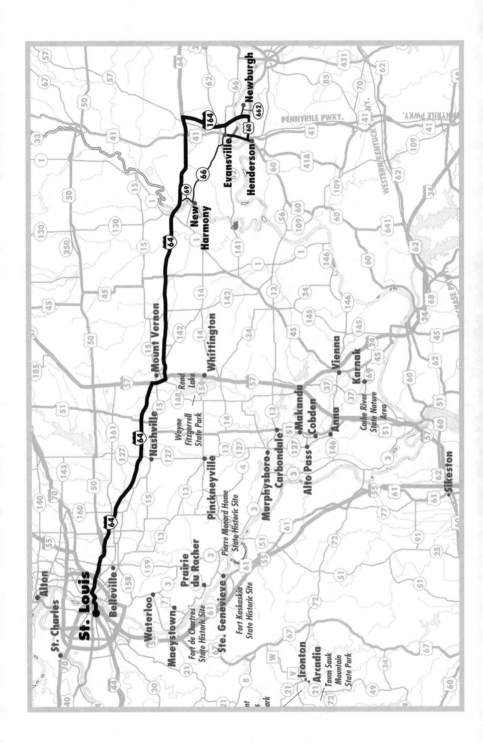

Audubon State Park, Museum, and Nature Center. For a different diversion visit Ellis Park Race Course for year-round thoroughbred horse racing.

Three towns, all different, with much to offer and only a three-hour drive from St. Louis.

Day 1 / Morning

Get an early-morning start. Go east on I–64 for 138 miles to exit 4 (Griffin exit); then go south on Highway 69 to Highway 66 West. In New Harmony follow the signs to the **Atheneum** on North and Arthur Streets; (812) 682–4474 or (800) 231–2168. At the visitor center watch the video to get acquainted with New Harmony and its history. Then take either a guided or self-guided tour of the log cabins, Harmonist homes, an opera house, and other sites. Rates: adults, $10.00; senior citizens, $9.00; children seven through seventeen, $5.00; families $25.00. For a self-guided tour, the Atheneum has books that will give walking routes and histories of each site. While you walk, look for the famous Golden Raintrees. Many can be found in Maclure Park at Raintree Street. If you visit in spring, you'll see a golden carpet of leaves around the thick trunks.

East of the Atheneum on North Street stands the **double log cabin** built in 1775, two log cabins with a walkway (referred to in these parts as a "dogtrot") in between. While it is pre-Harmonist, it is an example of how local materials were used in that period. The next house, the **David Lenz House,** is a typical Harmonist house, a simple, functional dwelling, similar to those of the Shakers. Across the street is the **Harmonist Cemetery,** enclosed by a brick wall. There are no gravestones because the Harmonists believed in equality in death, as in life.

Community House Number Two is one of four buildings built by the Harmonists for single members without families. **The New Harmony Workingmen's Institute,** Indiana's oldest library, was established by William Maclure of the Owen community in 1838. It also houses a museum, an art gallery, and historical archives. It's located at Tavern and West Streets; (812) 682–4806.

Visit the **Roofless Church,** North and Main Streets, an interdenominational church completed in 1960 and designed by architect Philip Johnson with the idea that the sky should be the only ceiling for all worshippers. The **Cathedral Labyrinth and Sacred Garden** (812–682–3050) provides a totally serene experience, especially for persons familiar with the labyrinth experience. Information on the labyrinth is available at

The Atheneum in New Harmony

the Atheneum. Another interesting building is the **Granary,** built to hold the Harmonists' abundant harvests. Be sure to notice the slits on the side that ventilated their stores.

LUNCH: At **The Bayou Grill,** 504 North Street (812–682–4491), you can choose from a great selection of sandwiches like old-fashioned chicken salad ($4.50) or a breaded-pork tenderloin ($4.95). For $2.25 extra you can add coleslaw and french fries. For heartier appetites the country-fried steak with cream gravy, homemade bread, salad, and vegetables ($7.50) should fill the bill—and the stomach. The Grill also serves an extensive Sunday brunch from 10:00 A.M. until 3:00 P.M.

Afternoon

Spend the afternoon browsing New Harmony's downtown and all the specialty shops, galleries, and craft stores. Start on Main Street at one end with the **Arbor House & Garden;** browse through their gardens and check out the garden and greenhouse accessories, plus collectibles, baskets, and art prints. Walking north, you'll come to the **Treasure Trove Antique Mall, Aunt Sallie's Soda Shoppe,** the **Christmas Cottage,** the **New Harmony Antique Mall,** and **Harmony Pottery,** with pottery made on-site. For a great selection of used books, visit the **Golden Raintree Bookstore.**

At the intersection of Church and Main Streets, you'll find the **Antique Showroom in the Mews;** the **Weave Haus,** featuring yarns and fabrics for knitting, weaving, and spinning; the **Red Geranium Bookstore,** where you can find information on local and regional history and the labyrinth; and **Heirlooms, Etc.,** not only a gift and flower shop, but a gourmet coffee bar with wonderful candies.

Walk into Aunt Sallie's Soda Shoppe and you will think you have walked back in time into the 1940s and '50s. Sit and sip an old-fashioned phosphate while looking at period decor. After quenching your thirst, take some time to visit the **New Harmony Gallery of Contemporary Art** on Main Street, featuring fine arts and crafts from local and regional artists. **Satterfield Fine Art,** next to the Red Geranium Bookstore, also has an extensive art collection by artist Stephen Satterfield.

Do not miss **Earthcare at the Depot,** on North Street, an environmental resource center focusing on organic gardening. You will find herbs, perennials, reading materials, and unique gifts.

DINNER: No visit to New Harmony would be complete without a meal at the famous **Red Geranium Restaurant,** 504 North Street; (812) 682–4431. Start with homemade crab cakes; then try the French onion gratinée soup or the spinach salad. Making a dinner choice is hard with entrees like Italian pepper steak, char-grilled duck breast, or chicken Kahlúa, to name but a few outstanding choices. Do not leave without trying their famous Lemon Shaker Pie. Moderately expensive.

LODGING: Where else would you get a good night's sleep but **The Wright Place** (812–682–3453)? An 1840-style saltbox house at 515 South Arthur Street, this bed-and-breakfast has a second-level suite with full private bath and TV/reading room, and a lower level room, also with full private bath. Guests can relax in the library and music room, which includes a grand piano. Within walking distance of all attractions. Rates: $95 to $150. Children and pets welcome.

Day 2 / Morning

BREAKFAST: At The Wright Place. Enjoy a full gourmet breakfast such as fruit and yogurt, ham and asparagus quiche, chocolate banana bread, juice, and coffee. If you have time, walk around the grounds, which used to be a Harmonist orchard. Laurie Wright, who, with husband Duane, owns the B&B, is the town's sole veterinarian. She can make a quiche and consult a frantic pet owner at the same time—amazing!

Leaving New Harmony, drive east on Highway 66 to Evansville, about 30 miles. Start your sight-seeing at the **Pagoda,** 401 Southeast Riverside Drive (800–433–3025), Evansville's visitor center. Built in 1912 as a Japanese park shelter, the restored building now houses the center and overlooks the Ohio River. While you're gathering material, pick up Evansville Foot by Foot, a walking guide to the Riverside Historic District.

Before you do the walking tour, visit the **Evansville Museum of Arts and Sciences** and the **Evansville Museum Transportation Center (EMTRAC),** 411 Southeast Riverside Drive (812–425–2406), which is next door to the visitor center. The museum has collections in art, history, anthropology, and science; a stroll-down-Main-Street exhibit; a hands-on exhibit for kids in the Science Center; and a stargazing show in Koch Planetarium. EMTRAC, a separate building next door, provides the history of transportation including railroad cars and engines, fire pumpers, and horse-drawn buggies. Hours: Tuesday through Saturday 10:00 A.M. to 5:00 P.M. and Sunday noon to 5:00 P.M. all year; closed Monday. Free admission to museum. Admission to EMTRAC: adults, $2.00; children twelve and under, free. Fees for planetarium shows. www.emuseum.org.

To get to the **Riverside Historic District,** go across Riverside Drive to Mulberry Street, and then left on First Street. Your guide pamphlet will show you various types of architecture to look for—Queen Anne, Italianate, and Georgian/colonial revival, among others. A house worth touring inside is the **Reitz Home,** 223 Southeast First Street; (812) 426–2179. An 1871 Victorian with tile and marble fireplaces, walnut wainscoting in Moorish design, and stained-glass window panels, this house has been recognized in many publications. Open Tuesday through Saturday 11:00 A.M. to 3:30 P.M. and Sunday 1:00 to 3:30 P.M. Adults, $5.00; students, $2.50; children twelve and under, $1.50. www.reitzhome. evansville.net.

Next, visit **Willard Library,** 21 First Avenue; (812) 425–4309. Opened in 1885, this library is the oldest public library in Indiana, and the Victorian Gothic structure is on the National Register of Historic Places. It also has the most comprehensive collection of regional and family history in the state, but more than that—it's haunted! In winter 1937 a custodian sighted the "Lady in Grey," and at various times since then, she has made herself known either by her perfume or by turning on water faucets. www.willard.lib.in.us/legends/firstsight.html.

Across the street from the library is the **Evansville Municipal Market,** 40 First Avenue; (812) 428–0956. Originally built in 1917 and recently restored, visitors can buy fresh flowers, herbs, and produce brought in by area farmers every Saturday from 8:00 A.M. to 2:00 P.M. The **Colonial Home & Garden Center** has fresh flowers plus bedding plants and gardening accessories. Open Monday through Friday 9:00 A.M. to 6:00 P.M., Saturday 8:00 A.M. to 5:00 P.M., and Sunday noon to 5:00 P.M. Walk around the **Festival Hall** to see such specialty shops as the bread maker, coffee connoisseur, a deli, gift shop, wine shop, and others. Open Monday through Friday 10:00 A.M. to 6:00 P.M. and Saturday 8:00 A.M. to 2:00 P.M.

LUNCH: You have no doubt worked up an appetite by now, and **Gerst Bavarian Haus,** 2100 West Franklin Street (812–424–1420), in the city's West Side, will take care of that. In the early twentieth century, nearly 40 percent of Evansville residents were either born in Germany or were first-generation German. The 110-year-old building was formerly a hardware store, but it's hard to imagine it as anything but a restaurant. The wooden booths, high ceilings, and planked floors will immediately put you in the mood for Gerst Wurst—or maybe marinated pig knuckles simmered and served with sauerkraut. If not, the Rindergulasch (goulash) over home-made spätzle is incredibly delicious. Or the smoked Mett Ring dinner, which is well-seasoned pork and beef. Finish off with Bavarian Apfel Strudel. Dinners from $8.95 to $14.95. Open Monday through Thursday 11:00 A.M. to 10:00 P.M., Friday and Saturday 11:00 A.M. to 11:00 P.M., and Sunday 11:00 A.M. to 9:00 P.M.

Afternoon

Cross over the Ohio River on Highway 41 to **Henderson, Kentucky,** to the **John James Audubon Museum,** Audubon Parkway; (270) 826–2247. The first artist to paint birds and animals in their natural surround-ings, Audubon began this task in Henderson. The museum has the largest collection of Audubon memorabilia in existence, including oil paintings, watercolors, and family heirlooms. The Nature Center has interactive dis-plays and a large observation room where you can see birds and other wildlife in a natural setting. Open year-round, 10:00 A.M. to 5:00 P.M.

daily. Closed Thanksgiving Day, one week during the Christmas holidays, and New Year's Day. Admission is free. www.kystateparks.com.

What's a trip without a zoo? Evansville boasts the largest in Indiana, the **Mesker Park Zoo & Botanic Garden,** 2421 Bement Avenue (812–435–6143), with more than seventy acres and 600 animals. Visitors can stroll 2½ miles of walking paths through the savannas of Africa and the Asian plains to North American forests. Discover the rain forest in the Discovery Center. Learn about lemurs in the Lemur Forest Exhibit. Open daily 9:00 A.M. to 4:00 P.M. Admission: adults, $4.75; children three through twelve, $3.75; children two and under, free. www.meskerpark zoo.org.

DINNER: RiverBend, 18 South Third Avenue; (812) 424–4300. For a taste of Louisiana in Indiana, this restaurant will satisfy. Try the fried-crayfish salad ($8.45), or if you're really hungry, Catfish Pecan topped with a Creole sauce ($13.95) or barbecued shrimp, with lemon, garlic, and herbs ($14.95). Lunch, Monday through Friday 11:00 A.M. to 2:00 P.M.; dinner, Tuesday through Thursday 5:00 to 10:00 P.M., Friday and Saturday 5:00 to 11:00 P.M. Sunday jazz brunch from noon until 4:00 P.M. www.riverbend evansville.com.

LODGING: The Starkey Inn Bed & Breakfast, 214 Southeast First Street; (800) 580–0305 or (812) 425–7264. Located in the Riverside Historic District next to the Reitz Home Museum, the Starkey has five large rooms with beds that beckon your tired bones. No children under twelve. No pets or smoking. Rates: $85 to $185. www.starkeyinn.com.

Day 3 / Morning

BREAKFAST: At The Starkey Inn Bed & Breakfast. Start your day of sight-seeing with a gourmet breakfast of cheese strata or French toast with peaches.

After breakfast, drive north on I–164 to Highway 66 and turn right into the little town of Newburgh. Then, make another right at State Street and go through the charming downtown district. Browsing the coffee shops, antiques shops, bookstores, and other enticing establishments will take more of your time than you probably planned, but it will be worth it. Stroll along the riverfront for one more peaceful moment before you head back home.

One more stop before heading home: **Angel Mounds,** located on the banks of the Ohio River, has two distinctions. It is one of the best-preserved Native American settlements in the United States and one of the best examples of Mississippian culture. The inhabitants, who formed a thriving culture between A.D. 900 and 1600, built eleven earthen mounds as platforms for their buildings. This culture is similar to that of Cahokia Mounds in western Illinois, outside St. Louis. The site includes reconstructed winter houses, a roundhouse, a summer house, and a temple. There's also an interpretive center with artifacts. Take the Highway 662 exit off I–164 and follow the signs. No admission, but a suggested donation of $2.00. Hours: Tuesday through Saturday 9:00 A.M. to 5:00 P.M. and Sunday 1:00 to 5:00 P.M.; closed Monday during winter months, mid-December through mid-March. (812) 853–3956. www.angelmounds.org.

Get back to I–164, then to I–64. Once there, head west to St. Louis, approximately three hours. You might want to take a lunch stop in Mt. Vernon at **Rural Route Country Cookin',** I–57 and I–64; (618) 244–2616. The barbecued-pork sandwich will hold you till St. Louis, but the plate specials, like chicken-fried steak, meat loaf, or pork chops are tempting. Inexpensive.

There's More

Evansville, Indiana

Burdette Park, Nurrenbern Road; (812) 435–5602. A 200-acre park offering a wide range of recreational activities for families. One of the biggest swimming pools in the Midwest, with four water slides. Campgrounds, fishing lakes, tennis courts, miniature golf course, and BMX racing track. Chalets rent for $70 a night and include fireplace, kitchen, linens, and a TV with VCR. Some units have whirlpool. Campground: Call (812) 435–5611 or (812) 422–1078. Rates: tent sites (two tents per site), $6.30 a night or $31.50 a week; RV hookups, $12.60 a night or $75.60 a week.

Casino Aztar, 421 Northwest Riverside Drive; (800) 342–5386. Gaming entertainment with all manner of games, five restaurants, and a 250-room hotel. Free concerts.

Vertical Excape Climbing Center, 1315 Royal Avenue; (812) 479–6887. If you're into rock climbing, or you would like to try it, this center has all the right stuff. Rental equipment and lessons for all levels. Call about rates.

Open Tuesday through Friday noon to 10:00 P.M., Saturday 10:00 A.M. to 10:00 P.M., and Sunday noon to 8:00 P.M. www.verticalexcape.com.

Wesselman Woods Nature Preserve, 551 Boeke Road; (812) 479–0771. A national natural landmark and state preserve with more than 190 acres of virgin hardwood forest. Hiking trails and a nature center with exhibits, wildlife observation areas, a library, and Chrysalis gift shop.

Henderson, Kentucky

John James Audubon State Park, US–41; (502) 826–2247. Hiking, camping, and golf. Golf fees: weekdays $5.00/nine holes, $10.00/eighteen holes; weekends $6.00/nine holes, $12.00/eighteen holes. Cart fees: $6.00/nine holes, $10.00/eighteen holes. Due to seasonal variations, call for cabin rates.

New Harmony, Indiana

Harmonie State Park, a 3,400-acre park 4 miles south of New Harmony. Features 200-site family campground with electrical hookups, rest rooms, and family cabins. Picnic areas, some with shelter houses and playgrounds. Hiking, biking, and horse trails of varying difficulty. Swimming pool and fishing. For cabin or bike rental, call (812) 682–4821. Cabin rates: $60.

Harmonist Labyrinth, Main Street, close to the south edge of town, a concentric circle of hedges with a circular stone building in the center.

New Harmony Theatre, Murphy Auditorium, 419 Tavern Street; (812) 682–3115. Professional equity theater presenting plays from mid-June through August. Adults, $18; seniors and students, $16. (800) NHT–SHOW; www.newharmonytheatre.com.

Special Events

April. Heritage Week. New Harmony. Craft demonstrations of early-nineteenth-century life in New Harmony. While it is open to the public, it is mainly for groups of fourth to sixth graders. Approximately 800 to 1,000 kids attend in the mornings. Adults wanting a tour are encouraged to come in the afternoon, to avoid the masses.

April through May. Herb Festival, Harmony Pottery. New Harmony. Seminars and workshops on such topics as medicinal herbs, soap making, macrobiotics, and many other topics. www.raggededgestudio.com.

May. Harmonie Hundred, a two-day bike tour through the New Harmony area. Riders can choose between a 16-mile or 50-mile trip. (812) 682–3453; www.nharmony.k12.in.us.

Tri-State Arts & Crafts Festival, Vanderburgh 4-H Fairgrounds, Evansville. Two hundred fifty booths in four buildings and outdoors, with festival food booths. (812) 425–0115; www.evansvillecvb.org.

June through July. Evansville Thunder Festival, 123 Northwest Fourth Street on the Evansville Riverfront. Watch Thunder on the Ohio, a hydroplane race, ending in an outstanding fireworks display on July 4. www.comsource.net/evvfreedomfest/.

July. Casino Aztar Evansville Riverfest. Held in downtown Evansville on the riverfront at the Casino, this festival includes entertainment, food booths, carnival rides, a 5K run, kids' corner, and talent show, plus much more. Free admission. (812) 424–2986.

September. Kunstfest. New Harmony. A fall festival of traditional German crafts, entertainment, and food including bratwurst, kuchen, brain sandwiches, and cabbage rolls. Demonstrators in period dress show hat felting, blacksmithing, rug braiding, soap making, and other crafts. Also Harmonist general store, historic tours, contemporary fine-art exposition, and more. (800) 231–2168; www.newharmony.evansville.net.

Tri-State Arts & Crafts Festival, National Guard Armory. Evansville. 150 booths, all indoors with food booths. (812) 425–0115; www.evansvillecvb.org.

October. Grey Lady Ghost Tours at Willard Library. Evansville. The tours are offered both during the evening and, for the faint of heart, during the day. Reservations are recommended. There is a nominal charge. Tours throughout the Gothic structure give details about "strange occurrences" with the ghost throughout the years and cover theories about who the ghost is, etc. Often these tours are given by library staff who have had an encounter. (812) 425–4309.

West Side Nut Club Fall Festival. Evansville. Held in historic West Franklin Street, this festival was born out of Evansville's German heritage. Besides music and entertainment, more than 120 food booths serve wonderful kuchen, dumplings, bratwurst, and other German fare. Then, there are booths serving ostrich burgers, brain sandwiches, and chocolate-covered insects! (812) 464–8347.

Other Recommended Restaurants and Lodgings

Evansville

Cool Breeze Estate Bed & Breakfast, 1240 Southeast Second Street; (812) 422–9635. Located in the Riverside Historic District, this 1906 Prairie School design has large rooms with high ceilings and private baths. Gourmet breakfast with homemade breads. Children welcome. No smoking. Rate: $85 per day. www.coolbreezebb.com.

The Jungle, 415 Main Street; (812) 425–5282. Fun restaurant with such items as Tarzan Tenderloin and Jungle Salad. Also steaks, seafood, and vegetarian offerings. Fat Cat's Lounge has fifty-seven different types of martinis. Lunches under $7.00, with dinners from $11.00 to $18.00.

The Old Mill, 5031 New Harmony Road; (812) 963–6000. Casual dining in rustic atmosphere with wood floors, a large fireplace, and an old waterwheel. Local cuisine such as brain sandwiches, catfish fiddlers, and wonderful fried chicken with mashed potatoes and gravy. Also German food. Most entrees $7.00 to $14.00. Open Monday through Saturday 4:00 to 11:00 P.M. and Sunday 11:00 A.M. to 10:00 P.M.

Newburgh

The Edgewater Grille, 1 East Water Street; (812) 858–2443. An eclectic establishment with hardwood floors, light walls, jazzy paintings, and lots of glass. Situated right on the banks of the Ohio River. Patrons can eat overlooking the river, which is always a plus. The signature pork loin stuffed with bread crumbs, spinach, onion, and eggs melts in your mouth, or try Franco's Zesty Rigatoni Matriciana. Entrees are $7.00 to $18.00.

New Harmony

Country Cottage Restaurant, 317 Church Street; (812) 682–4291. Family dining featuring plate lunches, sandwiches, salads, soups, and homemade fudge. Inexpensive.

The New Harmony Inn, 506 North Street; (812) 682–4491. Well-known inn located next to The Red Geranium Restaurant. Ninety guest rooms, some with kitchenettes. Swimming pool, spa; bike rental. Rates: $89.

The Old Rooming House, 916 Church Street; (888) 255–8256. Built in 1896, this comfortable bed-and-breakfast with four cozy rooms has been serving New Harmony visitors for fifty years. Bikes available to tour the town; books to read or board games to play for relaxing. Or just sit on the big, shaded front porch and swing. Three-room cottage also available, with bath and full kitchen. Local cafe within walking distance. Rate: $42 per night. www.oldroominghouse.com.

For More Information

The Atheneum, North and Arthur Streets, New Harmony, IN 47631; (812) 682–4474.

Evansville Convention and Visitors Bureau, 401 Southeast Riverside Drive, Evansville, IN 47713; (800) 433–3025; www.evansvillecvb.org.

Historic New Harmony Office, P.O. Box 579, New Harmony, IN 47631; (812) 682–4488 or (800) 231–2108; www.newharmony.org.

Walker's Guide to New Harmony's History, by Janet R. Walker, for a self-guided walking tour of New Harmony. Can be purchased at the Atheneum for $5.00.

EASTERN ESCAPE SIX

Indianapolis/Nashville (Brown County), Indiana

Big City to Country Living / 3 Nights

Four hours from St. Louis lies Indianapolis, Indiana. Known mostly for the Indy 500 and basketball, Indianapolis has more than enough to keep you occupied—besides the sports. Your problem will be budgeting your time once you find out all there is.

☐ Museums

☐ Historic town and shops

☐ State park

☐ Horseback riding

☐ Covered bridge

☐ Hiking

☐ Live entertainment

☐ Art galleries

The first part of the trip is mostly prairie—lots of prairie in Illinois and western Indiana. Indianapolis is Indiana's major city and it has made great strides in the convention-and-tourist business. Known as the "Crossroads of America" because of all the interstate highways converging there, Indianapolis has renovated its downtown, mixing old architecture with new. White River State Park, downtown, connects museums with the retail area by walkways and a canal. Conseco Fieldhouse, home of the Indiana Pacers and the RCA Dome, home of the Indiana Colts, both also downtown, bring in visitors who stay long after the games to enjoy the rest Indy has to offer.

After you leave Indianapolis for Nashville, which is known locally as "Brown County" (because *it* is Brown County), you'll start driving into wooded rolling hills with a charming little town right in the middle. A warning: Once you get to Brown County, leave your diets behind. You can't swing a dead cat without hitting a fudge shop, ice-cream emporium, or funnel-cake stand!

You will be able to walk off a lot of that fudge with all the galleries and shops Nashville has to offer. Or you can hike or play golf in the Brown County State Park.

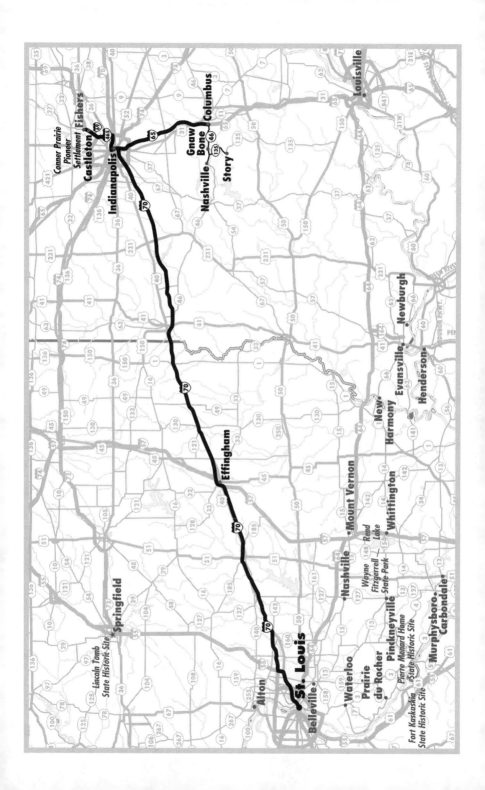

Day 1 / Morning

Get an early start, at least by 7:00 A.M. Indianapolis is 240 miles east of St. Louis on I–70—about a good four-hour drive. There are numerous places to stop for gas, snacks, or coffee along the way. Effingham, Illinois, marks the halfway point, with many fast-food restaurants and other places for quick stops.

If you drove straight through, you're probably ready for lunch. Continue to follow I–70 east to I–465 North to I–69 North to the first exit (Eighty-second Street at Castleton). Look for the big yellow airplane on the roof of your lunch spot, Loon Lake Lodge.

LUNCH: A most amazing restaurant, **Loon Lake Lodge,** 6880 East Eighty-second Street (317–845–9011), looks like a northern mountain lodge—with trees inside. A bear growls at customers; raccoons chatter at squirrels in the trees (not real). The menu has items like rattlesnake bites (real) and seasoned elk medallions. For the less adventurous diner, lunch offerings include a delicious and beautiful lime cilantro salad with grilled chicken breast, black beans, and sweet corn ($8.50) or shrimp poor boy ($8.25). The dinner menu is just as diverse and enticing. Open daily 11:30 A.M. to 2:30 P.M.; dinner, Monday through Thursday 5:00 to 10:00 P.M., Friday and Saturday 5:00 to 11:00 P.M., Sunday noon to 9:00 P.M.

Afternoon

For an afternoon during which you will learn and have fun, visit **Conner Prairie,** 13400 Allisonville Road (800–966–1836), an open-air, living-history museum where you can visit 1836 **Prairietown** and the **Pioneer Adventure Area.** There is also a large museum center with exhibits, a theater, a gift shop, and a restaurant. To get to Conner Prairie after lunch at the Lodge, take I–69 north to Fishers exit (116th Street). Go west on 116th to Allisonville Road, then north to Conner Prairie (a ten-minute drive from Loon Lake). There are lots of Conner Prairie signs, both on the interstate and along 116th Street, to guide you.

Inhabitants of Prairietown do not step out of character. Talking with them is a living-history lesson. Visit the schoolhouse, various homes, the innkeeper, doctor, or blacksmith and ask them about their lives and beliefs. Visit the Lenape Indian Camp and McKinnen's Trading Post. Explore a wigwam, grind corn into meal, and listen to Native American stories. In the adventure area you can plow, weave, wash clothes on a washboard, throw a tomahawk, and milk a sheep, all experiences of the 1800s. Admission April through November, $11.00, adults; $10.00, seniors; $7.00, children five to twelve; four and under are free. Farm Bureau and AAA members receive a $1.50 discount. Special prices January through March and in December. Hours 9:30 A.M. to 5:00 P.M. Tuesday through Saturday and 11:00 A.M. to 5:00 P.M. Sunday; closed Monday. Open Memorial Day, July 4th, and Labor Day. Visit www.connerprairie.org.

From Conner Prairie, drive downtown to **White River State Park,** 801 West Washington Street (800–665–9056), where you can either visit such attractions as the **Indianapolis Zoo** (317–630–2001), the **NCAA Hall of Champions** (317–916–4255), the **White River Gardens** (317–630–2001), a botanical wonderland, or the **Eiteljorg Museum of American Indians and Western Art** (317–636–9378). There's also an **IMAX theater** (317–233–IMAX) and the **National Institute for Fitness and Sport** (317–274–3432). You can wander along the **Central Canal Waterway** that runs from the White River through the park. Visit www.inwhiteriver.com for prices and hours of these attractions and more.

DINNER: From the penthouse floor of One North Penn Building, have a memorable dinner at **Magic Moments Restaurant;** (317) 822–3400. Not only do you get a spectacular view of the city, you have a magician entertain you between courses—and what courses! Try chicken marsala and a baked sweet potato with honey cinnamon butter or garlic pork roast with wild rice. Finish with a dessert such as white chocolate éclair cheesecake. Prices are a la carte, so with a salad, dinner, side vegetable, and dessert, you could spend upwards of $30 to $35 a person excluding drinks or wine; however, you will not forget this evening soon.

LODGING: For a family-friendly, reasonably priced hotel, try **Courtyard by Marriott,** 501 West Washington Street; (800) 321–2211. It's situated across from the city's urban state park (White River State Park). It's also within walking distance of the RCA Dome, Indiana Convention Center, Conseco Fieldhouse, and Circle Centre Mall. The Courtyard is a 233-room, full-service hotel. TGI Friday's restaurant. Free parking, outdoor pool. Rates $99 to $159, with an average of $129.

Day 2 / Morning

BREAKFAST: Le Peep, 301 North Illinois Street (317–237–3447), has been voted the place with the best breakfast and best omelet in Indianapolis since 1988. Specializing in unique breakfast and lunch creations including frittatas, French toast, pampered eggs, and ultra-healthy egg-white omelets. And a pampered egg is a happy egg. Average cost is $5.00 to $6.00. Open Monday through Friday 6:30 A.M. to 2:30 P.M., Saturday and Sunday 7:00 A.M. to 2:30 P.M.

Start your day at **The Children's Museum,** Thirtieth and Meridian Streets; (317) 334–3322. Ranked as the largest of its kind in the world, the museum features five floors of interactive exhibits and ten major galleries for physical and natural sciences, history, world cultures, and the arts. There's also the Cinedome theater, with a 76-foot screen. Other activities include a Victorian railway depot, SpaceQuest Planetarium, and Playscape, an area designed for infants to six-year-olds, which features a giant birdhouse, a tree house, a water table, and a race car. Open daily March to Labor Day from 10:00 A.M. to 5:00 P.M. Free from 5:00 to 8:00 P.M. on first Thursday of each month. Closed Monday from Labor Day through February. Museum admission: adults, $9.50; seniors, $8.00; children two to seventeen, $4.00. Museum/Cinedome combo: adults eighteen to fifty-nine, $15.00; seniors sixty and over, $13.50; children two to seventeen, $7.50; under age two, free. www.childrensmuseum.org.

LUNCH: For a more laid-back lunch, do **Acapulco Joe's Mexican Foods,** 365 North Illinois Street (317–637–5160), a true "locals'" place. Specialties are Mexican pizza and *chile con queso,* and if you get there at noon, you can hear the daily playing of Kate Smith's "God Bless America." Open 7:00 A.M. to 10:00 P.M. Monday through Saturday. Average lunch, $7.00.

Afternoon

Leaving Indianapolis, take I–65 south approximately 45 miles to Highway 46. This will be the Columbus/Brown County exit. Exit right and go west for approximately 18 miles to Nashville. With more than 300 art galleries, craft shops, specialty shops, and restaurants, you should have no trouble keeping occupied the rest of the afternoon.

A good way to start your visit in Nashville would be to take the **Nashville Express;** (812) 988–2308. You can get a good look at the whole town while the conductor points out shops, restaurants, and other points of interest along the 2 1/2-mile route. Hours are Monday through Friday 10:00 A.M. to 5:00 P.M., Saturday 10:00 A.M. to 6:30 P.M., and Sunday 10:00 A.M. to 6:30 P.M. Rates are $4.00 for adults; children four and under are free.

Most of the shops are located on Van Buren, the main street, but many little shops are hidden away in alcoves with walkways. So your best bet would be to stop first at the **Convention and Visitors Center** at the corner of Main and Van Buren Streets and get a map. Shops like **The Finicky Feline** (812–988–9264) and **Memories** (812–988–8422), both in Calvin Place, at the corner of Franklin and South Van Buren Streets, are much easier to find with a little direction.

If you want salsas, homemade jellies and preserves, and other gourmet items, look into **The Harvest Preserve,** 61 West Main Street (812–988–7606), with its shelves of peach, pumpkin, and apple butter with black-berry jelly, cherry preserves, and other yummies. For an uncommon number of hot sauces varying from mild to "you don't want to go there," visit **J. Bob's,** 16 North Van Buren Street (812–988–6844).

At **Ruth's Garden,** 44 Franklin Street West (812–988–0665), you'll find everything for the garden—flags, wind chimes, fountains, yard art, hummingbird feeders, and more—plus books to read about it and candles to light it! **Waldborough's,** Calvin Place (812–988–6900), offers unusual Perot dolls and Austin sculpture. It's never too early for Christmas, and you can get a head start at **The Holly Shop,** corner of North Van Buren and Mound Streets (800–860–4453).

At one of the more unusual shops, **Fourth Dimension Holo-graphics Gallery and Showroom,** 90 West Washington Street (812–988–9211), you can see amazing holograms done by Rob Taylor, who has the only camera of this type in the United States. Not mere photos, these holograms will last 200 or 300 years.

If ice cream sounds good, **Dag's Ice Cream Parlour,** 145 South Van Buren (812–988–4113), will fix you up with a super banana split or a dou-ble waffle cone. Fudge shops abound in Nashville, and the aroma of fun-nel cakes and fried chicken drift through the streets. It's hard to get your mind off food here.

The beauty of this little town is having the time to go in and out of the little stores. Sitting on a bench with an ice-cream cone and visiting with other browsers takes you out of this time and puts you into the era before cell phones and pagers. Enjoy it!

DINNER: With the aroma of sugar-cured, hickory-smoked ham or fried chicken drifting under your nose, you will have a hard time making a din-ner choice at **The Nashville House;** (812) 988–4554. But you would be truly remiss if you passed on the fried chicken, for which they are so well known. Your dinner will start with coleslaw, which is unlike any you have ever had. Then come their famous fried biscuits and homemade apple butter. Then comes the fried chicken with the trimmings ($15.25). They also have roast beef, barbecued ribs, ham, and roast turkey.

After dinner, walk through the **Old Country Store** in the same building. You can buy brooms, crockery, canes, biscuit cutters, fruit butters, lamp oil, and bag balm, plus much, much more.

Evening

If you're ready to relax and be entertained, the **Nashville Follies Theater,** 227 South Van Buren (800–449–7469), presents a variety of singing, dancing, and comedy shows from April through December sure to put you in the "Brown County" state of mind. Admission is $14.00 for adults and $5.00 for children twelve and under. Show time Friday is 8:00 P.M. and Saturday at 5:00 and 8:30 P.M. Throughout the season the actors also present weeknight, morning, and matinee performances. Visit www.nashvillefollies.com.

After the show, if you're not ready to head for bed, stop at the tavern inside **The Ordinary Restaurant,** 61 South Van Buren; (812) 988–6166. A cozy place to find the locals and hear the history of the area.

LODGING: Relax in one of Nashville's newest hotels, **The Hidden Valley Inn,** 201 North Van Buren Street; (800) 988–9000. The all-suite inn features bedrooms with king-size beds, living room, and fully equipped kitchenette including stove, microwave, and refrigerator. Large bathrooms with shower/tub. Also a complimentary continental breakfast in your suite—and truffles on the bed! No smoking or pets. Rates run from $89 to $219, depending on the season.

Day 3 / Morning

BREAKFAST: Hidden Valley puts coffee, juice, and luscious muffins in your room. If you want more, walk down to **Hobnob Corner,** corner of Van Buren and Main Streets (812–988–4114), for omelets, eggs, and traditional breakfast fare plus their most popular baked goods such as cinnamon rolls, bear claws, and other Danish (it's advisable to get there early because they go fast). Inexpensive. Open Sunday through Thursday 8:00 A.M. to 7:30 P.M., Friday and Saturday 8:00 A.M. to 8:00 P.M.

A beautiful start to the day would be a visit to the **T.C. Steele State Historical Site,** 4220 T.C. Steele Road, off Highway 46. A noted Indiana

Brown County State Park

artist and impressionist painter, Steel bought this abandoned farm in 1907 for his retreat. You can see the studio and house, then do a self-guided hike. Along the way you'll see the perennial gardens, lily ponds, and the cemetery where the Steels are buried. You might also see foxes, deer, skunks, and other denizens of the forest. Open Tuesday through Saturday 9:00 A.M. to 5:00 P.M., Sunday 1:00 to 5:00 P.M.; closed Monday. Call (812) 988–2785 for information.

From this site follow the signs and take the west entrance into **Brown County State Park,** which offers camping, picnicking, hiking, and horseback riding. There is also a snake exhibit, a bird-watching room, and other naturalist displays. You can climb to the top of the fire tower for a fantastic view of the whole area or drive to two lookout points.

Take a drive through two nearby covered bridges. One, the Ramp Bridge, is at the north entrance to Brown County State Park and is the only double-barreled two-lane bridge in Indiana. To get to the Bean Blossom Bridge, take Highway 135 north to Covered Bridge Road about 3.5 miles. Turn onto Covered Bridge Road and you will come right to the bridge.

LUNCH: Drive out Highway 135 south to **Story, Indiana.** This winding road might make you forget you're going for lunch, but you'll feel better.

Founded in the 1850s, Story is a story in itself. The general store now houses a gourmet restaurant, **The Story Inn,** 6404 South State Road 135 (800–881–1183; www.storyinn.com), where you can browse among the primitive antiques and read Story's history while you wait for your meal. The grilled artichoke served on a croissant with white cheddar cheese ($7.95) melts in your mouth. Or go for the Celtic Sausage Sandwich with fresh sauerkraut on whole-grain bread ($7.95). For a side, order the Story fries, plate-size shredded potatoes with herbed cheeses topped with white cheddar ($4.95). Breakfast is available all day. Open Tuesday through Friday 9:00 A.M. to 2:00 P.M., Saturday and Sunday 8:00 A.M. to 2:00 P.M. Open for dinner Tuesday through Sunday 5:00 to 8:00 P.M. Reservations suggested.

Afternoon

No visit to Brown County would be complete without browsing the flea markets at **Gnaw Bone, Indiana.** Normally, if you blink, you would miss this little town on Highway 46 east of Nashville. On weekends the parking lots of little stores are packed with tables overflowing with everything from Fiji masks to golf clubs, carnival glass to Pyrex. And that doesn't count the tents that hold even more. If you work up an appetite, food is not far away. **The Gnaw Bone Homebaked Bread Store** serves up wonderful apple cinnamon bread along with homemade jams, jellies, and preserves. The store is on Highway 46 before Nashville.

You could devote the rest of the afternoon to the art galleries located in Nashville. More than one hundred artists live in Brown County, and you can see their work at **The Brown County Art Gallery** (812–988–4609), **Waldron Gallery** (812–988–1844), **Honeysuckle Gallery** (812–988–0431), **The Brown County Art Guild** (812–988–6185), and other galleries in the little town.

If you like wineries, Nashville has two very good ones—**Château Thomas Winery** (812–988–8500) and **The Brown County Winery** (812–988–6144). The latter has an especially fine blackberry wine. The winery has a second location 5 miles east of Nashville on Highway 46.

DINNER: Right across the street from Hidden Valley Inn is the **Hotel Nashville Resort,** an elegant restaurant. With entrees like Neptune Filet Mignon with béarnaise and crabmeat ($24.95) and Chicken Oscar with béarnaise, crabmeat, and asparagus ($14.95), you can't go wrong. If they happen to have the special rib eye with Jack Daniels sauce ($17.95), go for it. A dessert tray with all homemade desserts that you can't refuse follows the meal.

Evening

If you're in the mood for theater of a different sort, **The Brown County Playhouse,** 70 South Van Buren Street, is known for its quality actors in performances such as *You're a Good Man, Charlie Brown* and *Sylvia*. Performances start at 8:00 P.M. Admission for adults, $14.50 (Friday and Saturday); children, $7.50 (Friday and Saturday); adults, $12.50 (Wednesday, Thursday, and Sunday); children, $6.50 (Wednesday, Thursday, and Sunday). (812) 988–2123.

LODGING: Hidden Valley Inn.

Day 4 / Morning

BREAKFAST: You would be hard-pressed to pick from good food in this town, but a good choice for breakfast is **The Artists Colony Inn and Restaurant,** Franklin and Van Buren Streets. A dining room with warm wood tables and chairs and large windows looking out on the street invites you to linger over coffee for quite a while. Whether you choose the steaming hot pancakes or the fruit bowl with an ample variety of fruit, you will not be displeased. Breakfast is served from 7:30 to 10:30 A.M. every day, with lunch and dinner 11:00 A.M. to 8:00 P.M. Sunday through Thursday and to 9:00 P.M. on Friday and Saturday. Moderate prices; wonderful atmosphere. (800) 737–0255; www.artistscolonyinn.com.

Time to pack up the car and head home. A stop in **Columbus** would be well worth the time. The American Institutes of Architects ranked Columbus sixth in the nation for quality, innovation, and design. World-famous architects designed more than fifty buildings, which makes this Midwestern city very special. For a guide to these buildings, call the **Columbus Visitors Center** at (888) 468–6568.

LUNCH: If you are in Columbus on a weekend, **Smith's Row Food & Spirits Restaurant,** 418 Fourth Street (812–373–9382), will serve you a lunch to hold you in good stead for your trip home. Try the grilled tuna Caesar salad ($6.75) or vegetarian grilled cheese sandwich ($4.95). Children also get an opportunity to try "adult fare" with Smith's unique children's menu, featuring kid-size portions of prime rib, chicken stir-fry and chicken Alfredo, along with the basic burgers and chicken fingers. In nice weather, you can dine on the outdoor balcony. Open Monday through Friday 11:00 A.M. to 2:00 P.M. Closed for lunch on Saturday and all day Sunday.

There's More

Indianapolis

Circle Centre, 49 West Maryland Street (317–681–8000), is Indianapolis's premier shopping complex, with Nordstrom and Parisian anchoring one hundred specialty stores. Experience the World Mardi Gras Entertainment Complex; (317) 630–5483. One cover charge ($5.00) gains admission to all four attractions: Gators (DJ tunes, dance music, Top 40); Brewskis (sports bar, wings); Flashbaxx (retro tunes of the '70s and '80s); and World Mardi Gras Music Hall (live bands). Also a nine-screen movie theater and Steven Spielberg's GameWorks Studio. www.worldmardigrast.net.

The Colonel Eli Lilly Civil War Museum, located on Monument Circle in downtown Indianapolis in the lower level of the Soldiers and Sailors Monument, depicts Indiana's history in the Civil War through documents, letters, diaries, and other items. Nine large screens create a multimedia experience with live reenactments of historical battles and common events. Free admission. Hours are Wednesday through Sunday 9:00 A.M. to 6:00 P.M. (317) 232–7615; www.indianacivilwar.org.

Indianapolis City Market, 222 East Market Street. Enjoy the sights, sounds, and smells of this historic market, built in 1886 to provide fresh meat and produce to city residents. Now an international pleasure with Asian, Italian, Greek, and Middle Eastern food choices. Open Monday through Saturday 6:00 A.M. to 6:00 P.M. (317) 634–9266.

Indianapolis Motor Speedway Hall of Fame Museum, 4790 West Sixteenth Street; (317) 484–6747. One of the world's largest collection of racing, classic, and antique cars. See a film about the history of the track and race. Gift shop (317–484–6760) with exclusive collector items. Open every day but Christmas, 9:00 A.M. to 5:00 P.M. Adults, $3.00; students six to fifteen, $1.00; children under six are free.

Nashville

Brown County Historical Museum, on Museum Lane. Visit an 1850 pioneer cabin, an 1879 log jail, and an 1867 doctor's office. See the crafts of blacksmithing, weaving, and other pioneer arts. Open May through October, Saturday, Sunday, and holidays 1:00 to 5:00 P.M. (812) 988–8547.

Family Fun Center, 216 South Van Buren Street, with eighteen holes of miniature golf, billiards, and an arcade for the kids—but great for adults, too! (812) 988–9490; www.glbvictory@worldnet.att.net.

Schooner Valley Stables, 2282 West Street (State Road 46). See Brown County in all its beauty from the back of a horse. Guided trail rides start at $15 for an hour. (812) 988–2859.

Special Events

May. The Spring Blossom Parade sponsored by the Brown County Chamber of Commerce, (812–988–9816) and the Antique Tractor and Farm Machinery Show. Call (812) 332–8398 for more information.

World-famous Indianapolis 500 Festival and Race. Downtown Indianapolis and the Speedway. Includes a minimarathon with 25,000 participants, Queen's Ball, the 500 Parade, and concludes with the race. These events occur during the entire month. (317) 636–4556; www.500fest.com.

June. The Bill Monroe Bean Blossom Bluegrass Festival. Bean Blossom, Indiana (north of Nashville). Band contest, children's workshops, workshop stage, and sunset Jam. (800) 414–4677; www.beanblossom.com.

The Brown County Artist and Craftsmen Studio and Garden Tour. Select studios and gardens are open to the public with demonstrations of weaving, basketry, woodworking, painting, and other crafts and art forms. For information and locations call (800) 881–1183.

September. Brown County Old Settlers Reunion. Bean Blossom, Indiana. Honors those venerable Brown County residents. Rides, food, and entertainment. (812) 988–2626.

Hoosier Story Telling Festival. Indianapolis Art Center, 820 East Sixty-seventh Street, Indianapolis. Storytellers from around the country tell stories from cultures including Hispanic, Jewish, and African American. (317) 255–7628.

October. Native American Harvest Celebration. Eiteljorg Museum of American Indians and Western Art, 500 West Washington Street, Indianapolis. (317) 636–WEST.

December. Enjoy a Brown County Christmas from the day after Thanksgiving, with the arrival of Santa Claus, through the weeks before Christmas. Free train rides with Frosty and the elves and holiday horse-drawn carriage rides. Strolling carolers, hot cider, and twinkling lights make Brown County a special place to be. Call (800) 753–3255 for more information.

Other Recommended Restaurants and Lodgings

Indianapolis

Iaria's Italian Restaurant, 317 South College Avenue, a family-owned establishment since 1933.Very popular with visiting celebrities. Good Italian food in a casual atmosphere with entrees under $20. (317) 638–7706.

Indianapolis Marriott Downtown, 350 West Maryland Street; (317) 822–3500 or (877) 640–7666. Indiana's largest and Indianapolis's newest hotel located in the heart of downtown within walking distance of shopping and sports venues. Spa, indoor pool, Circle City Bar & Grille, and Champion Sports Bar (with dynamite appetizers!). Rates: $129 to $229.

Jillian's, 141 South Meridian Street. A 45,000-square-foot, three-floor entertainment complex with sports video cafe and a bar with more than twenty giant screens. A game room with more than one hundred high-tech games and a nine-lane bowling alley. Entrees average $8.95. (317) 822–9300.

Slippery Noodle Inn, 372 Meridian Street. The oldest bar in Indiana, established in 1850. Open seven days a week with great food and live blues music. Also popular with famous gangster John Dillinger way back when. Moderate prices. (317) 631–6974; www.slipperynoodle.com.

St. Elmo Steak House, 127 South Illinois Street; (317) 635–0636 or (800) 637–1811. An Indianapolis institution since 1902 serving big and delicious steaks plus chops, seafood, and other steak-house fare. Famous for jumbo shrimp cocktail with an unbelievable hot sauce that you just can't quit eating! Intimate setting in beautiful dark wood decor. Entrees: $24 to $38. Hours: Monday through Saturday 4:00 to 10:30 P.M., Sunday 4:00 to 9:00 P.M.

The Stone Soup Inn, 1304 North Central Avenue. Built in 1901, the mansion is an impressive example of colonial revival architecture. Located in

Historic Old Northside (near downtown), the inn features large rooms with beautiful Mission and Victorian-era antique fireplaces, TV/VCRs, beautiful gardens, and comfortable sitting areas. Children are welcome. Rates range from $85 to $135. (317) 639–9550; www.stonesoupinn.com.

Nashville

You can stay at the Brown County State Park, either in the Abe Martin Lodge, sleeping cabins, or housekeeping cabins, completely furnished. Camping is also an option. (812) 988–4418 or (812) 988–6406.

The Cornerstone Inn, 54 East Franklin Street, features a spacious common balcony where you can sit and watch the Nashville hustle and bustle. Each of the twenty rooms is named after a Brown County ancestor. Amenities include queen-size beds and Jacuzzis. A complimentary breakfast buffet including coffee cake, eggs, and fruit is served in the dining room. Children welcome. Rates range from $115 to $175. (888) 383–0300; www.cornerstoneinn.com.

The Hotel Nashville, 245 North Jefferson, not only has a wonderful restaurant but also is an all-suite resort hotel with indoor swimming pool, sauna, whirlpool, and Jacuzzi suites. All rates are seasonal with many package plans. Prospective lodgers need to call (800) 848–6274.

The Overlook Fine Food and Spirits, State Road 46, overlooks (what else?) the Salt Creek Golf Course. Two miles east of Nashville, you can relax with such tasty fare as the Overlook Burger, barbecued ribs, steaks, or salads at moderate prices. (812) 988–7888.

For More Information

Brown County Convention and Visitors Bureau, Main and Van Buren Streets, Nashville, IN 47448; (800) 753–3255; www.browncounty.com.

Indiana Convention and Visitors Association, One RCA Dome, Suite 100, Indianapolis, IN 46225; (377) 639–4282 or (800) 323–INDY; www.indy. org. For one-stop hotel reservations and to check prices and availability, call (800) 556–INDY or book online at www.indy.org.

VisitIndy.info, located on the first floor of Circle Centre. Owned and operated by the Indianapolis Convention and Visitors Association. Great spot to get maps, brochures, and souvenirs, or to secure hotel, car-rental, and air reservations.

INDEX

M

About the Authors

Julie Gustafson is a freelance writer and lifelong resident of St. Louis. She has written numerous articles on subjects ranging from food and resorts to architecture and design.

Linda Jarrett is a St. Louis–based freelance writer whose work appears regularly in the _St. Louis Dispatch_ and the _Webster-Kirkwood Times._ Her travel and feature articles have appeared in local, regional, and national magazines. Linda is married and has three adult children.